FREE AND FRENCH IN THE CARIBBEAN

BLACKS IN THE DIASPORA

Founding Editors
Darlene Clark Hine
John McCluskey, Jr.
David Barry Gaspar

Advisory Board
Herman L. Bennett
Kim D. Butler
Judith A. Byfield
Tracy Sharpley-Whiting

FREE AND FRENCH IN THE CARIBBEAN

Toussaint Louverture, Aimé Césaire, and Narratives of Loyal Opposition

John Patrick Walsh

Indiana University Press

Bloomington and Indianapolis

This book is a publication of

Indiana University Press
Office of Scholarly Publishing
Herman B Wells Library 350
1320 East 10th Street
Bloomington, Indiana 47405–3907 USA

iupress.indiana.edu

Telephone orders   800-842-6796
Fax orders   812-855-7931

© 2013 by John Patrick Walsh

All rights reserved

No part of this book may be reproduced or utilized in any form or by any means, electronic or mechanical, including photocopying and recording, or by any information storage and retrieval system, without permission in writing from the publisher. The Association of American University Presses' Resolution on Permissions constitutes the only exception to this prohibition.

⊖ The paper used in this publication meets the minimum requirements of the American National Standard for Information Sciences—Permanence of Paper for Printed Library Materials, ANSI Z39.48–1992.

Manufactured in the United States of America

Library of Congress Cataloging-in-Publication Data

Walsh, John Patrick, [date]
  Free and French in the Caribbean : Toussaint Louverture, Aimé Césaire, and narratives of loyal opposition / John Patrick Walsh.
     page cm. — (Blacks in the diaspora)
  Includes bibliographical references and index.
  ISBN 978-0-253-00627-1 (cloth : alk. paper) — ISBN 978-0-253-00630-1 (pbk. : alk. paper) — ISBN 978-0-253-00810-7 (ebook) 1. Toussaint Louverture, 1743–1803. 2. Haiti—History—Revolution, 1791-1804. 3. Nationalism—Haiti—History. 4. Césaire, Aimé. 5. Martinican literature (French)—History and criticism. 6. Caribbean, French-speaking—History—Autonomy and independence movements. 7. Nationalism—Caribbean, French speaking—History. 8. Decolonization in literature. 9. Nationalism in literature. I. Title.
  F1923.T69W35 2013
  972.94'03—dc23
                                    2013002202

1 2 3 4 5   18 17 16 15 14 13

Je ne dirai pas que les faits ne sont rien. Sans eux il n'y aurait pas d'histoire. Mais le plus important en histoire, ce ne sont pas les faits, ce sont les relations qui les unissent, la loi qui les régit, la dialectique qui les suscite. C'est ce que, dans le cadre de mon sujet, j'ai tâché de saisir.

[I will not say that facts are nothing. Without them there would be no history. But the most important in history is not the facts, it is the connections that bring them together, the law that governs them, the dialectic that stirs them up. This is what, in the framework of my topic, I have attempted to grasp.]

—Aimé Césaire, *Toussaint Louverture: La Révolution française et le problème colonial*

Personne n'a mieux connu que Toussaint Louverture le théâtre sur lequel il avait à opérer, et le caractère des individus soumis à sa jurisdiction.

[No one understood better than Toussaint Louverture the theater over which he had to operate and the character of the individuals subject to his jurisdiction.]

—Pamphile de Lacroix, *La Révolution de Haïti*

Contents

Acknowledgments — *ix*

Introduction — *1*

Part I. Toussaint Louverture

1. Toussaint Louverture and the Family of Saint-Domingue — *25*
2. Under the Stick of Maître Toussaint — *46*
3. "Free and French": La Constitution de la colonie française de Saint-Domingue — *65*
4. Toussaint Louverture at a Crossroads: The *Mémoire* of the "First Soldier of the Republic of Saint Domingue" — *80*

Part II. Aimé Césaire

5. Césaire Reads Toussaint: The Haitian Revolution and the Problem of Departmentalization — *99*
6. Haitian Building: *La tragédie du roi Christophe* — *124*

Conclusion: Artisans of Free and French — *153*

Notes — *157*
Bibliography — *179*
Index — *189*

Acknowledgments

I AM GRATEFUL TO the many people who made this book possible. After years of graduate research on the history and literature of the French Caribbean, I arrived in Charleston for the fall semester 2007 and discovered its historical ties to Saint-Domingue. At the time, several institutions and communities were preparing to mark the bicentennial of the U. S. Abolition of the Slave Trade; the following summer, Toni Morrison came to Sullivan's Island, the point of debarkation for millions of slaves, to commemorate her "Bench by the Road" project. I had recently read Césaire's essay on Toussaint and decided to put aside another project to study the ties between the two men. My colleague Simon Lewis suggested that I locate Charleston not as a historical, southern city of the United States but as a northern port of a vast Atlantic and Caribbean economy. The director of the College of Charleston's program for the Carolina Lowcountry and Atlantic World, where I had the privilege to present part of an early draft, Simon has been a key interlocutor throughout its writing.

I am indebted to the generations of scholars of the history and literature of Haiti and the French Caribbean. Over the course of my research, I had the great fortune to exchange ideas with a number of individuals who have inherited this legacy. Special mention must go to Bernadette Cailler, who encouraged me to continue work on Césaire. Nick Nesbitt and Deborah Jenson generously answered many queries. Daniel Desormeaux and Gary Wilder read the original book proposal with great care and made invaluable suggestions for the core argument and structure. Daniel also provided assistance in locating various copies of Toussaint's memoir. I thank Jeremy Popkin and Françoise Vergès, who each read parts of the manuscript and gave direction at critical moments. Thank you to Aliko Songolo for including me in a panel on Césaire and to Cilas Kemedjio for his response to our panel. The final manuscript benefited greatly from the comments and questions of a team of readers. Thank you to Alex Crumbley, Lia Brozgal, Mylène Priam, Emily Beck, Téfo Attafi, Lisa Signori, and Morgan Koerner. These friends and colleagues made this a better book; any flaws are my own.

Several institutions and the people who animate them were essential to my research. I would like to thank the archivists at the Archives Nationales, in Paris, and the Archives Nationales d'Outre-Mer, in Aix-en-Provence; André Elizee and the staff at the Schomburg Center for Research in Black Culture at the New York Public Library; Susan Hamson and Tara Craig at the Butler Library of Columbia University; and the Manuscript Division of the Library of Congress. Outside of these archives, I could not have carried out research without the assistance of Michael Phillips and his team, especially Chris Nelson and Carolyn Savage, in the office of Interlibrary Loan at the College of Charleston's Addlestone Library.

Acknowledgments

I wish to thank Robert Sloan, Sarah Wyatt Swanson, and Tim Roberts of Indiana University Press for their help during the long transformation from manuscript to book. I am very appreciative of Sheila Berg's copyediting. I must also include four people who added their finishing touches to the book. Thank you to my brother, Kevin Walsh, for his editorial eye and for the index. Many thanks to Madison Smartt Bell, whose insight on the array of historical images of Toussaint was crucial to the likeness that adorns the book's cover. I am grateful to Steve Johnson for his drawings of Toussaint and Césaire, and to Doug Bell, of Kitchen Sink Studios, for his design.

A version of chapter 5 was published in *Small Axe* 34 (2010). I thank David Scott and Kelly Josephs, as well as Duke University Press, for granting permission to reprint a revised and longer chapter here. I also thank the anonymous readers for their extensive treatment of my article. I thank Claudine Michel and her staff at the *Journal of Haitian Studies* for permission to reprint a longer version of chapter 4, part of which appeared in volume 17, number 1 (2011).

I could not have undertaken research without the financial assistance of the College of Charleston. Two faculty research and development grants, as well as funds from the Department of French, Francophone and Italian Studies and the School of Languages, Cultures, and World Affairs, supported travel to various archives and allowed for the time necessary to complete the manuscript. I greatly appreciate the support of David Cohen, Shawn Morrison, Godwin Uwah, Robyn Holman, and Marilyn Tharp.

My mentors have left an indelible mark on this book. My gratitude to Tom Conley, in particular, is beyond measure. The depth and originality of his scholarship never cease to amaze me, and I cherish his friendship. I also owe an intellectual debt to Susan Suleiman, whose example continues to inspire me.

I would like to include a remembrance of Joseph Boromé, a lifelong scholar of Toussaint. After spending days combing through Boromé's papers at Columbia, I came upon a couple of letters he exchanged in the early 1970s with Sidney Mintz. In the attempt to find out more about Boromé, I emailed Professor Mintz, who had known Boromé during his time at Yale, when, he remembered, Boromé would come up from New York to visit and talk. Professor Mintz wrote back the same day with this warm recollection: "Such people prove by their behavior the intrinsic appeal of the past."

Finally, I dedicate this book to my family, especially to my parents, John and Ginger Walsh, who have given me everything; to Anaya and Tyan, my little readers; and to my wife, Shivika Asthana. This may not be the book for you, Shivvy, but it could not have been written without you.

FREE AND FRENCH IN THE CARIBBEAN

Introduction

SEPARATED BY NEARLY 150 years, the Haitian Revolution (1791–1803) and the departmentalization of Martinique, Guadeloupe, and French Guyana (1946) were defining events of the transatlantic connection between France and the Caribbean.[1] Historically, they have generally been thought of in opposing terms: the revolution marked a violent break from France, whereas departmentalization became, broadly speaking, synonymous with assimilation. An international conflict, the revolution sent shock waves around the Caribbean, north and south to the Americas, and across the Atlantic. In contrast, departmentalization, which became law soon after World War II, was a quieter, juridical transformation of colony to overseas department.

My point of departure is to question such received wisdom, especially as it has put considerable philosophical distance between the Haitian Revolution and departmentalization. In many ways, it is misleading to portray the fate of Saint-Domingue (the French colony that became independent Haiti in 1804) as distinct from that of the other "old colonies" of the French Caribbean. Doing so obscures the trans-Caribbean relationship of Saint-Domingue, Martinique, Guadeloupe, and French Guyana; furthermore, such a move reduces an understanding of the Haitian Revolution to an uncomplicated story of an army of former slaves overcoming their colonial masters. This is not to say that the story of emancipation should not be told, or that it no longer matters; rather, I propose a closer look at how two legacies of emancipation developed through narratives of revolution and ensuing nationhood that have been passed on to successive generations. The 1946 law of departmentalization was built on important antecedents, reaching back to the revolutionary nexus that tied France to Saint-Domingue. Therefore, the first of three central claims of this book is that a deep, historical connection exists between the two events. In order to develop this argument, I turn to the writings of the respective protagonists, Toussaint Louverture and Aimé Césaire. The second claim is that these iconic Caribbean leaders had much in common; through a series of close readings of primary texts, I examine the affinities of their projects as statesmen-authors. Both men left an abundant written record of the struggle to secure rights that the French Revolution had left behind as it sailed across the Atlantic; and, in fact, both men did much to define the complex relationship between autonomy and assimilation.

The history of the French Caribbean that I am concerned with is fraught with questions of universal rights, citizenship, sovereignty, imperialism, and nation building. These are questions that have crossed generations. Of particular interest here is the literature produced to address these issues, whether in the form of letters, reports, decrees, memoirs, essays, or plays. The third claim of this book—which ties together the first two—is that the study of these big questions too often neglects to take into account the kinds of narrative that carried and revolutionized them. This is a matter of pursuing an interdisciplinary approach that brings forward concerns of genre, textual production, and authorship to the practices of politics and historiography. Activated at the intersections of literature and history, and of literature and politics, the writings of Toussaint and Césaire call out to literary scholars, historians, and political scientists.[2] By reexamining the public interventions of Toussaint and Césaire under the light of their multilayered narratives, we, scholars and students of revolution and departmentalization, gain a deeper understanding of the historical and contemporary problem of "free and French" in the Caribbean.

La Gwadloup sé tan nou! / La Guadeloupe c'est la France

Having set up these core problems, I would like to take a step back and reapproach them by way of a recent crisis that shows just how much the projects begun by Toussaint and Césaire are relevant today. Because Part I treats part of the Haitian Revolution, it is tempting to examine the historical dimension of the earthquake that ravaged much of Haiti on 12 January 2010; it is even more tempting because the revolution itself was historically described by the French as a disaster that destroyed the slaveholding foundation of colonialism on Saint-Domingue.[3] If the earthquake exposed the calamitous consequences of disempowerment and impoverishment that followed the severing of colonial ties with the First French Republic, it also revealed a neocolonial relationship that has continued since independence. The destruction laid bare the tragic irony that France and the United States, countries largely responsible for two centuries of political isolation, military occupation, and economic exploitation, were now rushing to help. Much has been written about the earthquake, and I will not dwell further on attempts to make sense of the catastrophe, nor will I review the troubling reality of its man-made dimensions.⁴ What has not received anywhere near the same attention, however, is the general strike that paralyzed Guadeloupe a year before the earthquake.⁵

The crisis, which began in Guadeloupe in January 2009 and lasted for nearly two months, both magnified and minimized the distance between autonomy and assimilation, and had its origins in problems quite historical.⁶ The strikers' articulation of these problems disrupted the most simplified understanding of the logic of assimilation, which is that the overseas departments are integral parts of greater France. This does not mean, however, that the strike was a revolutionary call for independence. That being said, it is hard to ignore that in the past four years French leaders and their Caribbean citizens have exchanged words that have a familiar ring. On 9 January 2011, in a speech in Petit-Bourg, Guadeloupe, French President Nicolas Sarkozy reminded his audience: "Let it be clear among us, my dear Guadeloupean friends[,] . . . Guadeloupe is France, Guadeloupeans are French. And this is the territory of the French Republic."⁷ This affirmation belied the defensive posture that Sarkozy had assumed in order to resolve the crisis. The impetus for the speech—*the* reason, it could be argued, that the president declared 2011 the Année des Outre-Mer—was to repair the fragile ties between France and her overseas departments. That the French Caribbean was on shaky ground is patently clear in the admission that precedes Sarkozy's nationalist declaration:

> The last time I came to speak in front of you, it was during the Overseas Estates General, while we were in the process of finding ways, together, you haven't forgotten, to get out of a blockage that was paralyzing your territory. . . . Guadeloupe is a territory of turmoil. Guadeloupe is a territory of pride. Guadeloupe is a territory of combat.

Sarkozy's presence in Guadeloupe was part of continued efforts to respond to the general strike orchestrated by the Liyannage Kont Pwofitasyon (LKP; Alliance Against Exploitation). The massive mobilization eventually led to a series of negotiations, resulting in the signing of the Bino Accord (named for Jacques Bino, a union member killed during the crisis). The LKP, a coalition of forty-eight labor, political, and cultural organizations, delivered a long list of demands to the French government, which concerned low wages and the overall poor economic conditions of Guadeloupean workers but also extended to the high cost of staple goods, as well as housing and public services.⁸

This was, of course, not the first time an alliance of unions had presented a list of demands to metropolitan leaders: after the devaluation of the French franc in 1946, Césaire, then deputy from Martinique, demanded higher wages for workers. And, at once repeating historical responses and predicting future ones, the minister for the overseas departments disappointed Césaire.⁹ Sarkozy's attempt to persuade the overseas community was punctuated by a paternalistic rhetoric similar to that which laced his infamous speech in Dakar in July 2007.¹⁰ Before he declared with a flourish that Guadeloupe is "the territory of the French Republic," he acknowledged that it is also a "territory of turmoil." With this statement, Sarkozy also ended up ironically sounding a lot like Hugonin, the jester of Césaire's *La tragédie du roi Christophe* who declares that Haïti is a "country of commotion."[11] The subtle shifts in the president's language (from the possessive adjective to the indefinite article) seemed to betray not only a lack of confidence (overcompensated for by the president's penchant for repetition) but also the neocolonial reasoning that guides the entire speech. "I have understood your concern," Sarkozy assured them, "and your wish that the authority of the State be restored. I have heard your demand for a State that protects you, that accompanies you in the development of your territory. From now on, Guadeloupe needs stability and appeasement [*apaisement*]." Protection, stability, restoration of state authority, all building blocks of France's colonial mission (as I demonstrate in Part I), are evoked in the name of rebuilding a relationship with an overseas department.

But what did the LKP hope to rebuild? Beyond their immediate demands, the strike reflected the deeper desire of workers to topple the colonial structure of their relationship to France. As made clear in the preamble of the Bino Accord, the demand for better wages and an improved standard of living begins with the root of the problem: "the current social and economic situation existing in Guadeloupe results from the perenniality of the model of the plantation economy."[12] The strikers, who represented a broad swath of the Guadeloupean middle and lower classes, were well aware of their place in a long line of historical confrontations with the metropole: the leader of the LKP, Elie Domota, evoked the riots in Basse-Terre in May 1967, and in February 2009 the LKP marched to commemorate the strikers who were killed during a demonstration in 1952. The unrest was not just about high gas and food prices; for the LKP, it was a protest against the systemic exploitation of a society still operating on a colonial model.

This awareness was best captured by the double meaning of the Creole word *pwofitasyon*, which combines "exploitation" and "profit"; in a word, it accused the largely white business leaders on the island, the *békés*, of continuing colonial practices. The preamble goes on to decry the "obstacles to endogenous economic development and to social fulfillment" and calls for a new economic order and new social relationships. Although Sarkozy met the salary demands of the strikers and traveled to Guadeloupe to discuss additional reforms, the LKP refused to meet with him and denounced the judicial inquiry into Domota, as well as the prosecution of several union members.[13] In the view of Jean-Pierre Sainton, who took stock of the strike almost two years later in an interview with *Libération*, the LKP presented to France what amounted to a "cahier de doléances de 1788," a long list of grievances that were, in some sense, "impossible to meet." Impossible, Sainton argues, "because they affect everyday life, the very structures of Guadeloupean society, public services, etc."[14] Bonilla contends that even though the LKP wanted to put an end to *pwofitasyon*, they "did not have a parallel concept for political initiatives they wanted to implement" (132).[15] Clearly unhappy with the current state of political integration, the LKP nonetheless did not issue a call for independence. In the immediate aftermath, the French government took control of this middle ground, as evidenced by Sarkozy's strategic outline of steps taken to alleviate concern and to mark progress.

Four years later, little seems to have changed. While the Overseas Estates-General met throughout 2009 and various committees and workshops were formed to debate a series of reforms, the refusal of the LKP to participate in the process and the continued paternalism of the French state raise a troubling question: in the end, what did the strike achieve?[16] Furthermore, given the "disenchantment" of the people of Guadeloupe and their distance from a forum that has taken place mainly in France proper, did Sarkozy reinforce the francocentric logic of assimilation?[17] Or, does the defiant if ambiguous slogan of the strikers, "La Gwadloup sé tan nou / La Gwadloup sé pa ta yo" (Guadeloupe, it is ours / Guadeloupe, it is not theirs), still resonate in the face of President Sarkozy's insistence that Guadeloupe is France? And beyond the more abstract identification of a slogan-chant, how should we understand "ours" and "theirs"? It sounds like a territorial dispute leading potentially to a separation of metropole and department; it could also be heard as an internal dispute between the island's largely black workers and their white bosses. The ambiguity of this larger "ours" made its refusal both defiant and politically flexible, thus demanding radical change without, for the time being, seeking rupture from France.

Read this way, "La Gwadloup sé tan nou / La Gwadloup sé pa ta yo" contains an ambivalence similar to the historical articulations of the strikers' predecessors. To be sure, the push and pull between autonomy and assimilation has gone on since the leaders of the slave rebellion on Saint-Domingue (which included Toussaint) fought initially not for emancipation but for *libertés*, or a few days off during the week. The back and forth continued as Toussaint later issued a constitution centered on the conflicting union of "free and French." And a century and a half later, Césaire brought forward a law of departmentalization, only to push back against the dreary cultural assimilation it had become a short while later.

Free and French in the Caribbean

The forty-four-day strike, and the resulting impasse between the overseas communities and their French leader, is a cyclical problem of the French Caribbean. As a matter of politics, this means that the moment of impasse is also one of anticipation, of preparing the ground for a future articulation of the department-metropole relationship.[18] Understanding the strike also requires a critical historiography of the conflicting discourses put forward by the French president and the Guadeloupean protesters. It means going back to Toussaint and the Haitian Revolution and following his proclamation "free and French" forward to subsequent moments of fragile or fractured unity between colony/department and metropole. In this sense, the exchange between the LKP and Sarkozy compressed time between the eighteenth century and today and sets up the comparative structure of this book, which begins with an analysis of Toussaint's writings during the Haitian Revolution and then leaps ahead to Césaire's struggles with departmentalization.

Many have taken note of the similar political trajectories of Toussaint and Césaire. In some sense, the comparison became self-evident with Césaire's essay on Toussaint, a long work on which there has been a flurry of activity in recent years.[19] To my knowledge, this is the first book-length study to bring together the writings of the two men. The lack of a more thorough comparison has led to scant attention to the connection between revolution and departmentalization. Scholars had fairly criticized the "silencing" and "disavowal" of the Haitian Revolution and of the deeper ties between the *vieilles colonies* of the French Caribbean.[20] However, the past decade has seen an outpouring of scholarship on Saint-Domingue and the revolution that led to the founding of the first independent black republic.[21] The thesis of silence needs clarification, as it applied mainly to an omission in the European and American academies. Even this disclaimer feels inadequate, especially when one considers the writings of nineteenth-century historians, playwrights, poets, and abolitionists that presented a wide range of depictions of Toussaint.[22] For over a hundred years, beginning with Haitian historiographers in the mid-nineteenth century, Caribbean writers had not been silent about Saint-Domingue and Haiti.[23] The momentum continued between the two world wars and intensified from the late 1950s to the early 1960s, when a number of historical circumstances—the profound disappointment with departmentalization, the hopes for a federation of Caribbean states, the anxiety and fear of the violence in Algeria and Indochina, and the promising future of African decolonization—converged and brought a prominent group of writers, including C. L. R. James (with a second revised edition of *The Black Jacobins*), Jean Price-Mars, Édouard Glissant, and Césaire, to look back to Toussaint to offer a revised historiography of the troubling ties between republicanism and colonialism.[24] The rewriting of the past in this concatenation of texts considered alternatives to the present and future by repositioning the departments along a Caribbean spatiotemporal continuum.[25] And yet French commemoration of the second law of abolition in 1848 is representative of French political amnesia concerning Haiti, which has done much to erase the shared history of Saint-Domingue, Martinique, and Guadeloupe.[26]

In Part I I take time to draw out the protracted drama that was the Haitian Revolution. In order to ground this introduction it is helpful to begin with a summary. In 1791 a slave revolt broke out on the northern plain of Saint-Domingue, at the time the wealthiest and most productive colony in the world. Although their reasons for revolt differed significantly from the *gens de couleur libres* (a historical term meaning "free persons of color," i.e., persons of African descent, either born to free parents or freed by a master; many were landowners), who initially sought political equality with the white landowners, the slaves were soon joined by them, bringing the growing insurrection to the western and southern provinces. The revolt became a more organized rebellion that toppled the Spanish and British, the two main colonial forces that, along with the United States, vied to exert influence and to control trade routes in the Caribbean. Shortly after defeating the British in late 1798—Spain had signed a peace accord with France in July 1795—the army of Toussaint Louverture, the black general who controlled the northern and western provinces and who would soon annex the eastern half of Hispaniola (ceded by Spain to France in 1795, now the Dominican Republic), engaged in a brutal civil war with the forces of General André Rigaud, who controlled the southern province. Toussaint routed Rigaud, who fled to France, and found himself in control of the entire island. In a last great effort to retake control of their former colony, the French, then under Napoleon Bonaparte, sent a large expeditionary force in late 1801. The dramatic confrontation broke out into the final war of independence that led to the founding of the republic of Haiti.

Toussaint, then governor-general of Saint-Domingue, would not live to see independence; he died while held captive in France by Bonaparte. Having risen to the leadership of an army of former slaves fighting initially on the side of the Spanish, Toussaint joined the French Republicans in May 1794; upon defeating Rigaud six years later, he was the undisputed leader of Saint-Domingue. After his tragic confrontation with Bonaparte, Toussaint would become a world historical figure of mythic proportion. In one of his many proclamations of independence, Jean-Jacques Dessalines, the new governor-general and founder of Haïti whose troops defeated Bonaparte's army, acknowledged Toussaint as his "predecessor."[27]

Aimé Césaire, too, was exalted in mythical terms. While in Martinique during World War II, André Breton praised Césaire as a "great black poet."[28] Having recently published his epic poem, *Cahier d'un retour au pays natal*, Césaire gained literary renown that earned him political prominence in his election in May 1945 as mayor of Fort-de-France and, five months later, as deputy to the French National Assembly. A volatile mix of literature and politics defined Césaire's long life, which ended in his ninety-fifth year, in April 2008. With a brief interruption in 1957, he remained a deputy until 1993 and mayor until 2001. Like Toussaint before him, Césaire was honored as a forward-thinking leader at the crossroads of liberty and colonialism that has traversed the Caribbean from the eighteenth century to the present day.

I build on these brief biographies in the chapters that follow. However, this book is not a history of two men; it is a study of how they conceived and narrated the relationship between autonomy and assimilation. The primary materials under analysis are Toussaint's diverse body of writings (correspondence, reports, Constitution, and *Mémoire*) and Césaire's "Haitian texts," the essay *Toussaint Louverture: la révolution française et le problème colonial* and the play *La tragédie du roi Christophe*.[29] Specifically, I elaborate a narrative filiation between Toussaint and Césaire, one linked conceptually by the dichotomy "free and French," a resilient problem for persons of color who had to fight for their freedom despite it having been decreed for them.[30] Toussaint attempted to bring "free" and "French" together in his 1801 Constitution in an article that Bonaparte read as a rupture with France.[31] Césaire struggled with the gap between "French" and "Antillean" after the vote on departmentalization; he was all too aware that the legal rights sought by his fellow overseas citizens would not mean racial and social equality.[32] Césaire brought the "colonial problem" to the fore as the subtitle of *Toussaint Louverture*. Instead of bringing "free and French" together, he kept them apart: "At the moment of the colonial question, the French Revolution had started to come up against itself and, in confronting itself with the principles of which it had been born, to split, and thus to define itself" (110). For Césaire, the unresolved issue of race caused a split within the French Revolution, in which the declaration of "universal" rights was revealed to mask continued oppression.

Both Toussaint and Césaire understood that universal freedom had to overcome the profit-minded exploitation, the *pwofitasyon*, of European colonialism. Césaire recognized that the goal of universal rights remained unfinished, the legacy of two revolutions, a French precedent that Toussaint had fought to redefine and a Haitian example that Europe and the United States had done their best to silence. Toussaint's grasp of the limits of French republicanism and his multipronged repositioning of the doctrine of the rights of man over against national sovereignty is the analytic focus of Part I; Césaire's reading of Toussaint and his dramatic staging of the turmoil of the early years of the Haitian Republic is the central topic of Part II.

Historians and Literary Scholars in the Archives on Saint-Domingue

In *Haitian Revolutionary Studies* David Geggus made a startling observation: "One of the greatest servile rebellions in world history, the Haitian Revolution has been the subject of a great deal of writing and controversy but relatively little archival research" (43). As it turned out, this was a call to action to which scholars have responded in droves. As I have shown above, it is no longer the case that scholars of revolution ignore the "troubles in Saint-Domingue," leaving them hidden in the archives. A host of scholars have followed Geggus's lead, bringing forward archival evidence that is already having an impact on French, Haitian, and, more generally, Caribbean and American studies.[33] Geggus's extensive bibliography is an indispensable starting point for research in multiple archival sites; it is also a veritable genealogy of scholarship on Saint-Domingue and the Haitian Revolution, going back to historians such as the Haitians Thomas Madiou, Beaubrun and Céligny Ardouin, Joseph Saint-Rémy, Louis-Joseph Janvier, Pauléus Sannon, and Jean Fouchard, as well as to the French officer Pamphile de Lacroix, the abolitionist and legislator Victor Schœlcher, to C. L. R. James and the French historians Gabriel Debien and Pierre Pluchon.[34] Some of these accounts are imbalanced, susceptible as they have been to ideological currents or to the lack of a critical mass of documentary evidence. Nevertheless, they remain vital resources to the reconstitution of the archival trail.

There is no scarcity of literature on the French Revolution, yet it is rare for any of these texts to engage with the Haitian Revolution.[35] The paucity of sustained archival research is due in part to the dispersal of records. Geggus maps out multiple routes in the Caribbean, Europe, and the Americas; following such an itinerary certainly leads to more promising research, but it also demands a significant budget and creates no small amount of anxiety for the scholar embarking on the journey. Relying on the authority of the archives is not a straightforward matter: over the years, some documents were collected, passed censorial muster, and archived, while others were lost or went to private collections. The archives, therefore, are not the sole repositories of material on the Haitian Revolution. It is important to be aware of the censorship at work in the stamp of approval, by which local and national governments sanction a body of documents as an official record. The scholar who plumbs the silence provides a narrative that is an invaluable means of analyzing the record, for often what is missing provides a revealing counterpoint to what is present. Sibylle Fischer's *Modernity Disavowed* is a model of innovative scholarship that brings to light materials "lost" to the archives. Furthermore, most of the witness testimony on Toussaint comes from those who were not always friendly and, as Laurent Dubois states, "whose views about slavery and slaves profoundly influenced what they wrote" (6). A large majority of testimony comes from military officers, most of whom lived and breathed to see order reestablished on Saint-Domingue. For example, the ream of letters and reports submitted by General Kerverseau to Bruix, a French naval minister, was profoundly influenced by his deep mistrust of Toussaint: "I am nowhere near from sharing the unbounded confidence that many good citizens have in the virtues of General Toussaint Louverture and his attachment to the Republic."[36]

The sheer number and variety of documents strikes anyone who has spent time in multiple holdings pertaining to Saint-Domingue. The letters, decrees, reports, and proclamations are rich with implications for the study of the "Age of Revolution" in the Caribbean and Atlantic. The rhetorical power and attention to form of these documents calls out to scholars concerned with the daily lives of a wide range of colonial and metropolitan characters. In the past decade historians have turned to the archives and the early historiographical accounts to produce carefully researched analyses that have opened the door to collaboration with institutions and with scholars in other fields.[37] In addition, a number of researchers in other disciplines, including a growing group of literary scholars, have waded into these traditionally historical waters to respond to the connection between belles lettres and the revolutionary, transatlantic politics that characterized the French Caribbean.[38] These individuals have demonstrated less a desire to find new evidence—although that certainly remains within their purview—than the objective to analyze the literary, philosophical, and cultural dimensions of a diverse body of documents.

The cross-disciplinary approach of these scholars has left an indelible mark on this book. By turning to the archives to work through revolution and departmentalization, and the core problem of "free and French," I aim to speak to both historians and literary scholars. I argue that the latter, in particular, need to investigate archival sources but that both need to rethink the kinds of questions they have traditionally brought to the study of literature and history. Literary critics concerned with problems of narrative, genre, and authorship cannot ignore historical documents that address these issues; historians looking to follow the rise of Toussaint in revolutionary Saint-Domingue cannot simply hope to discover a document that would reveal his role in the years leading up to, and during, the slave revolt of 1791.[39] The depth of Toussaint's writing has been discounted; worse yet, his status as author has been called into question. Likewise, many have misread Césaire's essay on Toussaint as a biography, while still others have understood his multiple evocations of Haiti as mere substitution for his writing on negritude. Following Brent Hayes Edwards in *The Practice of Diaspora*, I am less concerned with the archive as a "repository" of the past of French republicanism than as a "discursive system that governs the possibilities, forms, appearance, and regularity of particular statements, objects, and practices" (7). In this sense, the "archive" is a dynamic set of documents penned by Toussaint that help us understand the language and forms of writing, from correspondence to reports to decrees and so on; moreover, it is a system in which boundaries of genre overlap and in which the subject or language of a letter changes or is changed by its reassertion in a report to a larger legislative body. This book treats archival sources as multilayered texts that ought to be analyzed in terms of the genres that frame them but that they also transform.

In an epigraph to this introduction I cite Pamphile de Lacroix, one of many military officers who left a memoir of service on Saint-Domingue. Lacroix draws attention to the "theater" of Toussaint's operation.[40] "Theater" refers not only to the military sense of "field of operation" but also to a dramatic awareness of words and actions, and of the place of Saint-Domingue as the staging ground of colonial desire. As narratives of historical events, the writings of Toussaint—and, in turn, Césaire's rereading of Haiti's beginnings—provide an ideal opportunity to rethink the narrative structure of history. Drawing on Hayden White's work on the deeper literary structure of historical representation, I give priority to rhetorical strategies, to the form of arguments, and to the links made between events.[41] For White, historians, too, operate over the theater of "data":

> History-writing thrives on the discovery of all the possible plot structures that might be invoked to endow sets of events with different meanings. And our understanding of the past increases precisely in the degree to which we succeed in determining how far that past conforms to the strategies of sense-making that are contained in their purest forms in literary art. (*Tropics of Discourse* 92)

White's premise is that it matters how historians "emplot" events, how they order them, and how they give meaning through literary devices. Earlier, in *Metahistory*, White had adapted a definition of emplotment from Northrop Frye: "Emplotment is the way by which a sequence of events fashioned into a story is gradually revealed to be a story of a particular kind" (7). Following Frye, White analyzes these stories in four genres: tragedy, romance, comedy, and satire. Later on, I discuss the implications of White's insistence on these "*archetypal* story forms" (8; emphasis in original); for now, I would like to stay with his most basic concern, which is the insistence on the literary structures that support historiography.

To open an archival box, crammed with disparate sets of faded documents, is to appreciate the many different kinds of narratives, and thus the many *histories* that can be written, on Saint-Domingue, Toussaint, and the Haitian Revolution. Budding historian that he was, Césaire understood this: in the introduction to *Toussaint Louverture*, he was clear about his method, which, by emphasizing the "connections" between "facts," could be read as a precedent for White. Césaire paid close attention to the forms of argument and to the context of discourse; he followed turns in speech from metropole to colony; he examined the political and historical circumstances that caused tension between the universal and the particular (the defining elements of "free and French"); and he read between the lines of public and private correspondence, especially that between Toussaint and Bonaparte. The turn to White that I make in this book is in the spirit of Césaire. That is, I do not question the authority of narrative, nor do I argue for an alternative approach to archival study. Rather, in my examination of two events, revolution and departmentalization, I explore the competing and often contradicting narratives through which they come into existence as "facts."

As will be clear throughout this book, my approach to a literary treatment of the archives is a restrained interpretation of White's metahistorical intervention. In an environmental history of the Great Plains, William Cronon explores the more far-reaching implications of White's theory.[42] Cronon points out that two historians will not only come to different conclusions about the same set of material; they will also tell two entirely different stories. Narrative directs the flow of past events while it also confronts the writer's own negotiation with embedded cultural constructions, the "hidden agendas" over which even the historian as author is not entirely in control. While apprehensive of falling down the rabbit hole of interpretive relativism, Cronon recognizes that narrative has the power to reframe and redefine the past. In his reading of Great Frontier narratives he underscores the connection between narrative choices and the subtext of the ideology of progress; in the stories of New Deal architects he observes the political will to shift stewardship of the natural environment away from the individual to a more centralized government. Framing devices, themes, tropes, and settings are, Cronon observes, "as literary as they are historical" and "compel us toward [a particular] conclusion" (1354).

Cronon's analysis of dust bowl narratives goes a long way to help us appreciate the profoundly different interpretations of Toussaint. Many have studied Toussaint's letters and found a revolutionary who broke completely with the old order and even sacrificed himself in the name of freedom for all people; others have uncovered a leader so in sync with his world that he manipulated people of all races to gain control of Saint-Domingue. The problem is not that one story is right and the other is wrong—these are things that capable readers can accurately discern—it is a question of how to escape the struggle over competing narratives. At this point, Cronon seeks a "safe harbor" so as not be to "rudderless in an endless sea of stories" (1371). He expresses considerable unease when faced with the space between narrative and the past as a historical object. The way out of this dilemma, according to Cronon, is the conviction that narrative power is limited in three ways: historical narratives are bound by evidence;

they must be plausible; and they must be kept in check by the communities for which they are written (1372–73). This argument gives direction to the narrative ship, as it were, by assuming a cohesive (though not necessarily homogeneous) community as a port of call. Fortunately, the surge of scholarship in the past decade demonstrates that a community of scholars dedicated to the history and letters of Saint-Domingue, Haiti, and the larger Caribbean exists. What has been missing, however, is an approach to Toussaint that wrestles with conflict and contradiction and downplays insight gleaned from biographical information, especially when the subject in question so relished the space between appearance and reality.[43]

Much of the research on the Haitian Revolution stakes its claim, for better or worse, by highlighting the central role of Toussaint Louverture.[44] The rise of the former slave from the plantation hierarchy of the ancien régime to the leadership of rebel slaves and to the military command of two governments speaks to an incredible if complicated transformation. A wide variety of historical accounts and literary representations from the early nineteenth century on have portrayed him as a scheming, brutal, and ugly warrior as well as a tragic, visionary hero. As his most recent biographer, Madison Smartt Bell, put it, "For two centuries, historians, biographers, playwrights, novelists, and even politicians have constructed whatever Toussaint Louverture they require."[45] Elsewhere Charles Forsdick adds, "This proliferation of representations of Toussaint—in different sites, at different moments, in different media, and with different purposes—reflects . . . the portability of Toussaint as well as the uneven, often contradictory nature of the representational processes to which he has been subject."[46] Forsdick finds that many scholars have focused too much attention on selected archival sources at the expense of "untapped material" and have thus carried out a "salvage operation" by leaning on oft-cited material to fit political or cultural imperatives instead of sifting through a critical mass of sources ("Situating Haiti" 22–23). Over time, competing representations of Toussaint have left us with an elusive historical figure, a theatrical persona, and a "shape-shifting" novelistic character (Forsdick, "Between History and Fiction" 203). The only sure thing, it seems, is that the historiographical "salvage operation" and literary reimaginings have been going on for some two hundred years.

The focus on Toussaint owes to an extraordinary life story and to the availability (however disorganized) of his extant writings; ironically, this has led to seemingly endless portrayals that have clouded our present understanding of him. A way out of this problem—and of the potential relativism of White's stance—is to marshal sufficient evidence to tell a balanced story based on his writings and those of his interlocutors. Such an approach would examine narratives through which Toussaint both (heroically) breached colonial authority and (less valiantly) reaffirmed mechanisms of colonial rule. In this manner, I suggest a return to the archives, not in the conventional attempt to recover another life story or to unearth new evidence, but rather to study Toussaint's voluminous correspondence and reports as a body of literature whose rhetoric exhibits a powerful range of purpose and meaning, from exhortation and inculcation to prosecution, defense, and lamentation. These genres carried the many voices of Toussaint and were, in turn, reappropriated by him, and it is through them as a whole that we can arrive at a more nuanced understanding of "free and French" on Saint-Domingue.

Reading Césaire: The Question of Legacy from Colony to Overseas Department

Aimé Césaire was no less extraordinary than Toussaint. Much has been written of his long life and of the monumental *œuvre* that came out of it. In early October 2008 a group of specialists came together for a colloquium, "Aimé Césaire à l'œuvre," the goals of which were twofold: to pay homage to Césaire, who had died just six months earlier, and to prepare a prospective for a new *Complete Works of Aimé Césaire*.[47] Under the aegis of the Centre National de la Recherche Scientifique, the editorial team set out to organize the totality of his body of work, including poetry, theater, essays, and speeches. The daunting task of such a collection has brought together scholars from around the world; as a result, it also has reminded us of (and, in a sense, institutionalized) the equally vast collection of critical writing on Césaire. In a recent essay that speaks in part to this reality, Mireille Rosello writes:

> Today acquiring new knowledge about Césaire means accepting not only that his work is no longer new, that the accumulation of critical knowledge filters our access to his poetry, but also that each new reading occurs in a new space and time, which means that we must negotiate the status of novelty and knowledge all over again.[48]

Reflecting on what she calls the "dialectics of old and new," Rosello describes a process of continuous mediation between, among other aspects of his writing (such as the play between clarity and opacity), a masterpiece like the *Cahier* and critical readings of it. Close observation of this exchange is essential to the more limited study of Césaire that I propose in this book. The "newness" that I attempt to bring out must come to terms with both the evolution of his writing—the various genres in which this transformation played out—and the changing circumstances of its reception.

Part II focuses on a particular optic of Césaire's writing, that which panned from Toussaint and Saint-Domingue to Christophe and a divided republic/kingdom. As such, it is imperative to raise two limitations of this section. These concern the relationship of the texts under analysis to other primary sources and the move away from the archives that predominates in Part I. First, this book is not meant to be an exhaustive study of Césaire, as is most evident in the decision not to include his poetry, which some will perhaps find problematic. I treat the dichotomy "free and French" as it passed through a crucial transition in his writing from the essay to the theater. Notwithstanding the difficulty of accessing some of Césaire's writings (notably the political essays), the second limitation in the weaker archival foundation for Part II is due to the fact that both *Toussaint Louverture* and *la tragédie du roi Christophe* are widely available.

Furthermore, both works have been the subject of much commentary, including new research that I discuss below. To be sure, the analyses herein would have benefited from access to personal archives, which remain largely inaccessible. Where possible, I bring forward a number of secondary works; however, as Hale and Véron observe, the scattering of public and personal archives on Césaire is a known problem.[49] Therefore, this book will not have had access to new material eventually provided by Césaire specialists still *à l'œuvre*.[50] Despite its more limited archival sources, Part II continues to stand on the principal method employed in Part I, which is that both literary scholars and historians must attend to the textuality of historical materials. In my readings of Césaire, the focus remains on the narrative forms (literary, political, and historical) of the exploration of Haiti's beginnings and the concomitant reflection on the (past, present, and future) problem of departmentalization.

If anyone understood the predicament of Toussaint's project for *la liberté générale* it was Césaire. Writing fourteen years after the law of departmentalization had passed, Césaire looked back to Toussaint to make sense of a perennial problem with the French interpretation of the rights of man. His analysis underscored the power of Toussaint's affirmation of the universal: "When Toussaint Louverture came, it was to take literally the declaration of the rights of man, it was to show that there is no pariah race; that there is no marginal country; that there is no outcast people" (*Toussaint Louverture* 344). For Césaire, the logic of the French Revolution contained universal principles that Toussaint had to enforce: "it was necessary to brutalize seriously the historical actor so that he would consent to play his role to the end" (216). Césaire puts pressure on the split between the particular (the French unwillingness to "play its role") and the universal ("there is no pariah race"). The title of the essay, which highlights Toussaint but also places him in apposition to the "logic" of the French Revolution and its colonial undercurrent, mirrors the tension between the particular and the universal. Césaire chose not to reject the French Revolution, nor did he celebrate it without qualification. He sought to bring a people into a new existence against a French discourse of rights and freedoms that continued to exclude them.

The period following departmentalization saw Césaire at the juncture of literature, politics, and history. For the politician it was a frustrating and exhilarating time, during which he both defended and lamented departmentalization just as several African countries moved to independence; during which he took often to the floor of the National Assembly to denounce failed attempts of the metropole to implement departmentalization; during which he published the scathing *Discours sur le colonialisme*, an essay that addressed directly the blatant contradiction between French colonialism and the liberation it celebrated in June 1944;[51] during which he broke with the French Communist Party in the concentrated prose of the *Lettre à Maurice Thorez*;[52] and during which he founded a new political party, Parti Progressiste Martiniquais (PPM), as well as its journal, *Le Progressiste*, in 1958. Césaire's close readings of revolutionary debates of the nascent French Republic led him to become a committed student of the French and Haitian Revolutions. If departmentalization was a move backward, then Césaire was determined to find motivation through Toussaint (via Schœlcher) in order to create a new political relationship with the French. In this sense, Césaire also looked ahead to a future configuration that he would help bring about by revisiting a revolutionary past.[53]

In one respect, Césaire's portrayal of Toussaint is evidence of his penchant for writing History through the eyes of the hero. His depiction of several historical Caribbean and African leaders is well known. In his poetry, he evoked Toussaint and Louis Delgrès (an officer in the French Army on Guadeloupe who rebelled in the face of Bonaparte's reestablishment of slavery); he wrote essays on Toussaint and Sekou Touré (his contemporary and the first president of Guinea); and, in addition to Christophe, he cast the Congolese leaders, Lumumba and Mobuto, in *Une saison au Congo*. The central roles that these statesmen play in Césaire's works is evidence of the cult of personality—the "decisive man," as he described Touré in the preface to the Guinean leader's *Expérience guinéenne et unité africaine*—that was part of Césaire's historical perspective.[54] And yet he did not represent these men in the same light. It would be an unfair simplification to state that Césaire witnessed historical events through archetypal figures alone. He was aware of personal, historical, cultural, generational, and geopolitical differences, and he attended to these moments of transition (*from* Toussaint *to* Christophe, as I demonstrate in Part II).

My readings of Césaire examine the interaction between literary exploration and political transformation, especially during the critical engagement with Saint-Domingue/Haiti, one that has taken a backseat to repeated criticism of the more problematic underpinnings of *négritude*.[55] Scholars have long appreciated Césaire's relationship to Haiti; with few exceptions, they have not given serious attention to his analysis of Toussaint's writings and of the passage to Christophe.[56] To be fair, many have focused on poetry and theater; nevertheless, Césaire's connection to Haiti has been downplayed as either an emotional draw or as part of his complicated relationship to Marxism. The claim I make here is that it is impossible to explore how Césaire charts the future of departmentalization, including his evolving projects of Caribbean autonomy and federation, without considering the historical mediation of his critiques of Toussaint and Christophe.

Toussaint and Césaire are, of course, the protagonists of this book, and they are, without doubt, heroic figures. However, by imagining them in a textual dialogue with each other, I bring their narratives to the fore and set them within the larger, interconnected stories of Caribbean autonomy and assimilation. This approach has the potential to find something new in Toussaint and Césaire, but it is also one around which a few problems accumulate. In order for the filiation between the two to illuminate the historical depth of the current discord between France and its overseas departments, it must take into account questions of time and space that delineate boundaries of colony (Saint-Domingue), nation (Haiti), and department (Martinique/Guadeloupe).

In addition to sifting through political differences across generations (Toussaint as governor-general, Césaire as deputy) and considering changes in narrative forms from the eighteenth century to the present (Toussaint's *Mémoire* and the modern understanding of memoir; Toussaint's letters and reports to French authorities, such as the *Refutation of Vaublanc*, and Césaire's *Discours sur le colonialisme* or the *Lettre à Maurice Thorez*), it is equally important to attend to the relationship between colonial past and postcolonial present.

Returning to the colonial past as a means of construing its relation to the present and future is a matter of great debate in postcolonial studies.[57] One obvious concern has been the question of proper historical boundaries. Critics point to errors that result from analysis of the colonial past in terms of the "postcolonial" present. Not only does this bring historical actors uncomfortably into the future, but, in the context of Western inquiry, it also tends to downplay cultures and literatures existing before European contact. Many have also questioned the linearity of the term *postcolonial*—written with some unease, often in quotation marks, or with a hyphen or a back slash—as if the period "after" (European) colonialism represented a clean break from the colonial.[58] It also suggests a center/periphery distinction, such that the "postcolonial" remains tethered to the colonial.

My own critical gesture, circumscribed around the French Caribbean and Atlantic from the late eighteenth to the mid-twentieth century, is a careful reading of the past in the attempt to make sense of these legacies today. I am inspired by the probing theoretical questions of David Scott in *Conscripts of Modernity*. Scott's overarching concern is the manner in which scholars tell stories of anticolonialism for our postcolonial present. Through a close reading of James's *The Black Jacobins*, Scott argues that the model narrative of a romantic, anticolonial overcoming no longer matters today. "I think we live in tragic times," he announces in a prologue that sets the mood of his provocative if somber analysis (2). Scholars who continue to present anticolonial struggles in a narrative of resistance are motivated, Scott argues, by a "longing" for movements that are part of the past. For Scott, this results in disjointed scholarship that neglects to rethink questions about the configuration of the past in the present. Like Scott, I am concerned throughout this book with taking a critical stance toward the narratives of Toussaint and Césaire that makes sense for the times in which we live. His theory of a "problem-space" is illustrative of the approach I have laid out here and helps me close this introduction.

A problem-space opens as a discursive intervention, a narrative argument composed of, Scott writes, "an ensemble of questions and answers around which a horizon of identifiable stakes (conceptual as well as ideological-political stakes) hangs" (4). Scott insists over and over that the kinds of critical questions asked about a historical landscape that has changed "must produce salient effects" so that they can be "worth responding to" (118). The call that Scott makes with no small amount of urgency—that "we" pay attention to the temporality of our questions and recognize that certain historical demands no longer hold meaning for "us" today—is one that scholars should heed. The problem at the outset, however, is that Scott is vague about who "we" and "us" are, and, therefore, about who decides the value of inquiry, or what is "worth responding to." Presumably, one community (of students, workers, artists, politicians, etc.) might decide that dramatic, anticolonial stories of the Haitian Revolution remain relevant and, as Bonilla argues, imaginative and forward thinking, while others might view them as an alibi for contemporary problems. The point is not that saliency should be determined by every imaginable community but rather that defining these communities and their stake in the particular story of revolution seems just as important as the value of the stories themselves.

Let me be clear, then, about the stakes of this book, written as it is for scholars and students of the literature and history of the French Caribbean. What is at stake is the continued relevance of the Haitian Revolution and the departmentalization of the French Caribbean; in particular, these events have much in common in the articulation of the conflict between freedom and sovereignty. What is at stake here is a literary-historical approach to the narrative arguments of Toussaint and Césaire; to be more precise, it is that a discursive filiation can reveal the attempts of both men to respond to the colonial foundation of French republicanism. From this line of inquiry, it is possible to imagine additional questions that deserve attention: How does the problem of political and cultural assimilation evolve between colonial Saint-Domingue and postwar Martinique? How does Toussaint's utterance, "free and French," differ from the ambiguous slogan of the LKP strikers in Guadeloupe? Following Scott, to answer these questions is to consider first and foremost their temporal dimensions, which are at once similar *and* different. "Problem-spaces alter historically because problems are not timeless and do not have everlasting shapes," he writes (4). The problem of freedom that Toussaint faced, for example, was not the same as the one that confronted Césaire in the winter of 1945–46: the return of slavery was a very real possibility for Toussaint, whereas for Césaire, it could be argued, it was a question of equality, and quite radical in its elimination of colonial law. The kind of shared sovereignty sought by Toussaint differed significantly from the juridical integration that Césaire pushed for in departmentalization. As obstacles to these projects, however, the problems of racial discrimination and imperial hegemony, while not of an "everlasting shape," certainly took on forms no less painful for Césaire than they had been for Toussaint.

It is no doubt true that new historical conditions tend to dim "old" stories of anticolonialism. Rather than lose sight of them, I propose to study the constitution of Toussaint's problem-space and Césaire's response to it in the new world of departmentalization. The context of language and narrative allows for reading between the lines, across time, of this filiation. This is not to suggest that the movement from one problem-space to the next is seamless; as an intervention, Césaire's revision is by definition a process that adapts and even contests. Despite important differences between the two, the bond between Toussaint and Césaire, as I have conceived it in this book, is only strengthened across time. The choice to construe their relationship as a filiation is also due to the French Republican conception of the metropole-colony relationship as a family, one in which France played the role of father to its colonial children. Under the First French Republic, the colonial family romance, which I take up in Part I, was driven by a paternalistic ideology that continued, to a great degree, in the hierarchical relationship between President Sarkozy and the people of Guadeloupe.

At the beginning of this introduction, I discussed the 2009 strike in Guadeloupe to illustrate the cyclical problem of the tenuous bond between "free and French." As a legacy, in which the past is inherited by, and has meaning for, successive generations, the particular bequest of "free and French" has been a tenacious problem. The French colonial legacy of racism, legalized by the *Code Noir*, shaped republicanism from the outset and left more division than unity. Emancipation, as Wilder has argued, created the problem of competing memories between French politicians eager to commemorate anniversaries of the 1848 abolition of slavery and their Caribbean counterparts, notably Césaire and Frantz Fanon, who decried the historical deferral of rights and the continued racism of European "Enlightenment."[59] Following Thomas C. Holt, Wilder examines the "problem of freedom"—whereby "it is only *after* emancipation . . . that race became an organizing principle of social relations"—as the colonial legacy with which Césaire attempted to come to terms ("Race, Reason, Impasse" 37).[60] Wilder further contends that "departmentalization in 1946 simply codified the link between Republican assimilation and colonial racism that had defined the long-term history of the francophone Antilles" (37). It is precisely the critique of this link that Toussaint handed down to Césaire. This is not to say that Césaire received it uncritically, or that his revisions were, in turn, praised universally. It has been all too clear, particularly in the history of the Caribbean, that a legacy has the power to divide and to fuel controversy. In fact, Toussaint's own children, Isaac and Placide, became embroiled in a legal dispute over the latter's attempt to claim a legal right to the Louverture name when he married. According to Isaac, Placide, who was actually his half brother, "usurped [his] filiation."[61] Among the heirs of Césaire, from Fanon to Glissant to the *créolistes* to Maryse Condé, there has been much disagreement (to put it mildly) over what each generation has inherited from its antecedents.[62] Therefore, the model of filiation that I propose herein must negotiate the inherent capacity of legacies to create both loyalty and opposition.[63]

It is precisely this inherent conflict engendered by legacy, caught between loyalty and opposition, that, I want to argue, best captures the tension in the declaration "free and French." The space of Toussaint's "loyal opposition" was, and remains, greatly misunderstood, even though he worked through it in thousands of pages and in an array of genres. It is not that Toussaint's expression of his predicament was poorly written; on the contrary, as many readers have concluded, including Césaire, it was ahead of its time. Therefore, given that the French government officially celebrated 2011 as the "year of overseas France" – the same year in which president Sarkozy commemorated

Césaire at the Pantheon – perhaps the time is right to inquire of the past and future of "free and French" in the Caribbean.

As I endeavor to bring together past and present, it is useful to lay out the structure of my book here. *Free and French in the Caribbean* is organized in two parts and six chapters. The first two chapters treat Toussaint's narration of family, and specifically the mediation between Saint-Domingue and the French metropolitan government. The first chapter, "Toussaint Louverture and the Family of Saint-Domingue," examines the literary dimension of letters and reports to representatives of the French government. The chapter reads his letters as both an apprenticeship and a lesson for those whose conceptions of freedom and sovereignty came into conflict with his own. Toussaint's vision was clear when it came to abolishing slavery but less transparent over the question of his attachment to the French Republic. This chapter follows his entry onto the narrative scene of Saint-Domingue and on the refocusing of the French colonial mission that occurred in the years between 1794 and 1798, or the period after he shifted allegiance from the Spanish to the French and before the proclamation of the 1801 Constitution. This is the crucial time when he defeated the Spanish, signed a treaty with the British, consolidated his power by defeating his rival, Rigaud, in the south, and opened negotiations with the United States. The second chapter, "Under the Stick of Maître Toussaint," studies the changing political landscapes in France and Saint-Domingue during the critical year 1797–98. It was at this moment, I argue, that Toussaint rewrote the colonial family romance and expressed doubt in the future of the extended family of France and Saint-Domingue.

The third and fourth chapters deal with the epic battle between Toussaint and Bonaparte. In Chapter 3, "'Free and French': 'La Constitution de la colonie française de Saint-Domingue,'" I read the 1801 Constitution as a pivotal document in which Toussaint both courts and defies the French. The Constitution recognized French sovereignty and that "all men are born, live, and die free and French"; it would also grant Toussaint the power of governor-for-life, an investment of power that Bonaparte read as a step toward independence. "Free," yes, but Bonaparte now more than ever questioned Toussaint's idea of what it meant to be "French." More important, Toussaint would attempt to articulate in the Constitution the fundamental problem of his leadership, the codependence of liberty and power. It is a layered narrative in which the abolition of slavery meets the necessity of governmental power and the restriction of freedom. The last document Toussaint would publish as a free man, the Constitution has been long dismissed as a work of political circumstance instead of a profoundly conflicted narrative that works through the meanings of universal freedom for a country of former slaves.

The Constitution was a short-lived experiment, as less than a year later Bonaparte captured Toussaint and shipped him across the Atlantic to a prison in the Jura. Chapter 4, "Toussaint at a Crossroads: The *Mémoire* of the 'First Soldier of the Republic of Saint Domingue,'" examines the transition from the Constitution to the writings during his incarceration, including several letters to Bonaparte and the crucial *Mémoire du Général Toussaint Louverture*. Misunderstood as a short, disappointing autobiography, the *Mémoire* is actually a report in which Toussaint, the wronged general in chief, defends himself to his superior, Bonaparte. The text begins with an expression of obligation to the French government, and thus hews, with important exceptions, to the classic genre of a military memoir under the ancien régime. After discussing the *Mémoire*'s place in the genre and bringing forward the complex etymology of the word *mémoire* itself, the chapter argues for the text's importance as a summary of key moments of his leadership, especially the priorities for the Constitution. Framed in a tripartite structure, the text offers a spirited defense but also recognizes a debt to the French, and reveals the contradictory stance of the *mémoire*, in which Toussaint delivers the skillful retort of "loyal opposition" to French Republican-Imperial ideology in the Caribbean.

The spirit of "loyal opposition" that found expression in Toussaint's Constitution and *Mémoire* resurfaced in the conflict between equal rights and French sovereignty during the departmentalization of the Caribbean. It was the moment when Césaire looked back to Toussaint to make sense of what would turn out to be a very unequal process of juridical integration into the French Republic. The transition to the second part of the book is the dialogue I imagine between Césaire and Toussaint. Chapter 5, "Césaire Reads Toussaint: The Haitian Revolution and the Problem of Departmentalization," opens with a comparison of Césaire's reading of Toussaint to that of James, whose second edition of *The Black Jacobins* came out just after Césaire's essay. The comparison of Césaire and James, mediated by the interventions of Scott and White, establishes the theoretical underpinnings of my literary-historical approach, one that pays close attention to questions of the temporality and the narrative art of Césaire's revisionist writing. The chapter gives shape to the historical and political contexts that shaped Césaire's first visit to Haiti, a six-month lecture tour from May to December 1944, followed by an analysis of the form of the essay. The historiographical and literary modes of the essay allow Césaire to revisit the connection between the French and Haitian Revolutions in order to negotiate political and cultural assimilation into France after departmentalization. Césaire works through the problem of assimilation, seemingly intractable in the postwar Caribbean, by bringing the writings of Toussaint out of the past in the effort to portray the revolution not as a historical impasse but as an ongoing, refractory process.

The sixth and final chapter, "Haitian Building: *La tragédie du roi Christophe*," shifts to Césaire's dramatization of the future of the Haitian Revolution in *Christophe*. It examines the shift from the essay to playwriting to argue that the interaction between genres is critical to Césaire's historical understanding of Toussaint, as well as the transition that occurred between revolution and nation building. The movement between the two is not entirely linear, and mirrors the cycle of birth and death privileged throughout the play. The chapter treats the relationship between the closed drama of the historical action and setting of the play and the forward-looking allegories of African and Antillean decolonization but is careful to underscore the Haitian optic of the play through several close readings of scenes that play out the drama of rupture and continuity, forces that define Haitian history. Finally, the chapter closes by reinforcing the Césaire-Toussaint connection through analysis of the crises of representation that leave the play, I argue, caught between the past and the future. These crises are at once literary, in the movement from the essay to the theater, and political, in the meditation on the struggle between freedom for the Haitian people and their continued suffering. Through the contradictory symbol of the Citadel, Césaire portrays Christophe, like Toussaint before him, as a tragic hero who attempts to build Haiti into existence from colonial rule.

PART I

TOUSSAINT LOUVERTURE

1 Toussaint Louverture and the Family of Saint-Domingue

THE HISTORIAN JOSEPH Boromé tracked down over sixteen hundred letters, reports, decrees, and proclamations by Toussaint Louverture.¹ These documents, now dispersed in public and private collections, represent one of the largest records of the Haitian Revolution and certainly the largest left by a man who had spent more than half his life as a slave in the French colony. Perhaps due to the sheer number of documents or to the years it took to locate them all, it appears that Boromé was never able to complete the biography he had planned, *Toussaint Louverture: A Life with Letters*.² Nevertheless, his tireless efforts led to a vital index of Toussaint's extant writings. Beginning with two letters in August 1793, while still fighting for royalist Spain, Toussaint announced his presence in an apparent show of support for general emancipation.³ These addresses were made just as Sonthonax, the French Republican civil commissioner on Saint-Domingue, abolished slavery and less than a year before Toussaint switched sides to France in circumstances that remain unclear, as Geggus has shown in his analysis of Toussaint's "volte-face."⁴ Almost ten years later, by then general in chief and governor of Saint-Domingue, Toussaint signed off in late 1802 by imploring Bonaparte for mercy. He died the following spring.

To date, the *Complete Works of Toussaint Louverture* does not exist.⁵ As Boromé attested in private correspondence, the attempt to recover nearly a decade's worth of documents, many forever lost and/or destroyed, is something akin to a Sisyphean task.⁶ Faced with such a vast and disorganized archive, I have given priority in the analyses that follow to selected letters and documents for close inspection, summarized or noted others, and left out some that perhaps should have found space here. I have followed up on Boromé's leads, where possible, in order to bring forward a limited perspective on three major phases of Toussaint's engagement with French republicanism and colonialism on Saint-Domingue: (1) the appropriation and development of French Republican discourse in relation to his positioning between Saint-Domingue and France, (2) the constitutional founding of his vision for Saint-Domingue, and (3) the final justification of his service. Toussaint's writing took shape in these overlapping periods of his tenure. In lieu of proceeding in a strictly chronological manner, I have elected to begin with a pivotal letter that he wrote to his sons as he consolidated power on Saint-Domingue during the summer of 1798. As I frame it, the letter addresses a family drama set inside the larger narrative of colonialism and republicanism, which the French themselves cast in terms of family. Toussaint penned the letter at a moment when the French government took a different approach to its colonial mission, one that included the education of Placide and Isaac Louverture.

My approach to a potentially unwieldy number of letters and documents is to give priority to Toussaint's narration of family and more specifically the mediation between his family on Saint-Domingue and his relationship to metropolitan French governments. The letter crystallizes the stakes of a family drama, a constellation of colonizer and colonized whose configuration can be traced by going back to the earliest recorded moments of his writings and by looking ahead to those moments that tutored him to proclaim the 1801 Constitution. My focus is on the narrative strategies in which Toussaint inscribed the abolition of slavery and the assertion of his leadership in a prevailing discourse of equal rights that continued to accommodate the needs of colonialism. I am interested in the structures of his responses to French governments and in the possible revisions to French discourse that came out of them. As such, the first two chapters explore the family romance of Saint-Domingue in the critical four-year period from 1794 to 1798. Here I analyze his entry onto the narrative scene and on the refocusing of the French colonial mission on Saint-Domingue. In the next chapter I zoom in on Toussaint's response to the changing political landscape in Paris during the critical year 1797–98. It was the time during which he rewrote the family romance and, as suggested in the letter to his sons, when he expressed doubt in the future of such family. By following the letter backward and forward and by reading it alongside a number of other documents, I intend to shed light on a set of interconnected histories of the Haitian Revolution. To set up my analyses, it is useful to review briefly the scholarship on the "families" that molded Toussaint and thus to attempt to capture a history of his formative years.

Prefiguring the Rise of Toussaint Louverture

What little is known about Toussaint's life before the slave revolt comes in snatches of documentary evidence; much of the story has been passed on from largely unverifiable sources, from a range of characters, both allies and enemies. These included generals, pamphleteers, biographers, and historians. To this group it would also be necessary to add Toussaint's son, Isaac Louverture, whose "Notes historiques sur l'expédition de Leclerc à St Domingue et sur la famille Louverture" were appended to Antoine Métral's *Histoire de l'expédition des français à Saint-Domingue*.[7] While Isaac has little information regarding his father before the revolution began, he relates much of Toussaint's activities leading up to the Leclerc expedition; furthermore, he cites his father frequently, so he must have had access to a number of letters and reports. Nevertheless, as virtually all scholars stipulate, it is nearly impossible to separate archival evidence from legendary story.

Toussaint was born a slave on the outskirts of Le Cap on the Bréda plantation, where, instead of being in the fields, he worked with the livestock before becoming coachman to the manager, Bayon de Libertat.[8] The blend of the factual and the legendary is at work even in oft-cited archival sources, including the dramatic account of Kerverseau, brigadier general and commissioner of the formerly Spanish side of Saint-Domingue and a determined enemy of Toussaint. In a report of 21 March 1801 to Bruix, minister of the navy and colonies, Kerverseau wrote, "Raised in the master's house by Baillon Libertat ... with a tenderness and care that in Europe one would hardly suspect that slave children had been able to find on Saint-Domingue, he responded to the kindness of his benefactor with loyalty, and distinguished himself by a superior intelligence and exemplary conduct."[9] According to Métral, Isaac wrote that Pierre Baptiste, a black man who had been educated by a missionary, taught history, French, and Latin to the young Toussaint.[10] From scarce archival material, Geggus crafts a back story that lays the groundwork for analysis of the future Toussaint, about whom the evidence is extensive. By way of calculated conjecture, Geggus contemplates the implications of Toussaint's time as a slave for his future as intermediary and leader:

> Despite his degree of acculturation, Toussaint did not lose touch with his African roots. He is said to have spoken fluently the language of his "Arada" (Ewe-Fon) father, who apparently was the son of a chief, and to have enjoyed speaking it with other slaves of his father's ethnic group. He seems also to have become skilled in the medicinal use of plants and herbs. Such slaves who lived at the interface between white and black society needed to know the ways of both worlds. To maintain their standing in both communities, they had to be shrewd observers of human nature and skilled performers in a number of roles. (16)

Geggus does what he can with the available material, careful to frame his analysis in the language of suggestion and to shift the weight of his conclusion from the singular, "he", to the plural, "such slaves." His account is convincing because it sets up a way to understand Toussaint's ability later in life to move easily between the different "worlds" of Saint-Domingue. It is readily apparent from hundreds of letters and reports that Toussaint had learned to belong to different communities and to communicate among them. Moving backward from this narrative evidence, one eventually reaches the space where the evidentiary meets the legendary, and where one has to imagine the young Toussaint navigating Creole (born in the Caribbean) and African cultural and linguistic boundaries, as well as the fields and the domestic quarters of the Bréda plantation. In any event, we know for sure that Toussaint was able to gain his freedom: he was manumitted by 1776, most likely by Bayon de Libertat.[11] As an *ancien libre*—freed before the 1794 abolition of slavery—Toussaint leased a coffee plantation and owned slaves, becoming part of a different class of freed persons.[12]

Toussaint left few archival traces during the fifteen years leading up to the August 1791 slave uprising. The large-scale revolt in the northern province would bring him to the fore. After nearly four months of fighting in the north, the black insurgents, led by Jean-François, Biassou, and, for a short time, Jeannot, sought not general emancipation but rather an increase in the number of "liberties" on the plantation and the release of fellow slaves, including Jean-François's wife and Biassou's mother. In the western and southern provinces, whites and the *gens de couleur* went back and forth between battles and tenuous peace agreements. In exchange for amnesty and an end to the insurrection, the black leaders attempted to work out a deal with Governor Blanchelande, the Colonial Assembly, and the newly arrived members of the First Civil Commission sent by the National Constituent Assembly.[13] However, the Constituent Assembly hemmed and hawed over the "colonial question" and debated at length colonial representation in the new government and the extension of political rights to free nonwhites. On 24 September, French legislators changed course from the May decree by ordering that the "laws concerning the state of unfree persons and the political status of men of color and free blacks" would be determined by the Colonial Assembly.[14] For James, this decision demonstrated that the Constituent Assembly, "standing to lose so much, allowed themselves to be frightened by the colonial deputies" (80). The commissioners also brought news of the Constituent Assembly's decree of 28 September that proclaimed a general amnesty for "acts of revolution" that, in theory, applied to the colonies.[15] The Colonial Assembly, composed mainly of planters, refused to grant amnesty to the rebellious slaves, a move that put them at odds with the commissioners, whose authority had been weakened by the decree of 24 September. The negotiations came to a standstill as the colonists further defied the commissioners by rejecting the initial demands of the black leaders. The commissioners continued to negotiate with the rebels to arrange for a release of white prisoners in a sign of good faith. As a delegation of leaders arrived in Le Cap under the protection of an escort that included Toussaint, the president of the Colonial Assembly, who had come to attend the meeting with the commissioners, continued to deny the request for amnesty.

Traces of Toussaint begin to materialize over the course of this political drama. The earliest known record of his role in the rebellion comes from a white magistrate, Gros, whose *Récit historique* is an account of his time as a prisoner of the black rebel leaders in late 1791.[16] According to Popkin, "Gros's work had more immediate impact than any other first-person narrative of the insurrection" (105).[17] Gros, who was not only a prisoner but also in service to the rebels as secretary to Jean-François, noted that

Toussaint was an aide-de-camp of Biassou at the time of the negotiations with metropolitan and colonial representatives. Through Gros's narrative, we learn that when the negotiations ultimately broke down after the prisoner exchange in Le Cap, it was Toussaint who "saved" the prisoners: "Toussaint, of Bréda, Biassou's aide-de-camp, braving all danger, attempted to save us, though he might have been himself victim to this monster's [Biassou's] rage. He represented to him, that we could not, and ought not to be thus sacrificed, without being imprisoned, and calling a Court Martial upon us" (cited in Popkin, *Facing Racial Revolution* 110). Gros juxtaposed the violence of Biassou to the reason and forward thinking of Toussaint. For Popkin, the depiction of Toussaint from the eyewitness, Gros, is one of a "skilled politician who would prove equally adept at dealing with blacks and whites" (110). Popkin's analysis would seem to confirm Geggus's categorization of Toussaint as a "shrewd observer and skilled performer." Gros's positive account of some of the black insurgents, and Toussaint in particular, offers a real glimpse of Toussaint's growing skills and capacity for leadership and goes a long way to explain his rise from the Bréda plantation to the ranks of the black rebellion, which included his own command."[18]

The Gros account does more than give a hint of Toussaint's skills in political mediation. For scholars of Toussaint, if the narrative is significant because it represents a voice from within the black rebel camps and explains the process of their communication with French representatives, it also suggests that Toussaint was involved in the production of addresses. In these addresses from Jean-François and Biassou to the Colonial Assembly and the commissioners throughout December 1791, the black leaders gave their reading of the decree of general amnesty, alternating between threats of more violence and offers to help contain the revolt by assuring a return to order.[19] Gros wrote of his consultations with both Jean-François and Biassou over the question of liberties, and when a dispute arose between the two he specifically mentioned Toussaint: "a host of insurmountable obstacles presented itself, and had it not been for the assistance of the Negro, Toussaint, belonging to Bréda, the conference would have terminated unsuccessfully" (cited in Popkin, *Facing Racial Revolution* 147). The Gros account provides evidence that Toussaint served as an intermediary between his superiors. Not surprisingly, it has led some to conclude that Toussaint actually had a greater authorial role. This argument is strengthened by the fact that he was a signatory to the major address that two deputies of the black leaders presented to the Colonial Assembly on 4 December.[20] Pluchon's interpretation of the Colonial Assembly's haughty and delayed rejection of the more moderate demands of the rebels is representative of many historians: "This refusal, as unrealistic as it was unwise, sounded the death knell of the French colony of Saint-Domingue."[21] The death knell coincided with the increased responsibilities undertaken by Toussaint.

In contrast to the more restrained analyses of Geggus and Popkin, James and Césaire read the stamp of political authority on the 4 December address as license for a more dramatic rendering of Toussaint's role at a turning point of the slave rebellion.

James concluded, "In its skilful use of both the moral and political connection between the mother-country and the colony ... the letter could have come from the pen of a man who had spent all his life in diplomacy" (105). In his analysis Césaire described the "moment" of Toussaint Louverture: "the moment of inspiring days ahead; the moment of consequence [*de la retombée*]; the moment of cold reflection that corrects errors and rights the ship [*redresse les méthodes*]" (*Toussaint Louverture* 195). These lines are the prelude to a lengthy analysis of the aforementioned negotiations. For Césaire, Toussaint's epiphany occurred at the conclusion of the drawn out attempts to deal with intransigent planters: he became "the first great anti-colonialist that history had known," one who would from then on fight for general liberty (205). This reading harmonized nicely with James, who had written nearly twenty-five years earlier, "Then and only then did Toussaint come to an unalterable decision from which he never wavered and for which he died. Complete liberty for all, to be attained and held by their own strength" (107). These hyperbolic analyses gloss over the more complicated view of general liberty held by Toussaint, yet they also contain a good deal of truth. Although James and Césaire wrote with considerably more flourish and historiographical license than Geggus, all three scholars emphasize Toussaint's skills at diplomacy. While Geggus stays close to the historical moment, both James and Césaire portray a world historical figure. The uneven historiographical record on the Haitian Revolution has shown that the historian's text, including that supported by ample archival evidence, is not necessarily free of ideological persuasion. This is not to endorse without question the less precise historiographical method that undergirds the dramatic prose of Césaire and James. As I discussed in introduction, what is at stake is an understanding of the narrative art of historiography and, therefore, of the implications for interpretation found at the juncture of history, literature, and, in the case of Toussaint, mythology.

This digression to the varied analyses of Toussaint's formative experiences, particularly in the rebel camps, offers two key lessons for reading his later writings. First, much of what scholars know, and have deduced, about Toussaint begins with a man who moved between worlds, someone who likely concealed the practice of power with the art of diplomacy. And second, in the absence of a more complete archive, to be able to arrive at any conclusion about Toussaint and his meteoric rise requires scholars to attend carefully to the narrative structures of history and mythology. Like Geggus, the scholar may draw reasonable conclusions strictly from the evidence; following James and Césaire, it is also possible to read into Toussaint's narratives an awareness of larger concerns that transcend the historical moment and extend into the future.

The attention to the concerns of history and myth is exemplified in analyses of Toussaint's adopted surname, Louverture. Or, to paraphrase Césaire, it is to follow how Toussaint of Bréda became Toussaint Louverture (*Toussaint Louverture* 204–5). Toussaint began signing "Louverture" in late August 1793: "I am Toussaint Louverture, my name has perhaps become known to you [Je suis Toussaint Louverture, mon nom s'est peut-être fait connaître jusqu'à vous]."[22] So begins the letter in which Toussaint famously took ownership of Louverture.²³ Since then observers and readers alike have had to pay attention to the power of both the man and the name. This doubling effect has led to a host of nicknames: Pluchon alternated between "the Dictator of Gonaïves," "the Black [*Noir*]," and "the Creole," unable to conceal his scorn and, despite himself, admiration for Toussaint. Boromé privately described him as a "double-dealer [*fourbe*]," while Geggus resigns himself to the mysteriousness of Toussaint: "The man remains, as ever, an enigma" (135).²⁴ It is perhaps impossible to avoid rendering judgment on Toussaint as a world historical figure. Perhaps the space between historical and mythical representation has collapsed in the figure of Toussaint. Yet it is clear that the biographical approach has led to competing representations.²⁵ For my purposes, it is necessary to appreciate historical renderings based on both archival evidence and well-supported imagination in order to read the "discursive opening" of letters and reports that begin in earnest in the spring of 1794.²⁶

The Haitian Revolution enabled the "literary orbit" of Toussaint Louverture (Dubreuil, 121). Dubreuil finds him a "character for himself and for others. King of tragedy, despotic and sublime," going so far as to attribute to Toussaint the distinction of the "opening of indigenous speech in French": "In many respects, Toussaint Louverture makes possible [*favorise*] the birth of francophone literature" (121). As others have done before him, Dubreuil plays on the polysemic dimension of "Louverture" to consider the ways in which his words and deeds "ring out" for the generations that followed him. There is no doubt that Toussaint was a "pioneer" in the critique of French colonialism, but it is important to nuance this declaration by looking more closely at the variety of writings in which he narrated his movement from the insurgent camps to royalist Spain and finally to the French Republic. To read Toussaint is to stay close to the documents but also to imagine listening to a gifted storyteller. It is to hear a former slave negotiate with colonists, to a military officer report to a superior, to a general exhort his troops, to a leader inculcate and, at times, strike fear in his citizen-laborers, and to a father instruct his sons.

10 June 1798–A Lesson for his Sons

I have received, my dear children, all of your letters. They gave me the greatest pleasure. I have been upset by one of them that Placide wrote to me, concerning Citizen Dufay. It is not proper to give such a lesson to a father, who cherishes, as much as anyone, his person, his honor, his duties, and his country. I want to believe that Placide, inexperienced as he is, copied this letter, without feeling its unpleasant expressions; as such, I do not make too much of it [*je ne lui en fais pas à lui un crime*]. Be on guard, my dear children, against unfavorable impressions that one might seek to give to you, write to me yourselves, borrowing neither the hand nor the style of anyone. Submit the letters you will write to me from now on to your teacher, never copy letters that would be given to you. I want to see in your letters, I want to find in them expressions of tenderness, of filial piety, and no expressions upon which your innocent youth is not yet able to reflect.²⁷

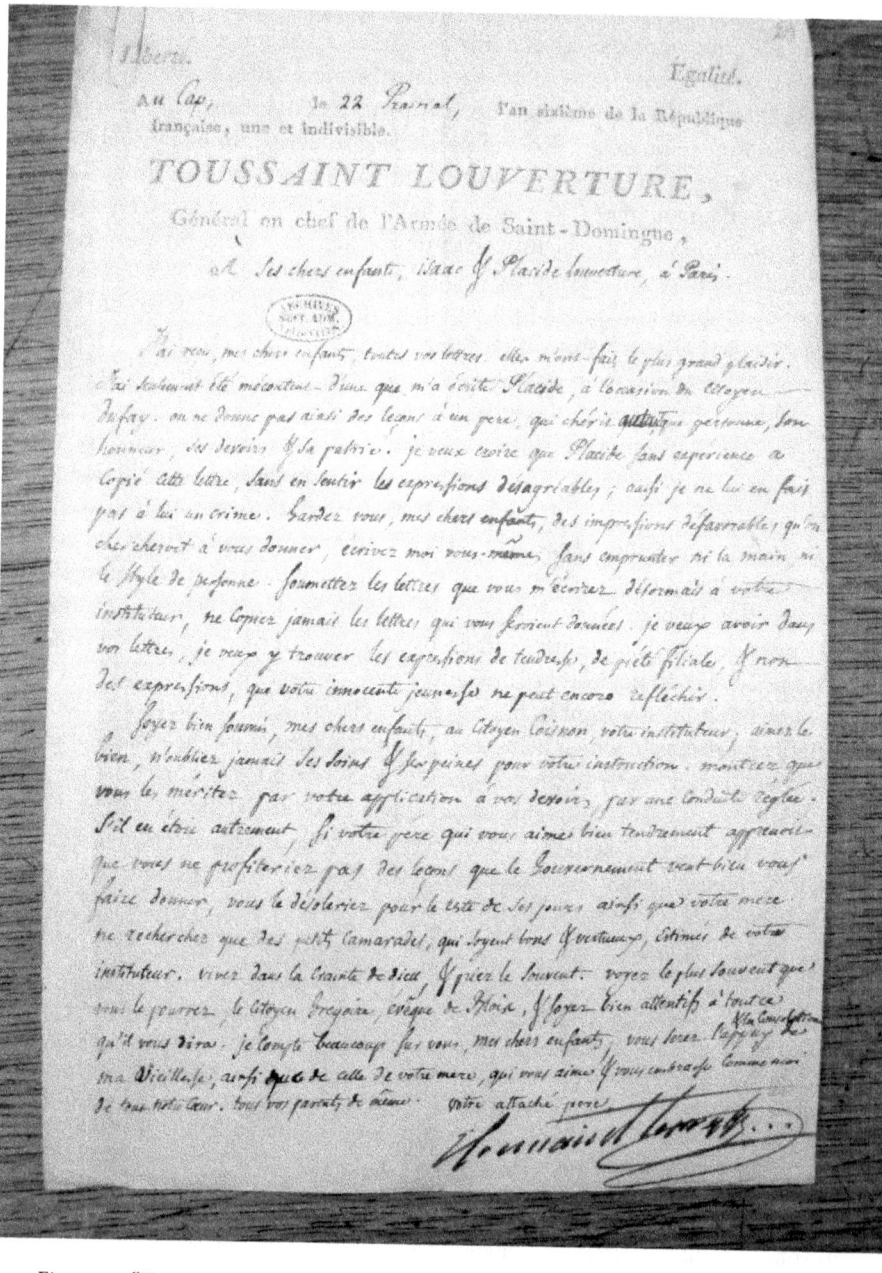

Figure 1.1. "Toussaint Louverture, Général en chef de l'Armée de Saint-Domingue, A ses chers enfants, Isaac et Placide Louverture, à Paris," Au Cap, le 22 prairial, l'an sixième de la République française, une et indivisible [10 June 1798]." AN, AF III 210, Dossier 963, folio 29.

Toussaint wrote the above letter to his sons, Isaac and Placide, when they were students in Paris at the newly created Institution Nationale des Colonies. Formerly known as the Collège de la Marche, the school was established in late October 1797 under the direction of the abbot Coisnon and the patronage of the French government as the centerpiece of a Republican project to educate the sons of colonial leaders.[28] The letter is part of a series of epistolary exchanges between father and sons, and between a father (Toussaint) and his surrogate (Coisnon), that took place over a period of almost six years, from June 1798 to February 1801.[29] Coisnon also communicated to the president of the executive council of the Directory, forwarding Toussaint's letters and reporting that he was working hard "to develop these young students [colons] into upstanding citizens, virtuous and grateful to the French Republic."[30] As far as is known, the letters came to an end almost ten months before Toussaint was reunited with his sons, who, along with Coisnon, had returned to Saint-Domingue with the French expedition led by General Leclerc that arrived in late 1801. The timing of the above letter—penned during the consolidation of Toussaint's power and changes in both the Saint-Domingue and metropolitan political landscapes—and the lessons it contains make it a key document. The role the sons unwittingly played as pawns in the gamesmanship between their father and Bonaparte finds significant space in many accounts of Leclerc's expedition.[31] However, few scholars have examined the Republican training of Isaac, Placide, and their classmates in light of revisions to the Constitution enacted by the French National Convention in July 1795, and fewer still have brought out the correspondence between Toussaint and his sons.[32] The new Constitution replaced the Convention with a bicameral legislature, the Council of Elders and the Council of Five Hundred, both supervised by an executive body, the Directory. Among the changes to the Constitution was Title I, Article VI, which declared that the colonies "are integral parts of the Republic, and are subject to the same constitutional law." In theory, the clause eliminated any administrative difference between the metropole and Saint-Domingue. While it was hardly a smooth transition, this rearrangement opened the door to new ways of thinking about the colonial mission, including the idea that developing public education in the colonies would serve the goal of integrating Republican values.[33] As evidenced in his varied responses, Toussaint was keenly aware of metropolitan debates and the changing political climate in Paris, and the above letter opens a window onto his dealings with an unstable French government.

Written four years into the period under analysis in this chapter, the letter allows for an ideal approach to read the multiple emplotments of Toussaint's conception of Saint-Domingue and its relationship to France. More than a lesson for his sons, the letter's instructions on writing and reading also serve posterity. In particular, the advice to Placide reveals not only Toussaint's method of reading but also how one might read him. By this, I mean to focus less on what the letter tells us about Toussaint the man—his paternal nature, his sense of loyalty, his distrust, even his cunning, personal qualities all perhaps discerned in the letter—than on the way he reads his sons' letters and teaches them how to write to him. In other words, in the space of a filial bond Toussaint constructed a discursive filiation between reading and writing. Before filling out the historical context, I wish to take a moment to tease out the lessons of the letter and to consider the implications for the larger interrogation of the French Republic.

Framed in a vocabulary of paternal pride, the letter offers an intimate look into Toussaint's state of mind and into the kind of father he was, both to his sons and to Saint-Domingue. The proud father expresses pleasure, whereas the authority figure conveys discontent. He cherishes his sons but also, ever the soldier, the code of honor, duty, and country. The letter juxtaposes a familial bond to the greater stakes of political power. In this sense, it addresses the obligation to country (*patrie*) as a moral imperative that goes beyond family ties. Toussaint had high expectations of his sons, including the expression of devotion to their father. "Filial piety," he admonishes, is something that should not be "copied" or expressed in a "borrowed" style. If Placide failed in his latest missive, it is because he "copied this letter." What is more, Placide neglected to hear or feel its "unpleasant expressions." To write, for Toussaint, is to find one's own voice; to read is to be on guard against "unfavorable impressions."[34] On the surface, one reads a father strengthening the bond with his sons; Toussaint teaches them to write to him in their own words and to gain experience by being truthful to themselves. Because they are passed on to his sons, these cautionary lines act as a legacy. On a deeper level, however, readers of Toussaint are also inheritors of the lesson. If "copier" is a charged verb in literary history, it is perhaps more so in a colonial setting, in which the colonized were perceived as children in need of education from the benevolent *mère-patrie*. The lesson is as much literary as it is political and ontological: Toussaint wrote to his Isaac and Placide as a father who no longer copied, who was very much the author of his own words and actions.

A fundamental aspect of this filial legacy concerns authorship and autonomy, and thus goes directly to the question of the agency of the colonized. The question of agency is a matter of great debate, one that sets the colonial representation of the colonized as adopted children against the capacity of these "children" to contest through a redirection of the very language and discourse granted to them. Toussaint's letter, I argue, goes to the heart of the issue: it displays a command of a colonial discourse, one in which he moved authoritatively through a wide range of rhetorical strategies to reimagine the family of Saint-Domingue. The letter is a rich document for the connection it makes between the confines of immediate family and its place in the greater families of Saint-Domingue and France. Toussaint wrote a significant number of texts and proclamations in the mode of family romance, a story that began in the August 1793 letter to his "brothers and friends," then took shape in the ream of letters he sent to General Laveaux, the Republican governor of Saint-Domingue whom Toussaint frequently addressed as his "dear father," and closed with the dramatic scene at Ennery in 1802 and his subsequent incarceration in France.[35] Since the French constructed the relationship between metropole and colony in familial terms, it is imperative to read Toussaint's letter to his sons as a colonial response to this larger Republican narrative.

A Family Romance from Metropole to Colony

At this point, I would like to flesh out theories of family romance to put Toussaint's narratives in a wider critical perspective. Because the term *family romance* comes from Freud, it will be necessary to explain how a European psychoanalytic model might be of service to social and political structures on Saint-Domingue. First, a brief exposition of Freud's essay, "Family Romances," which is an extension of his inquiry into the theories of wish fulfillment and interpretation of dreams.[36] Freud starts with the idea that a child's psyche develops in a family drama. Since parents are the "only authority and the source of all belief," he claims, the child's first and "most momentous wish ... is to be like his parents" (237). The child's early development soon becomes a deception, as he learns through comparison that his parents might be inferior to his original conception of them. The child then desires to liberate himself from the authority of parents, "of whom he now has a low opinion," and fantasizes of "replacing them by others, who, as a rule, are of higher social standing" (238–39). In this theory, the child's psyche reconstructs itself through a process of conflict and resolution to a reimagined family and resituates itself in a greater social order. In the case of "neurotics," Freud found the imaginative process to be characterized by strong feelings of "estrangement" and by "the motive of revenge and retaliation" (238–39). It is not entirely clear in the essay when "healthy" development ends and neurosis begins. The opening lines seem to announce this tension as Freud declares that the "liberation of an individual, as he grows up, from the authority of his parents is one of the most necessary though one of the most painful results brought on by the course of his development" (237). Later in the essay, Freud appears to hedge, as he argues that the "faithlessness and ingratitude" that motivated the liberation sought by the child were only "apparent"; therefore, the child completes the family romance not by separating but rather by "exalting [his father]" (240). In the end, it seems, the family romance is a conservative drama in that the child learns to reaffirm paternal authority.

The most influential reading of the Freudian family romance remains that of Lynn Hunt. In *The Family Romance of the French Revolution*, Hunt adapts Freud's psychological rendering of family drama for literary and political use.[37] Putting aside Freud's insistence on male authority and on the gender distinctions he made as a whole, Hunt takes away the idea that the family and the affective relations within it are constitutive of the founding of authority not only for private, immediate families but for larger social and political organizations as well. This move is crucial because it allows us, Hunt argues, to redirect Freud's psychoanalytic interpretation of family to wider use:

> The very mention of the name Freud by a historian is for some a red flag of danger. Among historians, psychoanalytic interpretation has been largely confined to the

analysis of individual biographies or, more rarely, to the analysis of group psychology in times of crisis. The connection between individual psyches and social and historical development is an interesting subject of research, but it does not directly concern me here. I do not, for example, offer an analysis of a figure such as Robespierre in Freudian terms. I am interested in the ways that people collectively imagine—that is, think unconsciously about—the operation of power, and the ways in which this imagination shapes and is in turn shaped by political and social processes. Central to this collective imagination are the relations between parents and children and between men and women. (8)[38]

I have cited this passage in its entirety because it underscores the move away from biography that I have set up in this book and, in so doing, opens up the reading of Toussaint's writings to something other than the psychological profiling that has prevailed. In her analysis of the French Revolution, Hunt develops the model of the child's fantasy into a reorganization of family and authority, one that can be read as "a myth of the origins of the social contract, or what might be called the original family romance" (6). Although Hunt does not address the implications of her work for the colonial setting, the argument that the familial and the political are connected is key to my reading of Toussaint.[39] Hunt focuses on the imaginative process as one of liberation from authority, or as a replacement of one political order with another, and neglects the play between separation and reaffirmation with which Freud closed his essay.

The idea that the language of French political authority, both monarchical and republican, derived from the unconscious imagination of a new familial order is a convincing argument. Yet how does it take into account the significant reordering of this new family in the colonial setting? If Freud's child imagined a new set of parents, in the "colonial relation," as Françoise Vergès points out, "it was a fiction created by the *colonial power* that substituted a set of imaginary parents, La Mère-Patrie and her children the colonized, for the real parents of the colonized, who were slaves, colonists, and indentured workers" (Vergès, *Monsters and Revolutionaries* 3; original emphasis). Vergès sees the colonial family romance as "the child of the French Revolution" (5) and as a complicated narrative that imported metaphors of "brothers" from the revolutionary credo of liberty and fraternity at the same time that it undermined the principle of equality by treating the colonized as children, or, as she writes, as the "little brothers" perennially indebted to France for the gifts of civilization and freedom. In the narrative of the colonial family romance the debt of the colonized is permanent and thus keeps them in a state of arrested development. And yet by giving the colonized access to familial metaphors, the French also gave them a discursive platform from which to reimagine and reinvent other kinds of families. The revised frame of the colonial family romance allows readers of Toussaint to appreciate the tension between French "parents" and the "children" of Saint-Domingue.

Toussaint's pedagogical intervention in June 1798 acknowledged a debt to France but also expressed distrust in the future of the extended French Republican family on Saint-Domingue. To grasp this challenge requires an awareness of where he stood at this moment; it is also necessary to look ahead through the four years leading up to his arrest in June 1802 and to recall the beginnings of his diplomatic movement in the growing insurrection. In broad strokes, the two years from 1794 to 1796 are when Toussaint joined the French, established his leadership by defeating the Spanish and digging in against the British; worked to quell a series of uprisings among various contingents of *nouveaux libres*, or blacks freed after the 1794 abolition of slavery; and wrangled internal rivals. From mid-1796 to late 1798 he proved his military mettle in a series of back-and-forth battles with the British that eventually led to their evacuation in October 1798. During this time, Toussaint showcased political savvy by working with, then outmaneuvering Republican commissioners and rival generals, and by justifying his actions in a series of reports to the French metropolitan government. Three events in particular highlight Toussaint's political acumen: in August 1797 he sent Sonthonax, the powerful commissioner who had first proclaimed the abolition of slavery four years earlier, back to Paris; in the summer of 1798 he was on the cusp of negotiating the end of the five-year British occupation of strategic positions on Saint-Domingue; and four days before sending the letter to his sons, Toussaint had just concluded a first meeting with the new French agent of the Directory, Hédouville, who had arrived at Le Cap one month earlier. Hédouville's mission was short-lived and ill defined, largely due to a political inclination out of line with Toussaint and to his powerlessness during the negotiations with Maitland, the British general who shunned the French metropolitan representative and opted instead to agree to terms with Toussaint. Upon Hédouville's dramatic departure barely six months after his arrival, Toussaint was, for all intents and purposes, alone in charge of the northern and western provinces of Saint-Domingue. As I have conceived it here, these scenes can be depicted more precisely in relation to Toussaint's decision to send his sons to France.

Conflict and Resolution: The Family of Saint-Domingue

In one respect, the education of the two boys—they were twelve and thirteen at the time—and the creation of the Institution Nationale des Colonies was a reward offered to Toussaint in recognition of his service to the Republican cause. To recall, the summer of 1795 was momentous for the French government and Saint-Domingue. The new Constitution was ratified one month after the Republic reached a peace agreement with Spain on 22 July. Under the terms of the Treaty of Bâle, Spain agreed to cede the eastern side of the island of Hispaniola to France. The next day, the Convention issued a decree, whose fourth article promoted Toussaint, Rigaud, Louis-Jacques Bauvais, and Jean-Louis Villatte to brigadier generals for their "defense of the Republic."[40] In October the French also instructed Laveaux to move the seat of his provisional governorship to Le Cap, where Henry Perroud, a local merchant, had been appointed by the Convention as intendant of public finances (James, 167). Villatte, who was an officer of color, resided in Le Cap and had already set up his own administration. His officers held important administrative positions and occupied houses abandoned by white émigrés. During the fight against the Spanish, Villatte and Toussaint had become considerable rivals, and their troops often defected to each other's contingents. In a letter to Laveaux on 18 June 1795, Toussaint wrote of the insubordination of one of his own officers, Joseph Flaville: "Upon my arrival [in Marmelade], I learned that the troops of Acul and Souffrière were on the move, won over by Joseph Flaville, who had become an agent of Le Cap and was looking to turn the citizens away from my command."[41] Laveaux's presence, which was not welcomed by Villatte and the inhabitants of Le Cap, only exacerbated the tension between the newly minted brigadier generals. When Perroud recommended to Laveaux that Villatte's officers pay rent on the houses they occupied, the situation came to a head in the controversial Affaire du 30 ventôse.

Culled from primary and secondary sources, the following is a summary of the incident that began on the morning of 20 March 1796. A group of "citizens of color" arrested Laveaux, apparently beating him and throwing him in prison along with Perroud. In a dramatic letter he wrote to Toussaint after being released two days later, Laveaux described his arrest:

> At ten in the morning, 20 March, I was alone in my bedroom, seated next to the table, talking with the chief engineer. Six or eight people entered the door of my office, one hundred in the living room, all citizens of color, not one black citizen, not one white. I thought it was about a dispute that they had come to ask me to resolve; I got up calmly; they made a circle around me, and I asked them: "What do you want, citizens?" At that moment, the one who was supposed to give the signal punched me in the face.[42]

Later that day, the municipal authorities of Le Cap declared, "In the name of the people, the Governor and Intendant have just been imprisoned; they have lost the confidence of the people. General Villatte has been named Governor of Saint-Domingue" (cited in Laurent, 354). However, one of Villatte's black officers, Pierre Léveillé, broke ranks to alert another officer camped outside of Le Cap, Pierre Michel, who, in turn, got word to Toussaint in Gonaïves. Toussaint responded immediately with a sharp letter to Adet, the French consul in Philadelphia, and then sent an address to his "brothers and friends" of Le Cap, in which he demanded that Laveaux be set free (354). He reminded them of the liberty that France had given them and asked, "What, then, will the mother-country say when she learns of your irregular procedures toward her representative?"[43] News reached Le Cap that Toussaint and his troops would soon arrive, joining with those of Pierre Michel and his allies. Laveaux wrote, "Thanks to their actions, thanks to the threatening letters you wrote them, the wicked men trembled and at five in the morning of 22 March, I got out of prison" (cited in Laurent, 353). While Laveaux left prison, Villatte fled Le Cap. Upon his arrival, eight days after Laveaux's arrest, Toussaint took control of the town to prevent further insurrection and to put down a rumor that Laveaux intended to reestablish slavery. In short, the affair transformed the personal and political future for Toussaint: he consolidated his power in the North as a key rival was displaced, and he reaffirmed his role as liberator, not only of Laveaux, the representative of France, but also of blacks and persons of color.

The incident has received a great deal of attention in historical accounts, a number of which arrive at different conclusions.[44] The variety of interpretations encapsulates the problem of historical representation that I raised in the introduction. That is, the conclusion depends to a great degree on the kind of story the historian wishes to write, the ideological climate in which it is produced, and the critical value of the questions the scholar puts forward. Following the summaries penned by Laveaux and Perroud,[45] the episode has been treated as a racial conflict between whites (Laveaux, Perroud), people of color (Villatte), and blacks (Toussaint).[46] Some, following Laurent, have read the event not so much as a "conflict of caste" but as a personal battle between the "commander of the Western Corridor" and "the commander of Le Cap" (351), and still others have understood it as a political clash between metropole and colony.[47] Dubois, for one, asks, "What role would metropolitan authorities have in Saint-Domingue?" and finds the more significant crisis to be one of governance that, in turn, exacerbated the frustrations of those in the colony who felt they deserved a greater political and economic role (202).[48]

All the above interpretations are plausible, but the evidence suggests that the theory of a racial conflict has been a historical smoke screen for the more convincing argument concerning political and personal tension. Laveaux's letter to Toussaint and Perroud's angry précis lend credence to the argument that they shifted their allegiance away from the people of color to Toussaint. On some level, it is not unfair for Pluchon to suggest that Toussaint manipulated the escalation of events, and to question why it took him a full week to arrive in Le Cap. To the extent that Toussaint came out of the affair with one less rival on Saint-Domingue and, as a result, gained considerable influence in Le Cap, the reasoning of Madiou and Schœlcher is sound. Finally, Dubois's assertion that the rivalry between Villatte and Toussaint ought to be understood in terms of the latter's "broader ambitions ... to secur[e] and consolidat[e] emancipation" is certainly valid (202). For my purposes, the event is a narrative turning point for the family romance of Saint-Domingue. That is, if there is a common ground in these analyses it is located in a sort of microdrama that epitomized the conflicting concerns of different leaders of Saint-Domingue. Interestingly, though Toussaint is "offstage" in Gonaïves, he directed two similar narratives of familial conflict for two different audiences, one for Adet, the French consul, in which he decried the attack on national sovereignty, and another for the citizens of Le Cap, which was a reprimand but also appealed to family unity. It is true that Toussaint backed up the second letter with the threat of considerable force. While his late arrival hinted at a possible manipulation behind the scenes, it could also have been a sign of his faith in the power of narrative.

Whatever conclusion one draws from the Affair of 30 Ventôse, it is clear that Toussaint crafted an outcome through a combination of military force and narrative persuasion. The entire incident is revealing for the manner in which he approached internal and external forces that both shaped and blocked his vision for Saint-Domingue. True to the workings of family romance—which includes the possibility of sibling rivalry—Toussaint removed Villatte from a place of prominence in the Republican family on Saint-Domingue at the same time that he extolled the *mère-patrie* in the letter to the citizens of Le Cap. Toussaint was also in the process of writing a colonial family romance, in which he created for himself the role of intermediary between France and the largely black laborers. If Laveaux as governor was a father to Toussaint, the laborers had a father in him. As head of the family of Saint-Domingue, Toussaint had to deal with rebellious "children" of his own. In fact, the Villatte Affair was sandwiched between two popular uprisings, the Datty Affair and unrest in the parish of Saint-Louis-du-Nord. In both instances, Toussaint was confronted with laborers who, while respecting him as their "father," placed greater trust in their local leader. The people harbored suspicion of Toussaint not only because he was a Creole but also because they had little evidence of the liberty and equality preached by whites with whom Toussaint associated. In a polyphonic account to Laveaux of the Datty uprising, Toussaint wove his voice with the protest of the workers: "Alas, General Sir, they want to make us slaves; there is no equality here, as it would appear to exist on your side; look how the whites and men of color, who are with you, are good and united with the blacks; it's as if they are brothers of the same mother; that is what, my General Sir, we call Equality; around here, it is not the same" (cited in Laurent, 316). Toussaint attests that he listened carefully, that he understood this legitimate complaint, but expresses shame in the laborers' greater crime of disobeying God and the law. Thus, he argued, the rebellion would only "prove [to the National Convention] what the enemies of our liberty have endeavored to make known to it, that blacks are not fit to be free" (317).

The paternal discipline offered to the workers in the Datty uprising is consistent with the aims of a leader on the rise. Once Villatte was out of the way, Toussaint turned his attention to the North and West in order to prepare against further British incursions into Saint-Domingue. He had balanced his subordination to the French with the cultivation of his own power. From the beginning of his command in mid-1794, he crisscrossed the northern and western provinces with the goal of establishing a patriarchal grip over various communities that risked being seduced by local chiefs or by the British. Those who threatened the unity of his family felt the mixture of indignation and paternal support reminiscent of the approach to Datty and his followers. It was in this context that, one month after the Villatte Affair, Toussaint addressed the citizens of Saint-Louis-du-Nord: "For how long will I have the pain of seeing *my stray children* flee the counsel of a father who idolizes them. . . . Have you forgotten that it was I who was the first to raise the flag of insurrection against tyranny, against the despotism that held us in chains?" (Laurent, 381; emphasis mine). Toussaint masterfully laid claim to paternity as well as the role of liberator. The narrative of family served to bridge the gap between bands of blacks, many of them African-born, and Toussaint, the more privileged *ancien libre*, and to make them "all of the same mother."[49] To keep his children in the fold, Toussaint strengthened the narrative's insistence on "the sacrifices of France for liberty, for happiness, for the felicity of men" (Laurent, 382)—which, as we have seen in the Datty affair, was a distant abstraction for the black workers—by focusing their attention on a more tangible truth: "There are more blacks in the colony than there are men of color and white men put together, and if some disorder were to occur, the Republic will take it out on us as blacks, because we are the strongest and it is up to us to maintain order and tranquility" (Laurent, 382). The explicit reminder of force reasserted Toussaint's position at the top of the familial hierarchy of Saint-Domingue while it also allowed him to flex his muscles with regard to the French Republic.

The Reeducation of the Colonial Family: The Institution Nationale des Colonies

The Datty Affair and the address to the citizens of Saint-Louis-du-Nord allow for a more complete vantage point from which to review the consequences of the Villatte Affair. It becomes apparent that Toussaint had gained the experience to compose two, parallel family romances. He played the father for black laborers camped throughout the North and West, while he convinced both Laveaux and the metropolitan government that he, as France's adopted son, had done a great deed. A grateful Laveaux called a public gathering in Le Cap to celebrate Toussaint and, according to Lacroix, apparently went so far as to compare him to the Black Spartacus predicted by Raynal and to declare that "he would only work together with Louverture."[50] The members of the Third Commission, who arrived in Le Cap on 11 May 1796, were quick to act on Laveaux's praise and capitalized on the Villatte Affair to bring together Titles I and X of the Constitution. In step with the provisions for public instruction, the commissioners issued a proclamation on 14 May, in which they announced that "public schools will be established in the entire colony, your children will go there to draw on this instruction, a sense of work and morals that must complete their whole regeneration. The Republic will take care of your children even further, as she desires that a certain number of them, who will have displayed the optimum disposition and willingness to be instructed, be sent to France" (Roussier, 207). In a sense, the commissioners preempted the Directory and forced its hand: the French government issued a decree on 17 August 1796 that made Toussaint a Général de division, a promotion that included the symbolic gift of a saber and a pair of pistols manufactured in Versailles (Schœlcher, 178).[51] More important, the Directory took direct responsibility for the education of Isaac and Placide: "The two children of this officer will be sent to France to receive education and training at the expense of the government" (Roussier, 208). The decree formalized what had already been in the works following the commissioners' proclamation of 14 May. In fact, Toussaint and Laveaux had written Truguet, minister of the navy and colonies, to inquire about the French education of a few black children, and apparently, near the end of May, Toussaint made a similar inquiry for his own sons (Roussier, 208). In one of the few remaining letters of Suzanne Louverture, the mother of the two boys writes that even though their departure will cause her pain, "I don't hesitate for an instant to send them to you, knowing that it is for their good, and that it will be very rewarding for us in another time to see them educated and to offer to our benefactors all our gratitude."[52] The language of all these letters confirmed the tone of the proclamation of 14 May, which, in the spirit of "regeneration," was to make education a means of attaching the workers to the *mère-patrie*.

Yet was there another motive for bringing the children to France? Investigation of an apparently harmless, logistical mishap is revealing of a deeper problem inherent to the new colonial philosophy. Having advocated, along with Laveaux, for the education of Toussaint's children, Sonthonax agreed to oversee their departure on 5 July 1796 aboard the *Watigny*. According to Sonthonax, the ship would be able to break through British lines, if necessary, "so that the children of one of the most resolute supporters of liberty would not be exposed to fall back into slavery" (Schoelcher, 188). Despite his quite ominous language, Sonthonax assured that their voyage to France would not be a reverse middle passage; however, there was a sense that Toussaint's willingness to send Isaac and Placide to France was meant to be a sign of his attachment to the Republic, and certain events on the way to France leave open this question. The *Watigny* dropped anchor at Rochefort on 14 August, and the arrival of the children appears to have caught the French government off guard, as there was still no plan for them. The students had to wait in Rochefort for two months, until the Directory issued a decree on 12 October to send the children to the École de Liancourt, a technical school founded in 1780 that was transformed by the Convention in 1795 to a national school for, among others, the "indigent children of soldiers who died in the defense of their country" (Roussier, 209). The children left Rochefort and arrived in Paris on 23 October, where they remained in the custody of Louis-Pierre Dufay, former deputy of Saint-Domingue to the Convention and member of the Council of Five Hundred.[53] In two letters addressed to the minister of the navy and colonies, dated 11 November and 2 December 1796, Dufay expressed "alarm at the dangers that these children encountered in Paris" and explained that he sent them an hour north to Liancourt.[54] These letters contain details about the place of the children in France and clarify the reference to Dufay in Toussaint's letter of 10 June.

Dufay's letters to the minister let slip another side of the Directory's desire to educate the Louverture children and their peers. As Roussier documents, the school at Liancourt was in a "deplorable state," and its students were malnourished and shabbily clothed (209). Presumably, such poor conditions, coupled with their inexperience in a cold climate, were too much for the students; as a result, we learn from Dufay that four students ran away, back to Paris: "Well! General, these little mutineers deserted, four of them, the four oldest, the two sons of General Toussaint Louverture and the two sons of General Pierrot, and arrived yesterday in the evening."[55] Dufay then reported that he received them and informed them that they could escape but that "we would then lose *precious hostages* who would confirm for us the loyalty of certain men who hold important command positions on Saint-Domingue."[56] He closed the letter by stating that he had the gendarmerie send the children back to Liancourt. It is possible that

Dufay made an offhand remark in a moment of surprise and frustration, and, given that this was one of the first impressions he made on Isaac and Placide, it goes a long way to explain their distrust of him. However, it does not dispel the idea that a more surreptitious reality lingered underneath the Directory's plan for educating its Creole wards.⁵⁷

Dufay's reference to "hostages" is an early and disquieting evocation of captivity, one that perhaps justified Sonthonax's fear of the children "falling back into slavery."⁵⁸ For Gainot, Dufay revealed a "practical motive, much different from the philanthropic argument invoked up until then to help the *nouveaux libres* benefit from instruction" (Gainot, "Un projet" 373). Nevertheless, as a result of Dufay's intervention, Truguet wrote to the director of public instruction that, given the conditions at Liancourt, the decision to send the children there was imprudent. The Directory decided to transfer custody of the children to Coisnon on 25 February 1797. The new approach seemed to bode well, as the abbot had been engaged at the start of the Directory in the cause of public education, of the kind proclaimed by the commissioners on 14 May. Along with Sonthonax, Julien Raimond, a commissioner of color, had pushed for the inclusion of black students in a tradition of the ancien régime by which the sons of wealthy planters (primarily whites but also of color) and local administrators would be sent to France for their education (Gainot, "Un projet" 373). For Raimond, the education of colonized children was a project for the long term, the only way to integrate and maintain Republican values in the colonies. In contrast to Dufay, who expressed concern for the political ramifications of the children's presence in Paris, Raimond and Coisnon clearly subscribed to a "philanthropic" colonialism. Their vision was on display at an award ceremony that marked the one-year anniversary of the Institute's founding: one of the young students spoke of being "adopted by a powerful and enlightened nation, brought back by its justice to our natural and primitive rights, from which our unfortunate fathers had been dispossessed by an unjust and barbaric force; . . . we have a country, we no longer have chains, we are beginning to think."⁵⁹ The mission of the school was to mark a new colonial era, one that disowned and condemned its past in the slave trade and instead, through a series of metaphors of family and enlightenment, looked to inculcate the colonized through the power of a wise French nation.

The new brand of colonialism, which coincided with the creation of the Institution Nationale des Colonies, was a Republican romance in that it aimed to regenerate a better family for its colonized subjects out of a damning colonial history. Drawing from French revolutionary debates leading up to the 1794 decree of abolition and the resurgence of these legislative debates under the Directory, Bernard Gainot refers to this period as a "new colonization" and argues that, in the desire to explain the problematic "colonial question" of republicanism, scholars have overlooked this phase.⁶⁰ Gainot brings to light the influence of the literary and political journal, *La Décade Philosophique*, founded in Paris by Jean-Baptiste Say and Pierre-Louis Ginguené, which provided ideological support for a more modern form of colonialism. "The journal was a laboratory of ideas," Gainot writes, and was motivated by the regeneration of the colonies based on the principle of general liberty ("La Décade et 'la colonisation nouvelle'" 100). As Gainot demonstrates, the articles published in *La Décade*, while not presenting a uniform thesis on a "new colonization," consistently promoted Republican establishments, like Coisnon's school, that shared their vision of the necessity of the development of Republican values over the long term. In an earlier article, Gainot recalled the forgotten project of departmentalization of the Antillean colonies, which became law under the "post-fructidor" Directory.[61] Adopted on 12 nivôse, year six [1 January 1798], the Law on the Constitutional Organization of the Colonies was, Gainot contends, an "organic law on the extension of the constitutional clauses concerning colonial territories" ("La Naissance" 51).[62] The law reinforced the administrative assimilation provided by Title I, Article VI, of the 1795 Constitution, which declared the colonies "integral parts of the Republic, and . . . subject to the same constitutional law." Before passing the law, the Council of Elders organized a committee to debate its merits and to consider at length the implications for, among others, the question of citizenship for the former slaves. The texts of these debates, including the published *Opinion* of Dufay, a committee member, reveal the desire of proponents of the legislation to take seriously the full extension of the 1789 Declaration of the Rights of Man to all people of color.[63] Having temporarily set aside financial and commercial issues, the members in support of the law fought hard to erase any legal distinction between "metropole" and "colony"—which, in the 1791 French Constitution, had turned on the particularity of the local (considerations of climate and race)—and even pushed to rename the colonies *départements d'outre-mer* with the aim of distancing the Republic from colonialism based on slave labor. The members ultimately decided to defer this nominal change, all the while devoting themselves to forging new ties with the colonies.

A larger question raised by the debates of the post-fructidor 1797 Directory and its proposal of a new social contract concerns the reconceptualization of the familial relationship between France and its colonies. That Dufay, the very committee member who espoused such "enlightened" ideas about citizenship, had also wondered what to do with the Louverture sons, the "precious hostages" of the French Republic, casts doubt on the alleged goals of the "new colonization." Dufay's contradicting views, along with the young Lechat's understanding of his relationship as an adopted son of France, laid bare the enduring ties between new and old forms of colonialism. French legislators believed that the former slaves had a right to general liberty but also saw republicanism as the sole guarantor of such freedom. The French continued to conceive of the metropole/colony relationship in the familial terms recited by their new students. In this view of colonial politics, it was a short step for Dufay to think of the runaway students as having escaped the boundaries of French control, and for him to betray the subconscious workings of the Republican romance: through the curriculum at the Institute, the children were trained to exalt the French father. In addition to keeping the students in line with Republican doctrine, the school doubled as a way to secure the loyalty of Toussaint, Christophe, Rigaud, and their subordinates on Saint-Domingue. The children were, effectively, hostages of fidelity.

Up to this point, I have brought forward the circumstances that helped frame the letter of 10 June 1798. Toussaint penned the lesson for his sons at the intersection of two families, one that he constructed on Saint-Domingue and another that he followed closely in Paris. It is now important to explore what he would do at such a critical juncture. Would he bring the families together, as one might expect of a man who had sent his children to France, or would he grow more suspicious of the new colonial program still very fragile in its nascent stages? The mixture of encouragement and caution that carries the letter speaks to the conundrum faced by the father of Saint-Domingue. As I discuss in the following chapter, in the turbulent year leading up to the letter, Toussaint and the French government and its agents jockeyed with each other, looking for common ground but straining to define the future of Saint-Domingue.

2 Under the Stick of Maître Toussaint

The inherent ambiguity in the Directory's colonial mission kept Toussaint on his guard. His actions and writings during this period reflect vigilance of the fractious political climate in Paris, one that continuously posed a threat to general liberty on Saint-Domingue. In this chapter I continue to delve into a clutch of Toussaint's letters and reports, in addition to the writings of several French representatives, who regularly promoted Toussaint, all the while struggling to contain his expanding power. The responses to Toussaint were inconsistent; since the Directory took the reins in mid-1795, the French government vacillated between the spirit that led to the 1794 ratification of the abolition of slavery and proslavery interests that still held considerable sway. At key moments the French failed to deliver a uniform message to the citizens of Saint-Domingue, and, accordingly, Toussaint restructured his relationship to the republic.

Political Theater on Saint-Domingue:
Laveaux and Sonthonax Exit Stage Right

On the same day the Directory formally provided for the education of his children, Toussaint wrote a letter to Laveaux, addressing him once again as "my father."[1] "I would like you to be named deputy [in Paris]," he wrote, "so that you may have the satisfaction of seeing your true country again . . . and I would be assured, and for all of my brothers, of having the most zealous defender of the cause for which we are fighting." The election of colonial deputies was to occur but one month after Toussaint penned the letter; in fact, shifting political winds in Paris were about to give royalist and planter factions a majority in both legislative chambers in the elections of spring 1797. Such an important political threat helps to explain the urgent tone of the letter. Two weeks later, Toussaint's grateful response to Laveaux leapt off the page: "Yes, my general, my father, my benefactor, my sympathizer, you alone can be the unshakable support . . . to inspire in all the electors, and for the happiness of all blacks, the utmost importance that you be named deputy."[2] The joy of the letter is weighted with religious terms, which add a measure of gravity and reflect awareness of the reactionary forces aligning in Paris; it could also be read as a sign of devotion to Laveaux and recognition of unselfish service. Despite the sincerity of these letters, this communication could very well be read as another maneuver. Toussaint kept Laveaux on his side by praising his continued support of the cause of general liberty but also removed a French authority figure.

After his election, Laveaux departed in October 1796 to take his seat in Paris. Toussaint was then alone to work with the civil commissioners, a group barely held together by a fragile alliance between Sonthonax and Raimond. The commissioners were under pressure from representatives of the planters in Paris to provide updates on the political and financial conditions of the colony. Although exiled planters had brought charges against Sonthonax and Polverel in summer 1794, requiring them to return to Paris for a lengthy trial, their prosecution ended in an acquittal. Two years later, planters and royalists in the French government, led by Viénot Vaublanc, again sought to remove Sonthonax from office. The political storm soon put pressure on an already growing rift between Sonthonax and Toussaint. Along with Laveaux, Sonthonax was elected deputy in September 1796 but extended his tenure on Saint-Domingue due to requests by the municipality of Le Cap and by Toussaint himself.[3] Petitions on his behalf are proof that Sonthonax had an important role to play as leader of the Third (his second) Commission: he was called on to reinforce the Republican administration of Saint-Domingue following the Villatte Affair, to manage the plantation economy, to oversee the military, and, in light of the Directory's program for public instruction, to establish schools. His ability to maintain order owed to his standing among blacks, particularly the *nouveaux libres*, who revered Sonthonax as a father figure. Schœlcher confirmed, through Madiou, that the former slaves were unwavering in their support because of his status as liberator following the decree to abolish slavery in August 1793 (Schœlcher, 191–92).

Sonthonax's influence on Saint-Domingue ran up against the rising power of Toussaint. Conflict arose when he intervened in matters that had been under Toussaint's sole control, especially the management of army personnel. In the request to reduce the ranks, Sonthonax encroached on Toussaint's power and raised suspicion of a possible racist motive: Sonthonax appeared to want fewer blacks defending Saint-Domingue than laboring on plantations. The commissioner also asserted authority over Toussaint's plans to allow white émigré planters to return and run their former plantations. In July 1797, he wrote a letter to Toussaint protesting the return of Bayon de Libertat, erstwhile manager of the Bréda plantation. Bell writes, "On July 4, 1797, Sonthonax sent Toussaint a remarkably hotheaded letter protesting Bayon's return to Saint-Domingue, with a copy of 'the law which condemns to death the émigrés who return to the territory of the Republic after having been banished, and condemns those who have aided or favored their return to four years in irons'" (150).[4] The threat of "four years in irons" was the last straw for Toussaint, who rode into Le Cap on 18 August, accompanied by several officers, including Christophe and Moïse, for a series of meetings with Sonthonax. These conferences took place in private, with Raimond acting as intermediary in separate, individual meetings with the two men. The end result was a letter that Toussaint and his officers wrote to Sonthonax.[5] Although his signature is on all copies of the letter (in the standard formula, "pour copie conforme"), Toussaint initially attempted through a collective voice to persuade the Commissioner to return to Paris: "today because order, peace, zeal for work, the reestablishment of agriculture, our successes against external enemies and their powerlessness, permit you to return to your functions, go tell France what you have seen, the prodigious feats to which you been witness, and be forever the defender of the cause which you have embraced." Framed as a group effort, the letter nevertheless bears the mark of Toussaint's rhetoric. The series of guarded imperatives delivers the command to leave not in terms of a personal conflict but in a logical progression of the larger interests at stake. The letter is a far cry from the personal tone that characterizes the correspondence with Laveaux; on the contrary, Toussaint once again coupled force and epistolary persuasion to dismiss Sonthonax, who finally embarked on the *L'Indien* on 24 August.

The letters to Laveaux and Sonthonax represent the continued and evolving efforts of Toussaint to remake the family of Saint-Domingue. It is no coincidence that these events occurred in parallel to the changes under way in Paris. Just as historians have referred to the removal of counterrevolutionaries in the Directory as the "Coup of Fructidor," we could also accurately describe the letters and reports concerning the dismissal of Sonthonax as the "fructidorization" of Saint-Domingue. In their letter to the commissioner, Toussaint and his subordinates defined themselves as "eternal soldiers of the Republic" in order to align themselves with the hard line against émigrés established by the post-fructidor Directory. Sonthonax attempted to delay his departure, going so far as to solicit support from Raimond, the municipality of Le Cap, and a coalition of officers, administrators, and various citizens. Toussaint did not budge: he called on the magistrates of Le Cap and Raimond to insist on the prompt departure of Sonthonax and wrote a report to the minister to explain the "causes of [Sonthonax's] necessary distancing" from Saint-Domingue.[6]

The public and private scenes of this drawn-out confrontation resulted in Toussaint's dramatic report to the Directory on 4 September 1797.[7] Delivered on the same day as the Coup of Fructidor in Paris, the report contains his version of private conferences with Sonthonax, Raimond, and Pascal (who was both Toussaint's son-in-law and secretary to the Third Commission) from 18 to 20 August. The text spans forty-four pages and is all at once report, indictment, and *pièce de théâtre*. Both Bell and Jenson read the theatrical elements of the play and provide insight into its production and dissemination. Bell reports that the day following the meeting with Sonthonax, "Toussaint summarized both halves of the interview to Raimond and Pascal, who set it down as a dialogue ten pages long. This *pièce de théâtre* may very well be fiction but it served as Toussaint's justification for pressing Sonthonax to leave the colony" (150–51). In an extensive analysis that puts the report in the larger context of Toussaint's media skills, Jenson points out that the report was Toussaint's "first document to be widely disseminated in the U.S. media" (*Beyond the Slave Narrative*, 94). She cites the English translation in the *Philadelphia Gazette* in early October (a date that, Jenson reasons, means that Toussaint wrote the report with a view to its publication in the press), in which Toussaint wrote, "To present this conversation to my fellow citizens with more precision and order, and that nothing may be omitted that was said, I have chosen the form of a dialogue. For the questions which were put to me were deeply engraved in my memory."[8] The report, then, was a preemptive defense of the dismissal of Sonthonax not only to the French government but also to a concerned international public. Jenson discusses at length the journalistic quality of Toussaint's correspondence and reports; in particular, she analyzes his writings in terms of public mediation. I will come back to the communicative power of Toussaint's writings in the next chapter, which treats the 1801 Constitution and its particular site of proclamation. For now, I would like to focus on the narrative structures of the report, which, following Jenson, created an audience of "virtual witnesses" in his public (*Philadelphia Gazette*) and private (French Directory) readers (Jenson, *Beyond the Slave Narrative* 95).

The text of the report showcases Toussaint's rhetorical agility as well as an awareness of the political implications of his writing. Indeed, more than a transcription from memory, like so many of his writings it rehearses and forecasts the representation of his role on Saint-Domingue. While some historians have belittled the text—Pluchon predictably described it as a "sketch comedy [*saynète*]" (189)—others have underscored the adaptability of Toussaint's writing.[9] On the opening page, Toussaint once again validates the family romance: "Full of gratitude for the nation, which was the first, to have raised my brothers and me to the dignity of free men, I would have been the most vile and most atrocious of men if I had been able for one moment to be guilty of ingratitude and if I had ceased to be faithful to the Republic that has adopted us." Five pages later, "concerning the motives that led him to dismiss Sonthonax from the colonies," Toussaint switches narrative gears, interrupting a first-person report with the play titled, *First Conference between the Commissioner Sonthonax and the General Toussaint Louverture*. He attempts to justify the expulsion of the commissioner by publicly revealing the latter's alleged plans for declaring independence. Toussaint accomplished a political feat by staging his role—a becoming "Toussaint" that was consistent with the theatrical and political dimensions of the adoption of "Louverture"—and by contrasting his voice with that of Sonthonax, the now-treasonous foil to the savior of Saint-Domingue:

> Sonthonax: What have I done to you? Do you have a complaint with me?
> Toussaint: Commissioner, I do not have a complaint with you personally. My criticism with regard to you concerns the Republic.
> Sonthonax: Explain what you have to reproach me for.
> Toussaint: Commissioner, you are the chief authority of the colony, yet you are not fulfilling your duty: instead of applying yourself to reconcile everyone, you seek rather to sow discord everywhere; you have spies and agents in all places to gain followers, and I know not why you have sent them near me to create unrest among my army; you bring blacks to get angry with whites, and at the same time you incite the people of color against the blacks; the unrest has thoroughly penetrated my army such that for some days I have been obliged to arrest sixty officers and I know that these are men sent by you who have brought about all this disorder.

In these lines and elsewhere, Toussaint deflected attention away from any personal animus to put into focus his unwavering support of Republican ideals. He solidified his image as a government servant beyond reproach by burning it into the text in the third person. The "play," which even includes stage directions—"with an impatience he could no longer hide"—is also evidence, as Jenson points out, that Toussaint drew on his awareness of "Saint-Domingue's unusually robust theatrical culture" (95). Although the rift between Toussaint and Sonthonax developed over a period of more than two years and was more complicated than the story plotted in the report, Toussaint clearly cast himself as the loyal soldier, while Sonthonax played the scheming *indépendantiste*. The accusation of the former liberator (and rival), set in the defense of the colony, is a tactic that Toussaint will employ in the *Mémoire*, and deserves to be cited at length here:

> Toussaint: I want nothing, I need neither gold, nor silver, nothing of the sort. You must leave, the salvation of the colony demands it.
> Sonthonax: Yet all is calm in the city, what do you have to fear?
> Toussaint: Not at all. You pretend to ignore what I know, that if the city is calm, it is against your wishes; I have sent men to preach calm, but you must leave. /
> [*with passion*] I have spoken to Commissioner Raimond to tell him that you must leave. He tried to get me to be lenient by encouraging me to foresee the detrimental consequences and the troubles that could arise in light of your character. Well, I take responsibility for this action; I will report my conduct to the Executive Directory, but you must leave.
> Sonthonax: So, you are determined to make me leave.
> Toussaint: Very determined.

The play is set as a tragedy in the inexorable movement ("you must leave") to banish Sonthonax: it is a story of greed and of the downfall of a once-beloved father figure.

But this report was more than political theater: it is also, as Dubreuil observes, a kind of Socratic dialogue. As one of two main characters, Toussaint leads the other to a

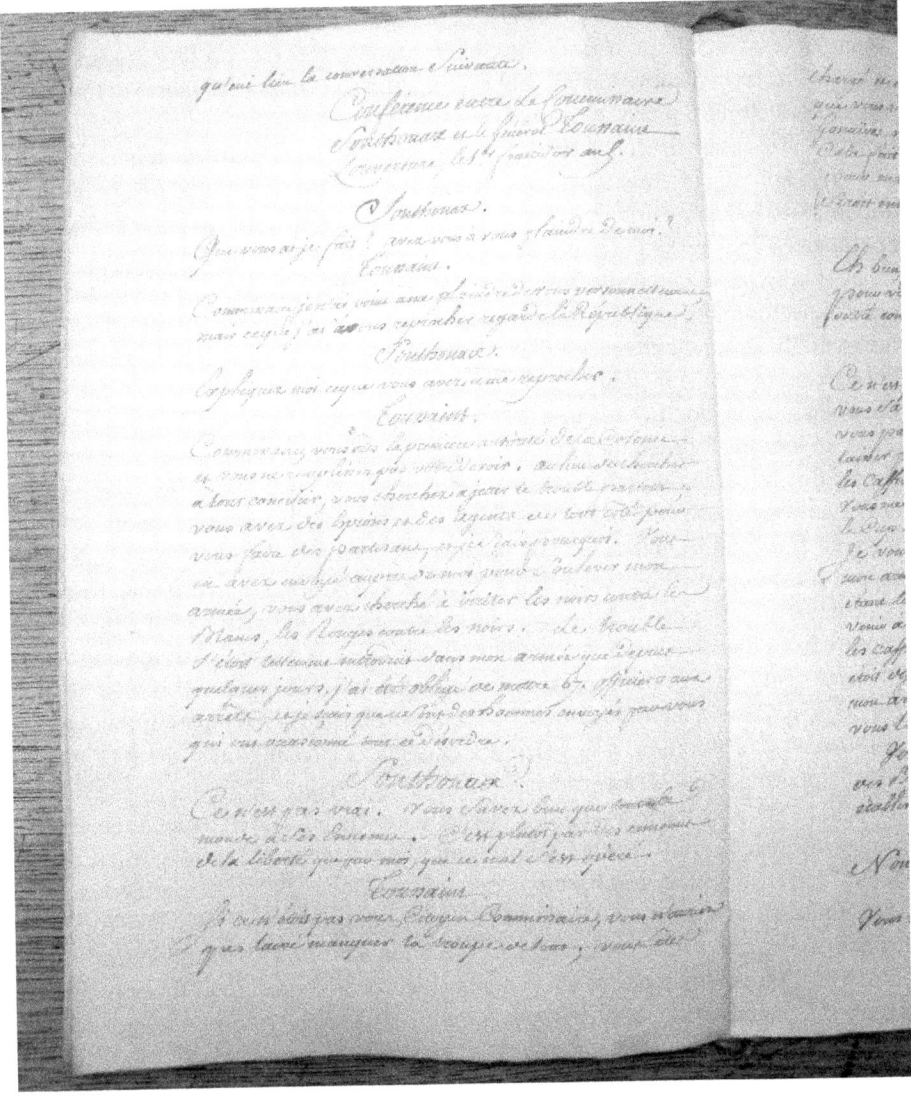

Figure 2.1. Toussaint Louverture, "Rapport au Directoire Exécutif, Toussaint Louverture, Général en Chef de l'Armée de St.-Domingue, Cap français, le 18 fructidor, l'an 5 [4 September 1797]," AN, AF III 210, Dossier 961, folio 1. This report contains the "play/dialogue" that Toussaint wrote concerning his conferences with Sonthonax.

logical if simple and inevitable conclusion: Sonthonax must depart for the good of the colony. Several exchanges are indicative of Toussaint (as Socrates) responding to a series of questions from his interlocutor and leading him to reaffirm the moral of the "play." The rhetorical effect, moreover, is that the Directory, represented by their *agent particulier*, must also accept the conclusion. However, Sonthonax, who until his arrival in France remained ignorant of the extent of the accusations, read the narrative as a show of smoke and mirrors. When he first learned of the indictment in early January 1798 in Bayonne, Sonthonax wrote to the Directory to request a suspension of judgment, closing the letter by stating those who had accused him "waited until his departure to stab him in the back."[10] At this point, he had also learned that the political upheaval on Saint-Domingue mirrored the dramatic changes in Paris. In the spring of 1797 the royalists had annulled his election to the Council of Five Hundred, yet by the fall he had been reinstated after the Coup of Fructidor. In early February 1798, Sonthonax counterattacked by addressing a special session of the Council of Five Hundred with his "Observations," a summary of service during his second mission to Saint-Domingue. Five days earlier he had presented a written copy of the address, a seven-page refutation of the report "written under the name of Toussaint L'Ouverture."[11] He pointed out several inconsistencies in Toussaint's report, most notably the dates of the alleged conspiracy to declare independence. On the contrary, he wondered, how could he have proposed the massacre of whites and a rupture from France when Toussaint himself had written two letters to the minister of the navy *after* this time in support of his work on Saint-Domingue? In addition to finding holes in its logic, Sonthonax went on the offensive against the report; it was, he said, a "ridiculous conversation" that portrayed him "like a student, under the stick [*sous la férule*], spouting nonsense and causing himself to be reprimanded by his teacher." In the move to a personal attack, Sonthonax (perhaps unconsciously) fell back on the colonial family romance to argue that it was Toussaint, the former student, whose transgression had turned the familial relationship between Saint-Domingue and France on its head. "Certainly, if someone should perhaps be suspected of independence," he wrote, "it is without a doubt he whose political life has been but a continuous revolt against France. Toussaint L'Ouverture is one of the Vendéen chiefs of St.-Domingue." To strengthen his argument, Sonthonax associated Toussaint with the Vendéens, those who had recently rebelled against French Republicans; in other words, by assuming the role of teacher, Toussaint should be suspected of revolt.

Sonthonax's "Observations" are a chilling reminder of the lingering effects of the "old" colonialism still very much a part of the French Republican project on Saint-Domingue. During his testimony on the legislative floor in Paris, the commissioner struggled to take the logical high road, as the former lawyer compromised his integrity from the very beginning by insinuating that the general in chief, a former slave, could never have conceived of the plan to remove a civil commissioner on his own:

> He is a narrow-minded soul, as lowly as his original state of a slave who took care of livestock; he usually speaks Creole and hardly understands French. Born to be

governed, his fate is to be beholden to a foreign impulse. His profound ignorance has made him entirely subordinate to the priests, who, in Saint-Domingue as in France, seize any occasion to overthrow liberty.

The statement is a lead-in to a counteraccusation of a larger conspiracy of priests and émigré planters. The more complex and problematic argument remains the ad hominem attack. Sonthonax repeated the indictment of ignorance later in the address, underscoring, for him, the utter irony of Toussaint as *pédagogue*: "I read this miserable brochure, vile production of intrigue and imposture; I have but two words in response: it is that Toussaint only speaks Creole, that he barely understands French, and is perfectly incapable of holding the language that one attributes to him." The counterattack turned on the question of authorship and on its connection to the agency of the colonized as uneducated child. Toussaint may have had Sonthonax's defense in mind when he wrote the letter to Isaac and Placide a short four months later. The cautionary tale of the 10 June letter—"be on guard," he warned them—is that the only way to preserve general liberty is to wrest control of the language and discourse that had been deployed to colonize them.

Toussaint, Authorship, and Authenticity

Thus far, I have argued that Toussaint's lesson for his sons goes to the larger question of literacy as a form of agency for the colonized. It was a lesson that he had learned along the way to his command of Saint-Domingue, and that one can read in the reappropriation of the multiple discursive forms available to him. Sonthonax's questioning of the possibility of his authorship—"he barely understands French"—has been a source of doubt in scholarship on Toussaint that remains to this day. It is a doubt that needs to be put to rest, precisely because the study of the process by which Toussaint produced his documents—and by extension his agency—is emblematic of authorial voice on Saint-Domingue.

Was Toussaint a forerunner of francophone literature? To what extent do the correspondence, the decrees, the reports to French governments, the Constitution, and finally the *Mémoire* display an understanding and reappropriation, rather than imitation, of French discourse? His political mastery of Saint-Domingue came about, in part, due to an ability to adapt (to) French language along with the formulas and genres of military and governmental practice. As a slave Toussaint may have had some instruction in reading and writing; as far as is known, he also taught himself, although his writing was largely phonetic, with seemingly arbitrary syllabification and punctuation.[12] As we have seen, Toussaint moved shrewdly between worlds, and his authorship was both a function and a result of having learned to mediate them. The possible formal education he received as a slave, the practical skills he picked up in contact with various secretaries (both white and persons of color) in rebel camps, in Spanish and French armies, and in administrative hierarchies, all have in common forms of mediation. To some extent, this mediation mimics that between speech and text, except that

Toussaint was actively involved in a method that combined dictation, transcription, and revision of the written word. This process was a sort of mimicry of European discourse that nevertheless depended on the originality of Toussaint's voice.[13] In addition to his handwritten texts, Toussaint became an author of mediated texts, in which these mimetic and defiant voices operate in concert.

Despite the strong case to be made about Toussaint's authorship, it continues to be called into question. The central accusation is that the secretaries *produced* the text, which disputes the idea that the kind of mediation engaged in by Toussaint was properly textual. And this despite accounts to the contrary. M. E. Descourtilz, like Gros, another prisoner eyewitness, wrote of Toussaint's *pénétration littéraire*:

> I saw him in few words verbally outline the summary of his addresses, rework [*rétorquer*] poorly conceived, poorly executed sentences; confront several secretaries who presented their work by turns; redo ineffective sections; and cut out parts in order to place them better elsewhere; in a word, making himself worthy of the natural genius predicted by Raynal, whose memory he revered, by honoring him as his precursor. (Descourtilz, 3:245–46)

Throughout his account, Descourtilz does little to mask an intense dislike for Toussaint, yet in one short paragraph he pays homage to the talents of an adversary. In the reference to the abbé Raynal's widely read *Histoire philosophique et politique des établissements et du commerce des Européens dans les deux Indes* (1770), Descourtilz connected Toussaint not only to Raynal's prediction of the rise of a Black Spartacus, but more important to a tradition of French Enlightenment literature (Raynal collaborated with Diderot) in which Toussaint would find a prominent place as a literary *successor*.

The dialogic process was authentic to Lacroix as well, who wrote, "He never would have signed a letter that he did not conceive or for which he did not weigh each word; if a secretary used one that he did not know, he had this letter redone several times, by different secretaries, until they had found the turn of phrase that fit the expression of his thought" (355). Although this testimony gives weight to the active role of the secretaries, the final expression belongs to the man who "conceived and measured" each word.[14] A military officer with his own access to secretarial assistance, Lacroix understood the authorial practice of men of Toussaint's standing. As Daniel Desormeaux points out, "To say that Toussaint is not the author of his *Mémoires* because he did not write them himself would be tantamount to considering all his official correspondence apocryphal because he dictated it" (135). Lest one forget, Bonaparte, too, issued a memoir, *Le Mémorial de Sainte-Hélène*, on which he collaborated with Las Cases, who wrote the text by dictation and listening to Bonaparte recount his life stories.[15] To question Toussaint's authorship would be to impose a modern view of writing and authorship on a historical period when dictation and redaction were the norm.[16] It is important to read these mediated texts as the product of a new kind of literacy, one that confronted the "pedagogical" mission that now defined the colonial relationship between France and Saint-Domingue.

Literacy in the Tropics: The Rebuttal of French Republicanism

The historical questioning—and, in many cases, slandering—of Toussaint has never been simply about his ability to write and read French. Neither was it a coincidence that Sonthonax's accusation occurred shortly after the Directory refocused their efforts to settle the colonial question by founding the Institution Nationale des Colonies and by passing the first law of departmentalization. The "new" colonialism required an armed coup and was defined by its struggle with the "old" view of ignorant, Creole students, who dared to replace their French masters and put them "under the stick." As evidenced by its Royalist and Republican factions, the French legislative body had to deal with its own sibling rivalry, between those who sought to maintain general liberty and those who wished to restore slavery. Just as Toussaint's children were seen as "hostages to fidelity," French republicanism was always already hostage to its fundamental connection to a discriminatory colonialism. The doubts about Toussaint, and specifically the refusal to acknowledge his literacy, speak to this contradiction. Toussaint's consolidation of power took place when he seized the "agency" of Saint-Domingue, when he refuted royalist claims, and when he refused to acknowledge any future *agent particulier* sent by the Republic.

The kind of "literacy as agency" that I put forward here attempts to build on Srinivas Aravamudan's theory of the "tropicalization" of the Enlightenment.[17] The title of his study, *Tropicopolitans*, is a neologism, uprooted from its botanical meaning and grafted to a new stock composed of the literary (trope), the geographic (tropic), and the political (polis). The tropological "activates" the tropicopolitan, or "a name for the colonized subject who exists both as a fictive construct of colonial tropology *and* actual resident of tropical space, object of representation *and* agent of resistance" (4; original emphasis). Following Hayden White, Aravamudan points to the linguistic function of "trope" as a "turn," or slippage, that reveals the shifting spaces between the data of discursive fields and the adequacy of language to analyze them. In the example of the word *slave* Aravamudan recalls the "forgotten ... ethnogeography" of "Slav," an "ethno-linguistic particularization," which then traveled to "slavery," or the general conditions of African labor in the historical Caribbean and Americas, to its metaphorical application in the discourse of French revolutionaries. "Tropological recursions," he continues, " ... allow slavery to trope, or turn through various contexts" (5). The movement of ideas and words from Europe to the colonial Caribbean brought about their "tropicalization," by which Aravamudan means the mediated and "motivated" change of these ideas by the colonized. In this theory, literacy is also a kind of trope, in that it involves the capacity for reading colonial representations and relationships and then being able to reconceptualize them. Aravamudan calls this "metaliteracy," which takes off from scenes of reading (real or imagined), such as the legendary account of Toussaint finding inspiration in Raynal (289). Metaliteracy, then, is the awareness that allowed Toussaint to work through the colonial underpinnings of French republicanism.

The colonial tropology of the family romance also turned to the physical movement of children from Saint-Domingue to a new school in Paris. Toussaint had initially requested their departure under the protection of Sonthonax, but as his relationship with the commissioner soured, he seized control of the family hierarchy on Saint-Domingue. Following Aravamudan, it is possible to read these scenes as a "tropicalization" of the paradigm of the colonial family, in which Toussaint the colonial object (as student) moved dramatically to powerful teacher (Sonthonax's *pédagogue*). As I have demonstrated in my readings of the Datty and Saint-Louis-du-Nord Affairs, such tropicalization was a process that developed as Toussaint mediated the turn between French and Saint-Dominguan paradigms. I have argued that the pedagogical letter to Isaac and Placide is evidence of an awareness of this shift: it is the sign of the space of metaliteracy that he occupied. And yet, as Aravamudan cautions, criticism that looks back on Toussaint's reappropriation of French discourse ought not to "reify agency from the position of *other* or *subaltern*" (15; original emphasis). Quite simply, agency means different things in the different contexts (cultural, historical, geopolitical, linguistic) in which it turns. Toussaint's particular reappropriation of French models—especially the constitutional mode of governance—could not be the basis of a universal example of "decolonization," nor could it serve as a template of heroic, contested agency. Toussaint's agency resisted but also reinforced; it was just as much an overcoming as it was a taking over. The appeal of the theory of tropicalization and its connection to plural reading practices is that it allows one to follow the "discursive redeployment" particular to Toussaint and the setting of Saint-Domingue (15). It recognizes that how he acted as teacher and as patriarch was something unique to him and the worlds in which he moved.

In the remainder of this chapter, I turn to two encounters with representatives of France that, like the "play" created to justify Sonthonax's necessary departure, signaled Toussaint's redirection of the figure of the "hostage of fidelity" in a deft refutation of French colonial agency. Pluchon proposed that the dismissal of the commissioner was to "appease the royalists" (203), an argument similar to that put forward by Césaire, who wrote that the move "cajoled [*amadouait*] the mulattos" (*Toussaint Louverture*, 251). In both analyses, Toussaint deployed a stall tactic to give him the time to react to the rise of Vaublanc. Toussaint's retort to the incendiary speech made by Vaublanc was indicative of his resistance to those who sought to dissolve general liberty on Saint-Domingue. Similarly, his dealing with Général Hédouville, the French agent appointed by the French legislative body during the short phase of a royalist majority but later approved and dispatched by the post-fructidor Directory, provides insight into his growing resentment of mistreatment by the metropolitan government.

On 29 May 1797, not three weeks after Toussaint was promoted to general in chief, Vaublanc, who owned property on Saint-Domingue, took the floor of the Council of Five Hundred. Citing reports of the commissioners and letters from military officers, in particular, General Rochambeau, who had arrived on Saint-Domingue with the

Third Commission, Vaublanc stated, "This ill-fated island has reached the last degree of misfortune."[18] He decried that the colony was governed by "ignorant and crude negros [*nègres ignorans et grossiers*], incapable of discerning unbridled license from austere liberty, bending to laws." In the end, the planter-legislator argued that the rule of law was not understandable to former slaves and that the restoration of order necessitated the return to plantation life "before the revolution." Vaublanc's heavy reliance on Rochambeau rendered his plans unambiguous: the French general wrote in a *Précis sur la colonie de Saint-Domingue*, "The foundation of the Restoration of St. Domingue is a more rigorous slavery of blacks [*l'Esclavage de noirs*] than in the past."[19] Toussaint learned of Vaublanc's speech by way of his agents in the United States and replied in late October, after the Directory called on General Augereau to remove reactionary elements in the legislative body. Toussaint followed the theatrical report of his conferences with Sonthonax with a methodical refutation of Vaublanc.

In its deconstruction of the flawed planter logic, the fourteen-point refutation is masterful: the new *magister* of Saint-Domingue corrected the former slave masters. Toussaint wrote of being "profoundly affected" by a royalist-inflected republicanism because it allowed former slaves "to believe that the Representatives of the French were their enemies." The questioning of republicanism begins subtly enough but expands in rebuttal of Vaublanc's assertion that the "blacks [*noirs*] under Jean-François swore a fierce hatred of true Frenchmen." Toussaint conceded the undisciplined violence of Jean-François but took Vaublanc to task for confusing liberty with a narrow view of nationality:

> Does he mean by this designation the traitors paid by England, those who, following such odious treason, allowed this perfidious nation onto the territory of liberty? In this case, we are honored not to merit this honorable name; but if the friends of liberty classify under this respectable denomination men subject to the heart and soul of the French Constitution, to its beneficent laws, the men who cherish the French, friends of their country, then we swear that we have and will always have the right to be called French citizens. (Toussaint Louverture, *Réfutation*)

As he will do in the 1801 Constitution, Toussaint made a distinction between liberty and nationality, underscoring the universal quality of the former, its founding in the rule of law, over against the latter, a "respectable denomination," if susceptible to political manipulation. He took apart the logic of an adversary through irony: "we are honored not to merit this honorable name." This withering sentence contains more than just the classical playing off of the literal meaning with its opposite. The (barely) unstated intention behind "the honor in refusing the honorable" is the willingness to separate from the French if necessary. Toussaint was careful to intertwine the principles of general liberty with the raison d'être of the French Constitution itself. This interpretation came through loud and clear in the final passage of the refutation:

> [Despite] all that the enemies of the principles that the mother country decreed for Saint-Domingue will say to you to weaken in your eyes the inviolable attachment

to France and its Constitution, the black and colored generals will never infringe upon the oath they took to live free and French: they will always choose to bury themselves in the ruins of their country rather than relive slavery; rather than be ruled by a country other than France, who declared them free; one may slander them, but they will never change their principles; and, sure of those principles that you profess, they will look down upon their slanderers.

This is the loudest declaration of "free and French" before its articulation in the Constitution. The dichotomy of freedom and sovereignty was a trump card for Toussaint, one that he played in dramatic fashion, because the symmetry of "free" and "French" depended on a balanced movement between the two. In the *Réfutation*, however, the valence of the two principles shifted between the power of what was stated (our attachment to France is inviolate) with what was implied (we will fight France if necessary). Moreover, because the irony of the previous passage (honored not to merit the honorable) remained intact, the *Réfutation* was a charged discourse that dissembled the professed attachment to France with the threat of the unsaid.

A week later, Toussaint included part of the *Réfutation* in a longer report to the Directory, one that showed, according to James, that he had lost confidence in France. He reiterated the willingness to defend liberty by force and raised questions about the presence of his sons in France: "I would tremble with horror if it was in the hands of the colonists that I had sent them as hostages; but even if it were so, let them know that in punishing them for the fidelity of their father, they would only add one degree more to their barbarism, without any hope of ever making me fail in my duty" (cited in James, 196). Although the Directory had deported sixty-five royalists to French Guyana, the executive leaders had a bigger problem: they were clearly alarmed by the forceful rhetoric of Toussaint, who, moreover, appeared nonplussed by the expulsion of pro-slavery legislators. The Directory chose to proceed with the July 1797 appointment of General Hédouville, the "pacifier of the Vendée," as the new agent on Saint-Domingue. In a chapter titled "Mission to Undermine [*de sape*]," Césaire noted that Hédouville "was by no means a subordinate officer [*homme de second plan*]" (256). That Hédouville was celebrated for having put down the rebellion of the Vendée—and for having conserved it for the Republic—was, for Césaire, an ominous sign that the mission was to weaken Toussaint's authority. If Sonthonax had raised the analogy of the Vendée uprising during the French Revolution with the "revolt" of Toussaint, the comparison now joined the pacification of the Vendéens with the restoration of order on Saint-Domingue. During Hédouville's journey from the Vendée to Saint-Domingue, the analogy of revolt made a geopolitical turn and acquired a new meaning that threatened the freedom of the former slaves.[20] The French government gambled on a risky move: intent on assuaging Toussaint of any concern of slavery, it nevertheless instructed an agent with experience in restoring order to revitalize the plantation economy.

Toussaint's defensive maneuvers in response to Hédouville, along with a flurry of offensive attacks on British positions from late 1797 to early 1798, suggest that he was preparing the ground for alternative political options with France, Britain, and the United States. Hédouville arrived on the Spanish side of the island in April 1798 to consult with Roume, a member of the Third Commission, and with General Kerverseau, who by then had been on the island for almost three years. Kerverseau alerted the new agent to the power that Toussaint had accumulated and to the fundamental distrust that defined his character. Hédouville was well aware that he was about to engage in a delicate negotiation with the general in chief. In the eight months since the departure of Sonthonax, Toussaint had defeated the British in several key battles, to the point where, as he wrote Laveaux in late September:

> It is enough to tell you that the success of the Republican Army was so rapid that three months after our last campaign, we have already conquered Mirebalais, Le Grand Bois, the mountains of Arcahaie, and the Spanish part occupied by the English, and that the latter, pushed everywhere, were soon forced to evacuate Saint-Marc, Arcahaie, and Port-au-Prince. It was at the moment when I received their proposals for evacuation that I learned of the arrival of Agent Hédouville in Santo Domingo.[21]

True to the form described by Kerverseau, Toussaint waited a month after Hédouville's arrival in Le Cap on 8 May before meeting with the French agent. One of the reasons for the delay was that Toussaint had been in active negotiations with General Maitland, who earlier in the spring had taken over the helm of British forces on Saint-Domingue. Due to a series of defeats and to the staggering loss of British soldiers to yellow fever, the British commander had orders to end their occupation.[22] In order to preserve a British presence in Jamaica and to maintain control, along with the United States, of trade routes, Maitland also sought to create a rift between Toussaint and the Directory. At first, he worked openly with Hédouville and Toussaint but ended up negotiating secretly with the latter. Moreover, Toussaint agreed to terms with the British that included amnesty for some French émigrés, contravening French laws that Hédouville had every intention of upholding. In the late spring and summer of 1798, Toussaint left the French agent in a diplomatic lurch and, in so doing, defied the hierarchy of rule.

As foreshadowed by the *Réfutation* of Vaublanc and in the November letter to the Directory, the greater family of Saint-Domingue had begun to break up in the summer of 1798 due to a deep sense of mutual distrust. On 6 June Toussaint and Hédouville had their first meeting, one that both men remembered differently in after-action reports. Hédouville wrote of Toussaint's false protests of attachment to the French republic and of "oaths of loyalty entirely belied by his actions."[23] For his part, Toussaint described the agent's disrespectful entourage of young soldiers, who taunted him with royalist slogans.[24] In his *Précis historique des annales de la colonie française de Saint-Domingue depuis 1789*, Pélage-Marie Duboys, a colonial magistrate and contemporary witness, provided insight into what was, by all accounts, a doomed relationship:

> Reason appeared to establish itself between them, if, on one side, Hédouville had known how to handle the ambition and prejudices of the General in Chief, and if,

on the other, the haughty and suspicious temperament of Toussaint Louverture had not left him susceptible to the slightest impression. The enemies of the colony were skilled in sowing the seeds of division. (Tome II, 4)[25]

Duboys put additional blame on Toussaint for the "spirit of native domination in a country of slaves," a view that coincided with Hédouville's assessment (6). In light of his diminishing power, Hédouville, following orders from the Directory (and apparently refusing to learn from the example of Sonthonax), resolved to downsize the army and to revise Toussaint's agricultural regulations. He also attempted to restore civilian authority, which led to unrest in the North, where many of Toussaint's generals were in charge. Before long, a complicated incident involving the French agent's attempt to arrest Moïse, Toussaint's nephew, brought the conflict to a head. Toussaint countered with an order for Hédouville's arrest, but, in late October, before Dessalines could arrive in Le Cap, the pacifier of the Vendée had fled for France. Before departing, however, Hédouville attempted to create lasting division between Toussaint and Rigaud by officially vesting the latter with authority in the South, a move that would exacerbate the tension between the two leaders on Saint-Domingue and ultimately lead to a civil war.

Where Kerverseau and Hédouville saw a usurpation of power, Toussaint couched his authority in terms of the necessity of maintaining general liberty. Three years later, the commingling of liberty and power will become the philosophical core of his Constitution. In the report to the Directory on 22 brumaire [12 November] Toussaint wrote of the threat to "public tranquillity" posed by Hédouville. He detailed the measures he took, as well as those of Hédouville, and attested, once more, to his attachment to France. In this respect, the combination of the justification of a course of action with the reiteration of an oath of loyalty is similar to the composition of the *Mémoire*. The report accused Hédouville of being the instigator of the discord; the situation had become so dire, Toussaint stated, that he was forced to step in for the good of the public well-being. In fact, Toussaint had written an earlier letter, "Au Général et agent particulier du Directoire à Saint-Domingue"—it did not include a name or a specific date, but in all likelihood was meant for Hédouville—that set up the thesis of the November letter to the Directory.[26] The letter was one of the few written in Toussaint's own hand, perhaps because he was without a secretary (he hinted at this possible circumstance in the brief heading, "coming and going [*nallant et venant*]"). I would like to include a transcription of the phonetic French in its entirety here, followed by my translation, because its signature language prepares us for the prison writings to Bonaparte:

> Enmi de la chose publique, Enmi de lordre et la tranquilité, de homme pour leur in te ré par ticulier, de homme, an bisieux. veut fer pa cé lé mal pour le bien, et le bien pour le mal, on faite, pa cé les tenebre pour la lu mier, et la lu mier, pour les tenebre. Il veut que ce qui et dous soi amer, et que ceu qui et a mer soi dous, il et dous leureux pour de homme don neur, trété de la sorte, conte Citoyen a gent, sur Toussaint Louverture et sa parolle. Les remed pallia tife né fon que fla té le mal, et il fau ta lé a la source, pour le guérire, comme vous ne conné ce pa la colonni, je crin con vous de

tourne de tou votre Bonne in tan tion pour le bien de la republique, et an coura gé vos subordonné qui périron mille foi pour les salut de la colonni, et les xecution de zordre du Directoire quil nou ce ra trans metre par vous,

Salut et respec,
Toussaint Louverture

[The enemy of the public thing, enemy of order and tranquillity, of men for their particular interest, of ambitious men, wants to make evil pass for good, and good pass for evil, in fact he passes darkness for light, and light for darkness; he wants what is sweet to be bitter, and what is bitter to be sweet. It is painful for men of honor to be treated in this manner. You may count, Citizen Agent, on Toussaint Louverture and his word. Palliative remedies only flatter the disease, and one must get to the source to heal it. As you do not know the colony, I fear that you are being turned from all your good intentions for the good of the republic, and are encouraging your subordinates who will perish a thousand times for the colony and the execution of the orders of the Directory that will be transmitted to us by you,

Salutations and respect,
Toussaint Louverture]

The letter begins with an anaphoric, nominal sentence that refers to an impersonal "enemy of the public thing." In her translation, Jenson brackets "chose publique" as "republic," because it is possible that Toussaint translated the Latin original, *res publica* (*Beyond the Slave Narrative* 80). This is an astute observation, not simply because it is another possible indication that Toussaint had received some education as a slave, but, more important, it could be a pedagogical move consistent with earlier letters. Written in the third person, it allowed him to express anger at the French agent without addressing him directly and to offer a warning, softened here through binary metaphors, about the kind of men who would destroy the colony. Toussaint then switched to the second person in a gesture of reassurance but still referred to himself in the third person, as if to remind the agent of his larger-than-life persona. He then mobilized a dual discourse of pain and healing, in which he both suffers from and heals the "disease" that threatened Saint-Domingue, an evil that had even corrupted the "good intentions" of the French agent. Following his own lesson, Toussaint initially "flatters" the agent only to move quickly to the warning that is the final sentence: if you stay on your current path (of jeopardizing public tranquillity), we will "perish a thousand times" (to preserve liberty).

The handwritten letter to the French agent encapsulated the concerns of the "public thing" for which Toussaint had prepared for nearly five years and for which he was now ready to perish. As he underscored in the first line, the "public thing" meant "order and tranquillity" for the family that he led on Saint-Domingue. Instead of simply writing "republic," Toussaint chose to remind his French interlocutor of the etymology of the word: in the colonial setting of Saint-Domingue, the "public thing" conveyed meaning

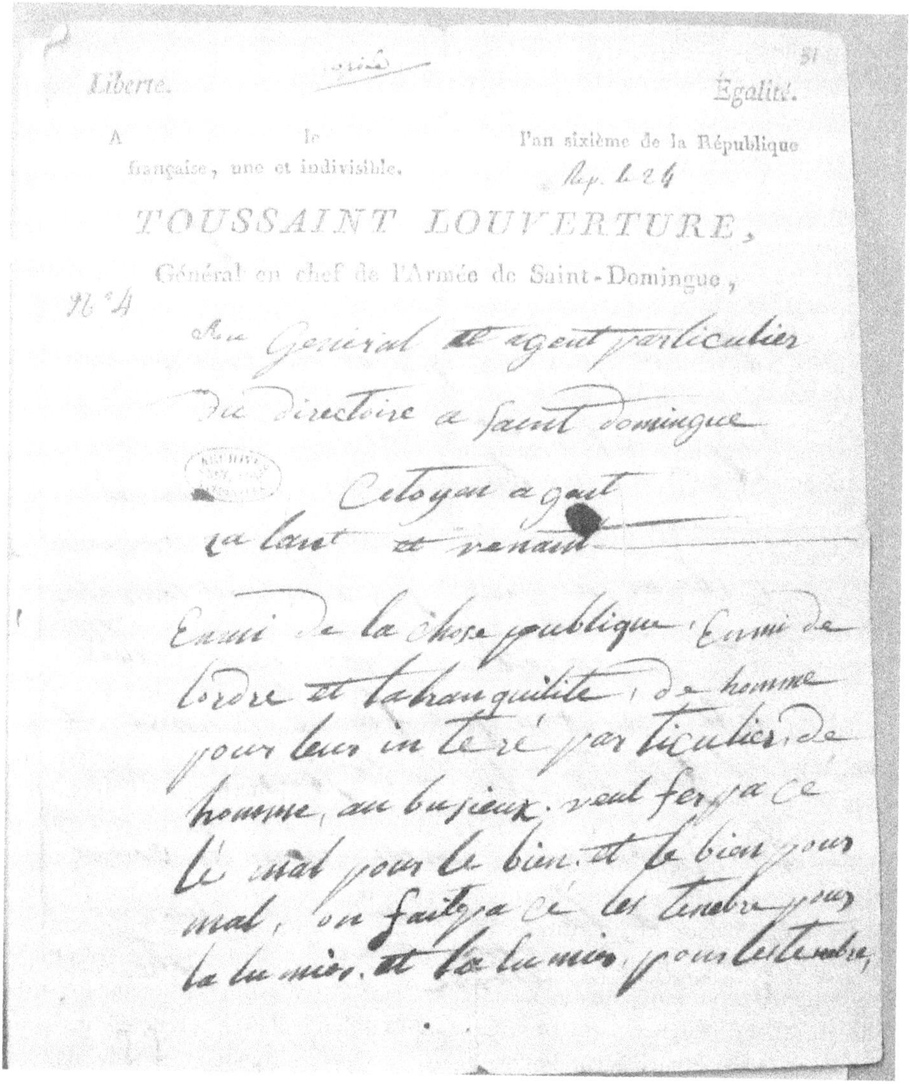

Liberté. Égalité.

A le l'an sixième de la République française, une et indivisible.

TOUSSAINT LOUVERTURE,

Général en chef de l'Armée de Saint-Domingue,

N° 4

Au Général et agent particulier du directoire a saint domingue

Citoyen agent

Ca lant et venant

Ennemi de la chose publique, Ennemi de l'ordre et tranquilité, de homme pour leur interé particulier, de homme, au bujieux, veut fer ya ce le mal pour le bien et le bien pour mal, on faitya ce les tenebre pour la lu mier et la lu mier pour les tenebre,

Figure 2.2. "Toussaint Louverture, Général en chef de l'Armée de St.-Domingue, au Général et agent particulier du Directoire à Saint-Domingue, l'an sixième," AN, AF III 210, Dossier 962, Folio 30. The first page of the three-page letter.

in stark *opposition* to the private matters for which the planters continued to fight vehemently. In colonialist logic, slaves were property; for Toussaint, the revolution was a radical redefinition of property rights. The meaning of "public thing" held by the family of former slaves was fundamentally about a general liberty that would always trump rights of private property. If Hédouville and the Directory conceived of "republicanism" in this manner, Toussaint reasoned, they could "count on his word" for a call to arms.

The hard line that Toussaint took with Hédouville became an even greater gamble in the consequences it would entail for the family he had assembled on Saint-Domingue. The departure of Hédouville and the weak agency of his temporary successor, Roume, whom Toussaint summoned and then imprisoned, left a vacuum of governance in the north and the west that only Toussaint could fill. A conflict ensued with Rigaud in the South, and the colony was enflamed in a civil war that ended with the latter's exit and Toussaint in sole possession of Saint-Domingue. The result was a crisis of power between the general in chief and the French government, now under the Consulate of Napoleon Bonaparte. As I move to subsequent steps taken by Toussaint to present the case for "free and French" to Bonaparte, I would like to return once more to the story of Toussaint, Isaac, and Placide, and to the relationship between a father and his sons and their place in the family romances that both Toussaint and the metropolitan leaders had crafted in the attempt to keep everyone together. Toussaint's ability to restructure the family of Saint-Domingue, coupled with the Directory's inability to be consistent with the more altruistic goals of the Institution Nationale des Colonies, would also have consequences for the Louverture sons in Paris.

Following the multiple historical accounts, the scene at Ennery could be described as a dramatic family reunion wrapped inside the greater story of the moment that sparked the war of Haitian Independence. According to the sensational account of Métral, it was the scene "where the love of country triumphed over the father's heart" (II, 60). In his narrative, Métral stayed close to Lacroix, who related Toussaint's unwillingness to accept the offer to become first lieutenant to Leclerc. Instead, according to Lacroix, "he was ready to sacrifice his children for his color [il était prêt à faire à sa couleur le sacrifice de ses enfants]" (313). If the Institution Nationale des Colonies was founded to educate the notable sons of Saint-Domingue as a way to inculcate Republican values—and most important the "public thing" of liberty for all—then the scene at Ennery, which cast Isaac and Placide as hostages to the loyalty of their father, proved that the mission of the French Republican school had reverted dramatically in four short years. Or had it? A report in year eight [1799–1800] from the minister of the navy and colonies to the Consuls of the Republic summed up the founding of the school and revealed two political goals that called into question its altruistic basis.[27] The report is worth citing at length:

> The utility of this establishment had been served and recognized by the Executive Directory. Reasons of Politics and Justice came together on its behalf. . . . By calling the children of Toussaint Louverture, Rigaud, and their chief lieutenants, to give

them a free education, the Directory had had as its goal not only to consolidate by Enlightenment and Instruction the work of liberty but also to assure itself, in the person of these children, hostages of the fidelity of their fathers, who have become by the force of circumstance the absolute Masters of the colony.

In other words, the school served largely as an insurance policy, and not only for the loyalty of Toussaint et al., but also for white planters, whom the Directory would be able to indemnify "as much as possible, the losses they experienced."

Toussaint's writing between 1796 and 1798 increasingly highlighted the impossible position in which he found himself. He had sent his sons to France because he believed in the educational mission; he was also wary of "unfavorable impressions" they might receive. The letter of 10 June expressed faith in French republicanism, at least its constitutional support of the principle of general liberty. At the same time, the words for Isaac and Placide were marked by a distrust of the instability of French institutions. The Institution Nationale des Colonies was shut down in the summer of 1802, not five years after it opened and shortly after Bonaparte reestablished slavery in the decree of May 1802.[28] In this light, the cautionary lesson he gave his sons was a logical postscript to the rebuttal of Vaublanc and was consistent with the warning to Hédouville.

As I will attempt to show in the next two chapters, Toussaint's ultimate downfall, ironically, may have been due to his failure to heed the warning in his own letter. That is, he attempted to occupy the space between his self-representation as servant *and* leader, son *and* father.[29] The colonial metaphors that I have developed thus far, namely, those of family and pedagogy, took a specific turn between Saint-Domingue and France. And as they shifted, they reached the point where they were brought together in the colonial idea of the *mère-patrie* educating her adopted children. The result of this uncomfortable union—a metaphorical space enforced by a literal threat—was the forced and paradoxical figure of speech in the "hostage of fidelity."[30] Forced and paradoxical because the French gesture to bestow the Institution Nationale des Colonies as a place for teaching and learning was also a proving ground of loyalty to France, a sort of imprisonment for an always deferred French citizenship; forced and paradoxical because the "new" colonialism under the Directory had allowed the planter lobby to hijack its mission and because even the "fructidorized" legislative body could only belatedly and temporarily dislodge slaveholding factions. The slippery representational power of the catachrestical structure works, as Aravamudan notes, as a play between surplus and lack. The colonial representation allowed Toussaint to be the both general in chief and loyal Creole servant. When he disrupted the dichotomy by dropping the role of servant, the French expressed confusion or, via Sonthonax, outrage. Toussaint himself displayed a similar impatience with the "wayward children" among the former slaves who labored under his rule. His particular "tropical" agency operated in the seizing of the colonial figure (of pupil, of family) and in the remaking of the greater family of Saint-Domingue.

3 "Free and French"
La Constitution de la colonie française de Saint-Domingue

23 August 1802, *Au cachot*

On 7 June 1802 Toussaint was taken hostage by French troops and soon thereafter shipped to France aboard *le Héros*, a vessel whose nomenclature suddenly conveyed a simple irony for his captor, Napoleon Bonaparte.[1] It must have been a theatrical scene: a hero of the protracted drama of the Haitian Revolution was on his way to a tragic death. Toussaint arrived in the harbor of Brest by mid-July. Nearly two weeks later, Bonaparte decreed, "The so-called Toussaint Louverture will be transferred and held prisoner at the Fort de Joux. He will be held in secret, with neither the ability to write nor communicate with any individual other than his servant."[2] Bonaparte's minister of war, General Berthier, relayed these orders to the local prefect, Jean De Bry, and inquired about the security of the fortress in the Jura, the mountains of eastern France on the border with Switzerland. De Bry responded to his superiors on 15 August: "I have inspected the premises myself, and I can assure you in advance that there will be no difficulty in carrying out the complete execution of the will of the government."[3] Unfortunately for De Bry, the ink had barely dried on his letter when two prisoners at the fort, General d'Andigné and le Comte de Suzannet, escaped in the middle of the night.[4]

According to d'Andigné, news of Toussaint's imminent arrival had actually hastened their plans to break out. Their escape brought about draconian security measures.[5] In his memoir, d'Andigné recalled that while on the lam he encountered Toussaint: "We entered Fontainebleau just as he had stopped there to dine; fifty dragoons made up

65

his escort" (Fortuné, II:118). Toussaint arrived at the fort one week later, on 23 August. Bonaparte's leniency to d'Andigné and Suzannet makes his treatment of Toussaint that much more brutal. The First Consul allowed the Vendéens to dictate the terms of their internal exile: "Bonaparte let us be the ones who chose the cities that would be most convenient. But he demanded," d'Andigné clarified, "our word of honor to stay there." (II:121). As Toussaint made clear in his *Mémoire*, there was no honor accorded him by Bonaparte. Upon learning of the evasion of the daring *chouans* (Royalist insurgents), Bonaparte issued a further instruction to his aide-de-camp, General Caffarelli, on 9 September: "You shall go to the Château de Joux. You shall carry out an investigation into the escape of d'Andigné and Suzannet. . . . You will advise that they not let up on the strict surveillance we must enforce to prevent a man such as him to escape."[6] His mission complete, Caffarelli reported back to Bonaparte on 16 September. The response is less important for the confirmation of tighter security at the prison than it is for his impression of Toussaint: "This man is master of himself, and he repeats the same things so exactly, at one to two day intervals, that one has to think either he is telling the truth or he is a profound liar whose story has been told for a long time."[7] Caffarelli's letter predicts what many biographers later concluded about Toussaint. Despite having brought Toussaint across the Atlantic and having whisked him in a closed carriage to a damp, dark cell in the Jura, Bonaparte still feared that his captive might escape.

Such fear was understandable given the power of Toussaint's adopted name, *Louverture*, in which the literal and metaphorical both find space. Bonaparte went so far as to make sure that his prisoner would never leave. Many have called attention to the torturous conditions of his incarceration at the Fort de Joux, while still others have elided the fact of his slow execution.[8] The most direct and most poignant description comes from Toussaint himself in a testimonial to the conditions of his capture and imprisonment. Once again, I provide a transcription of the original document, followed by a translation:

> A re te abitrerement sans montandre, ni me dire pour quoi, an pa re toute mésavaire, piÿer toute ma famille, an general, saisire mé pa pié, et les garde, man bar qué, an voyer nu comme ver de ter, re pan dre de calomni les plusatros cer mon conte, da pré cé la, je sui an voyer dant les fon du ca chau, nes ce pa coupe la janbre dun quie quin et loui dire marché, nes ce pa coupé la langue et loui dire parlé, nes ce pas an teré un homme vivant?[9]

> [To arrest arbitrarily without hearing me, nor telling me why, taking away all my affairs, pillaging my entire family, in general, seizing my papers and keeping them, embarking me, sending me naked like an earthworm, spreading the most atrocious calumny about me, after that, I am sent to the depths of a cell, is this not to cut off the leg of someone and telling him to walk, is this not to cut out the tongue and telling him to speak, is this not to bury a man alive?]

In this moving plea we read a poetic and almost clinical self-evaluation, a combination strikingly similar to the letter written to Hédouville. A series of rhetorical questions, chained together by dramatic language, barely conceals the literal register of physical deterioration and impending death. The dispassionate autopsy report only intensifies the voice in the *Mémoire*.[10] The above passage highlights Toussaint's attention to the literariness of an otherwise formal complaint and defense of conduct. The clinical analysis is a testimony to the dehumanization wrought by the French empire; Bonaparte's response was a tragic coda that, paradoxically, ensured the immortality of the symbol of escape evoked by *Louverture*.

Toussaint's Constitution recognized French sovereignty, but it also granted him the power of governor for life, an investment of power that Bonaparte read as a sure step toward independence. A little more than a month after the Coup of Brumaire [9 November 1799], by which Bonaparte took power from the Directory, the First Consul made his inaugural public address to the "Citizens of Saint-Domingue": "If there are ill-intentioned men in the colony of Saint-Domingue, if there are those who maintain relations with enemy powers, brave black men, remember," he declared, "that the French people alone recognize your liberty and the equality of your rights."[11] The proclamation, which spoke to a key consular constitutional revision that I discuss below, professed to uphold general liberty for blacks, yet was rendered fragile by the explicit warning it contained: surrounding slaveholding regimes pose a threat to your freedom. Furthermore, the emphasis on sovereignty that one reads in the distance between "French people" and "your liberty" will have implications for Toussaint's Constitution. Following his orders, General Caffarelli arrived at the Fort de Joux to interrogate Toussaint. "In talking with him," Bonaparte commanded, "you will inform him of the enormity of the crime of which he has made himself guilty by bearing arms against the Republic; that we had considered him a rebel the instant he had published his constitution" (VIII:30). He had already indicted Toussaint for the treasonous act of writing the Constitution de la colonie française de Saint-Domingue.[12]

I have begun this chapter with the final moments of the epic confrontation between Toussaint and Bonaparte—as well as a preview of the *Mémoire*—because these arresting images speak volumes to the fatal consequences of Toussaint's mastery of Saint-Domingue and of his signature interpretation of "free and French." In order to fully appreciate the agony of a man buried alive, it is necessary to examine first the 1801 Constitution and its rearticulation of the dichotomy of freedom and sovereignty. In what follows, I discuss the circumstances that led to the proclamation of this founding document and analyze Toussaint's constitutional vision for the family of Saint-Domingue. I am concerned with the relationship between freedom and slavery that was unique to constitutions of the time, particularly those of France and the United States. How does Toussaint attempt to constitute the principle of universal freedom for the former slaves? And how does he affirm this freedom in relation to not only his role as governor for life of Saint-Domingue but also Bonaparte's menacing assertion of metropolitan power?

As I frame it in this introductory discussion, the metaphorical opening of Toussaint's proposal of "free and French" was forever closed by Bonaparte's literal insistence on the supremacy of French sovereignty. The conflict between the two men was the result of a profound disjunction, similar to the split that occurred within French republicanism, between its Declaration of the Rights of Man and its colonial interests. As Toussaint argued in the *Mémoire*, it was also fundamentally about race. His constitution put pressure on the connection between the new discourse of rights and the power of the budding nation-state to bestow these very rights.[13] Toussaint sparred with Bonaparte, moving between loyalty and subversion, and created a guarded, double awareness that would place him on one of the first crossroads of the black Atlantic.

8 July 1801—Toussaint Proclaims Liberty

> "Oh you, my fellow Citizens, of every age, every class and every color, you are free, and the Constitution delivered to me today, must render Liberty eternal."[14]

After fighting and negotiating his way to the stage, Toussaint publicly celebrated the new Constitution in Le Cap. Having convoked a General Assembly on 4 February 1801 (not coincidentally the anniversary of the National Convention's abolition of slavery in 1794), Toussaint charged this body to elect ten of its members to draft a constitution to be submitted for his review and approval. The *Constitution de la colonie française de Saint-Domingue* was completed on 8 May and approved by Toussaint on 3 July.[15] The three years from the departure of Hédouville, in October 1798, to the summer of 1801 saw Toussaint take a circuitous route to this proclamation. After signing a secret treaty with the British and negotiating to open trade with the United States—whose consular general, Tobias Lear, was in attendance in Le Cap (according to the *Extrait des registres*)—he defeated Rigaud in the South and annexed the Spanish side of the island. Therefore, it is imperative to understand the rhetoric of "eternalizing liberty" as part of a calculated plan that took shape over time. Those investigating the 1801 Constitution generally fall into two camps: either Toussaint aimed to declare a de facto independence or he intended to keep Saint-Domingue under the French Republic. Where Pluchon reads in Toussaint's writing and actions a series of "plots [*complots*]," tied to *intrigue* and *duperie*, or "attempts to deceive" (234), I continue to analyze the sequence of emplotments, or how Toussaint put together his proposal to Bonaparte. The search for motives too often dismisses the narrative strategies in which he envisioned Saint-Domingue's relationship to metropolitan France.

A constitution is a narrative of foundation, composed of articles that establish laws of a sovereign country and the fundamental rights of its inhabitants. The 1801 Constitution merits closer analysis for its unique declaration to abolish slavery, for the precedent it set for future Haitian constitutions, and for its relation to European and American discourse on rights and sovereignty. The publication of this Constitution occurred at a liminal moment, engendering an imaginative reappropriation of the goals of both Republicans and planters (Republicans or Royalists). As his tumultuous relationship with Sonthonax demonstrated, Toussaint was not the only figure on Saint-Domingue who could be accused of harboring aspirations of independence. Dubois is instructive on this point: "In strengthening the autonomy of his regime, Louverture was preparing not to break with France, but to renegotiate its relationship with the colony. Ironically, his regime represented the fulfillment of some of the dreams of autonomy enunciated by the planters of Saint-Marc years before" (Dubois, *Avengers of the New World* 226). Dubois calls attention to the fact that for some time French planters (whites and *gens de couleur*) had lobbied and fought for local autonomy. Unlike Toussaint, their explicit reason for doing so was to maintain the profitable, colonial status quo by retaining slavery and the slave trade. The early constitutional debates following the French Revolution saw legislators assign to the overseas colonies a separate legal status. The first French Constitution of 1791, whose preamble included the *Déclaration des droits de l'homme et du Citoyen de 1789*, purposely excluded the colonies from its jurisdiction: "The French colonies and possessions in Asia, Africa, and America, although they form a part of the French Empire, are not included in the present Constitution."[16] As I have pointed out, four years later, in July 1795, the National Convention closed this loophole in a new constitution that redefined colonial possessions as "integral parts of the Republic ... subject to the same constitutional law." However, powerful, pro-slavery factions maintained considerable control of the French Republic's colonial mission and kept Saint-Domingue at some constitutional distance. As the reports of Toussaint and the agents sent to work with and against him reveal, the legal space between metropole and colony enabled continued exploitation.

Ironically, Bonaparte had actually created an opening for him. Returning to the First Consul's address to the "Citizens of Saint-Domingue" on 25 December 1799, we see that, a year and a half before Toussaint, Bonaparte, too, proclaimed a new constitution: "Citizens, a constitution that could not support itself against multiple violations is replaced by a new pact destined to strengthen liberty. Article 91 states that the French colonies shall be governed by special laws" (*Napoléon* VI: 42). The new consular law nullified the Directory's revision of 1795 and reaffirmed Article 8 of the Constitution of 1791. "This measure," Bonaparte continued, "derives from the nature of things and the difference of climates. The inhabitants of French colonies situated in America, in Asia, in Africa, cannot be governed by the same law. The difference of habits, customs, interests, diversity of soil, agricultures, production, all require diverse modifications" (42). This language of difference, which drew heavily on legislative debates a decade earlier, was part and parcel of a historical colonial discourse that was also cyclical. Unlike the lengthy deliberations that occurred before each of the major constitutional reforms in the nascent French Republic, including the debates leading up to the First Law of Departmentalization in January 1798, Bonaparte wasted no time relegating Saint-Domingue to a subordinate status. He declared liberty and equality sacred but only because granted by the French. In an attempt to rein in Toussaint to the French national cause, Bonaparte left Saint-Domingue outside of metropolitan jurisdiction; it was a reopening of a legal loophole that Toussaint circumvented with his own constitution.

How should we read Toussaint's proclamation of "eternal liberty" in relation to French antecedents? First, it is necessary to take note of the publication of the 8 July proclamation in the minutes [*procès-verbal*] of the official *Registre*, which, as an attestation of the ceremony, bore the stamp of authority and served to validate, in some sense, Toussaint's remarks. The governor general's speech is set inside the register and is both prefaced and followed by the speeches of Citizens Borgella (president of the Central Assembly) and Fouqueau (president of the Civil Tribunal of Le Cap). To be sure, the municipality of Le Cap and the Central Assembly were under Toussaint's control; as a result, one cannot read the legitimacy inherent to the register without taking into account the power that Toussaint exercised and orchestrated. Indeed, it is possible to read this influence in the opening remarks of Borgella:

> French colonists and you, brave soldiers, Saint-Domingue has aspired for a long time for the well being of a local Constitution. One faction after another has come from the Metropolitan Government, propagating subversive principles on this distant Island, and [each] has suffocated the just claims of its unfortunate Inhabitants, and has degraded their dignity as free Men.

Borgella rehearses the concerns made by Toussaint both in the *Réfutation* to Vaublanc and the letter to Hédouville; by citing the French Constitution of 1795 and its inclusion of the colonies as "integral parts of the Republic," Borgella also set up Toussaint's forthcoming justification of the Constitution of Saint-Domingue. In fact, before ceding the podium to Toussaint, Borgella made reference to the new consular constitution proposed by Bonaparte and asked rhetorically, "Was it made for you? . . . No." Although he made sure to acknowledge what France had done for the inhabitants of Saint-Domingue, Borgella closed his remarks, laden as they were with dramatic praise to Toussaint, by underscoring the "long silence" of the metropole and the "absence of Laws" on the island (*Extrait des registres*). In sum, the ceremony was not simply a day of pomp and circumstance, it was a script designed to prepare the historical and political ground for the 1801 Constitution.

Borgella primed the audience for Toussaint, whose speech celebrated freedom but left considerable space between Saint-Domingue and France. At first glance, the remarks are consistent with the more conservative rhetoric of family peculiar to Toussaint. He praised the "reign of good morals and the divine Religion of Jesus Christ," magistrates as "Fathers and Defenders," and the values of "integrity and uprightness"; he exhorted his "brave troops" to "respect discipline and authority, develop agriculture, obey superiors, and defend and uphold the Constitution against all enemies foreign and domestic, who would seek to attack it." The language was far from radical; and yet, in front of an international audience, and to a public, whom he addressed as "the People of Saint-Domingue," to proclaim a new Constitution was revolutionary. As Nesbitt suggests, it was as if he addressed a "newly formed nation" (*Universal Emancipation* 156). The proclamation was audacious, especially as it is only in his last line that he explicitly mentions France: "Long live the French Republic and the colonial Constitution!" In the end, despite the final toast to the French Republic, the speech was far from a gesture of unity with the metropole.

Beyond the circumstances of the proclamation of the Constitution—which, it cannot be understated, was carried out *before* Toussaint sought Bonaparte's approval—the text itself exposes the rift between Saint-Domingue and France. According to Sibylle Fischer, the earlier Haitian constitutions, including Toussaint's, were "fictions" because "they did not correspond to the legal and political reality" (228). These realities include the establishment of racial taxonomies and the prevalence of slaveholding governments in and around the Caribbean and Atlantic. Therefore, Fischer points out, to abolish slavery and hierarchy based on race (as did Dessalines's 1805 Constitution) was to give these documents an "illusory character" (228). To say that Toussaint's Constitution (and, for that matter, those that followed) was a declaration of political desire, however, does not mean that it was unmoored from political and social reality. To place undue emphasis on the Constitution as an aspirational text is to ignore the fact of Sonthonax's abolition of slavery in 1793 and its subsequent ratification by the National Convention in 1794. In the same vein, to begin with the premise that Toussaint's Constitution was a "fantasy of statehood" means that the French Declaration of the Rights of Man, too, must be read as a "foundational fiction" (Fischer, 229). The problem with this analysis is that it would require dismissing much if not all of Toussaint's writings up to this point. As we have seen, these letters and reports express a mixture of belief in, and distrust of, the French Republican discourse of rights.

What the Constitution does, I would argue, is set a precedent for the conflict between freedom and limits imposed on it by sovereign nations. Many of these restrictions came from Toussaint himself; like his successors, he counterbalanced the articles on universal rights with measures that created a martial-like state. These articles have received much attention over the years, and it is not surprising that Duboys deemed the Constitution "a monster" or that Dubreuil, more recently, found it "shameful."[17] Before discussing its authoritarian dimension, it is important to acknowledge its revolutionary laws, especially when compared to the constitutions of France and the United States. After delimiting the territory of Saint-Domingue, which "is part of the French Empire, but is subject to particular laws" (Article 1), the Constitution states, "There can be no slaves on this territory, servitude is forever abolished. All men are here born, live, and die free and French" (Article 3). While the Constitutions of France and the United States addressed the question of rights in a Declaration or Bill of Rights, which continued to permit slavery and were subject to periodic amendment, Toussaint inscribed abolition and equality of rights into the first articles of the text. The Constitution immediately reinforces the universality of his particular government in the language of the next two articles: "Every man, regardless of his color, is eligible for all employment.... The law is the same for all, whether it punishes or protects." Freedom does not depend on race or citizenship, the very same obstacles to universal rights that would impede the French and United States Constitutions for some time to come.

As radical and unequivocal as they are with respect to the eternal abolition of slavery, these opening articles retain the ambiguous link between universal freedom and nationality. Following the response to Vaublanc and the letter to Hédouville, the question remains, what do we make of the movement between "free and French" in the Constitution? For Doris Garraway, one of the "paradoxes of the emancipatory project . . . [was] the fact that when this struggle was defined in universal terms, it became indissociable from a claim to belonging within the French Republican social body" ("'Légitime Défense'" 67). This reading would seem to stake the claim, "free and French," to a goal of assimilation within greater France, or at least security under the protection of France. In doing so, however, it dims Toussaint's vision for Saint-Domingue, which had already cast an international glow, to a more nationalistic perspective, in that one would perceive an inseparable bond between "free and French." Following this logic, we remain arguably stuck inside the vicious circle of universal rights and national sovereignty. Garraway reads in Toussaint's Constitution a "rhetorical nationalism" in that the freedom he proposed would be ultimately provided and protected by the French. This analysis is similar to the one offered by Césaire, who argued that Toussaint was proposing a sort of Commonwealth. This was a "brilliant intuition," Césaire commented, the only problem being that it was "ahead of its time, and by a good century and a half" (*Toussaint Louverture* 283). The *Discours préliminaire* to the Constitution could be read another way: it describes a symbolic renovation of the French colony into which a new foundation is poured: "the former edifice cleared of its ruins . . . seemed to have marked the propitious moment when it was necessary to put down a foundation." The revolutionary implications of such a stance result from a narrative that walks a fine line between assimilation and autonomy.

As we have seen in its opening articles, the Constitution underscores the problem of sovereignty, as both France and Saint-Domingue seem to exercise control. The first two articles concern the question of "Territory," listing the administrative units of Saint-Domingue as well as its place in the French empire. The same clause ends, however, by relieving the empire of command of Saint-Domingue because it is "subject to particular laws." The second section, "Of Its Inhabitants," makes clear that Toussaint places liberty above, or on a par with, sovereignty. These initial articles create the fundamental contradiction in the Constitution between the universal abolition of slavery and the question of territory, or the only particular, geographic site on which the ban can exist. As Nesbitt points out, "Its ontological ground (the universal ban on slavery) necessarily refers back to its own (empirical) ground" (*Universal Emancipation* 160). It is from this seemingly irresolvable contradiction that Nesbitt arrives at the oxymoron, "singular universal," to make sense of the extraordinary circumstances under which

Toussaint and his Assembly deliberated. Nesbitt's argument is convincing as a new way to think about this founding initiative because the contradiction between universal freedom and sovereign law was both a political and an ontological problem.

The Constitution left the French government effectively powerless. Bonaparte was all too aware of this and responded four months later in a letter to Toussaint in which he argued, "The circumstances, where you found yourself surrounded on all sides by enemies, with the metropole unable to come to your aid, nor to feed you, legitimated those articles of this Constitution which could otherwise not be so."[18] These circumstances removed, Bonaparte reasoned, meant that Toussaint must submit to French sovereignty. The contingency of Toussaint's abolition of slavery was that it could only be constituted on Saint-Domingue. In all other respects, the foundation of universal freedom was not based on circumstance. To this end, Toussaint clearly foresaw a geopolitical and legal repositioning of powers and assertion of rights and freedoms. The attempt to reconcile the conflict between "being free" and the familial obligation to the "public order" is what made Toussaint's constitutional vision so new.

Ultimately, being "free" seems to have had little to do with being "French." The legislative and military powers of the "French colony" of Saint-Domingue were henceforth subject to Toussaint and his Central Assembly. The language of Title VII, "On legislation and legislative authority," is unambiguous: "No law relative to the interior administration of the colony may be promulgated if it does not bear this formula: The Central Assembly of Saint-Domingue, on behalf of the governor, delivers the following law . . . " After Title VII, the Constitution includes but two nominal references to the French government, and neither states what its authority shall be. From "The Government," to "Tribunals," "Municipal Administrations," and "Armed Forces" through to "Finances" and "General Dispositions" the absence of French authority is palpable. Most provocative is the clause in the seventy-seventh and final article, in which Toussaint, reiterating Borgella, stamps his authority in the "absence of laws," as if France no longer laid any claim to Saint-Domingue. In his letter to Bonaparte written nine days after the ceremony in Le Cap, Toussaint introduced the Constitution to his ostensible superior and restated that its necessity arose out of an "absence of laws."[19] In seeking approval of a document that moved nearly all authority away from France to Saint-Domingue—and, in so doing, liberated rights from a national referent—Toussaint made a powerful gesture that stunned Bonaparte.

Liberty and Power on Saint-Domingue

The Constitution is remarkable not only for the revolutionary positioning of rights and sovereignty but also for its regressive, authoritarian measures. Title III, which establishes Catholicism as the state religion (banning the practice of Vodou); Title IV, which forbids divorce; and Title VI, which regulates agriculture and trade—all had the potential to crack the foundation of universal liberty. While it is tempting to explain away the articles concerning agricultural labor (14–18) as part of the daunting task of rebuilding Saint-Domingue after a decade of war, to do so would ignore the harsh underbelly of Toussaint's work regime. Each plantation is the "quiet sanctuary of an active and constant family, whose owner or his representative is necessarily the father" (Article 15). The Constitution legalizes the ideal of the hierarchical family unit that Toussaint developed in his lengthy correspondence with Laveaux and during his efforts to quell rebellions among black laborers. If these earlier writings and addresses hinted at Toussaint's paternal role, the Constitution explicitly defined the incarcerating conditions of "family" life: Article 16 states that "any change of domicile on the part of the laborers brings about the destruction of agriculture. . . . [T]o repress a vice as fatal to the colony as it is contrary to public order, the Governor undertakes all policing measures of [the decree] 20 vendemiaire year IX [12 October 1800], and the proclamation of the following 19 pluviose [9 February 1801] of the General in Chief Toussaint Louverture."[20] Such domestic imprisonment was not the most controversial clause: perhaps the most damaging, Article 17, concerns the introduction of additional laborers, who were "indispensable to the reestablishment" of the agricultural economy. For Pluchon, this was nothing less than the renewal of the slave trade; Schœlcher had arrived at a similar observation, denouncing the euphemisms that hardly mask the authorization of an "execrable traffic of his 'brothers'" (296). As a whole, this sequence of articles would seem to call into question the universality of freedom on Saint-Domingue.

Despite being in the impossible position of having to create a government and society based on universal freedom at a time when the rest of the world was not ready for it, Toussaint threatened to undermine the Constitution with these restrictive measures. His investiture for life (Article 28), the censure of the press (Article 39), and the establishment of the governor's extrajudicial powers (Article 40), all combine to worrisome effect. "The kings of the France of yore," Schœlcher lamented, "had no more power than was granted to Toussaint by this Constitution" (297). Moreover, the language and policies put forth to regulate agriculture re-created the servile constituency that had brought about the revolution in the first place. Nevertheless, Césaire read the Constitution as a "work of circumstance" (283) and argued that it was so revolutionary as to require the authoritative measures that Toussaint put in place: "It is the exceptional situation, revolutionary as it was, that imposed the dictatorship" (279). In this analysis, the Constitution provided Toussaint with the means necessary to found a country that was surrounded by slave-based economies. Césaire's take on this contradiction paralleled the reasoning of Bonaparte in the 18 November 1801 letter to Toussaint. If for different ends, both read the Constitution as a political necessity.

One solution to the apparent conundrum between politics and principles is to remember that, although he drew on French and American precedents, Toussaint was firmly committed to creating a government for the people of Saint-Domingue not based on slavery. Did political and agricultural realities necessarily undo the principle by which "servitude is forever abolished"? That his Constitution abolished slavery and gave everyone access to employment distinguished it from the founding documents of France and the United States. The ban on slavery was only politically motivated insofar as it moved the discussion of rights out of France itself and into the Caribbean and Americas. An additional way to understand the document would be to tease out the ontological from the political.[21] This argument is effective if one focuses more on the critical and original ban on servitude that grounds the document and less on the measures taken by Toussaint to rebuild and defend Saint-Domingue. Nesbitt argues that "overpersonalizing the Constitution" as a reflection of Toussaint's "indubitable power" is to equate the authoritative measures with the revolutionary principle and, thus, to weaken unfairly the foundation of universal freedom (*Universal Emancipation* 158). In this line of reasoning, it matters less that it was Toussaint who embodied the contradiction between principles and political means in order to wrangle the elusive universal right to freedom; it is the enduring battle for freedom and the power that attempts to restrain it that deserves our attention.

The gulf between the articles that establish freedom and those that restrict it appears to make the Constitution a flawed document. Moreover, the power that the Constitution gave Toussaint, under the guise of protecting the people, came at a price. The proclamation of the Constitution ultimately led to his arrest, imprisonment, and death in France. Therefore, he was powerless to carry out any reform of the Constitution, aside from the memoir he left in a cold cell in the Jura. Before I move to the reflection that takes place in the *Mémoire*, it is important to work through Toussaint's understanding of just how the former slaves had earned their freedom and what they would be expected to do with it. In the short term, Toussaint had to prepare for the possibility of a future invasion and the reestablishment of slavery. This involved opening trade with the United States for much-needed arms and munitions.[22] In order to defend Saint-Domingue for the long term, however, he needed to help the citizens rebuild their lives and the economy. This meant educating the former slaves to see themselves as active and willing participants in the project of Saint-Domingue. As we saw in the proclamation of the Constitution—where he encouraged the laborers, "flee idleness, it is the mother of all vice"—Toussaint acts to shape their freedom from the very beginning. It is a discourse of inculcation not unlike that penned to his sons three years earlier: he exhorted the people to think about responsibility, about discipline, and, very practically, about getting back to work.

Beyond these general terms, however, Toussaint gave the masses little to no chance to appreciate their freedom. He deprived them of ownership of land and forbade them to leave the plantation. The plan was to operate Saint-Domingue from the top down, delegating enforcement of agricultural regulations to his military officers and even encouraging former white colonists to retake possession of plantations. If he came to personify the liberating force of revolution, Toussaint also assumed the mantle of a militarized, centralized power on Saint-Domingue and incarnated the codependence of liberty and power. This dual embodiment recurs in his eventual successor in the North, Christophe, who had thousands of workers suffer to build the Citadel, which doubled as a physical and symbolic fortress.[23] Under the leadership of Toussaint, the emancipatory project of the revolution gave the slaves their freedom, but it actually replaced one form of suffering with another.

Despite his defeat of the Spanish and the British, and his unquestionable role as revolutionary leader, Toussaint struggled to reassure the people that a life of servitude was a thing of the past. Popular unrest was not uncommon under his regime and actually became such a problem that in November 1801 Toussaint had his own nephew, Moïse, executed for his alleged role in an uprising in the North, where he was the chief agricultural inspector.[24] That Toussaint severely restricted the liberty of his workers and diminished their role in his familial paradigm of governance should not be understated. However, it is imperative to explore how such a drastic turnaround was even possible. The starting point must be in the foundational space of the Constitution, which narrated the moment when the story of the greatest overcoming of slavery collided with the immediate necessity of imposing limits on the newly emancipated. In other words, the Constitution not only grounded the principle of universal freedom but also took measures to contain it and give it shape: it was composed of two narratives that both complemented and contradicted one another.

The tension in the 1801 Constitution between liberating black laborers and demanding their continued service to Saint-Domingue created a core, philosophical problem concerning freedom before and after abolition that has been the subject of major historical works. In general terms, "the post-emancipation problem," forms a genealogy of historical research, most notably from Eric Williams, *Capitalism and Slavery*, to David Brion Davis, *The Problem of Slavery in the Age of Revolution, 1770–1823*, and finally to Thomas C. Holt, *The Problem of Freedom: Race, Labor, and Politics in Jamaica, 1832–1938*.[25] While each of these studies takes a different approach, they are all concerned with the motives that led to the transition from, and links between, the abolition of slavery (in terms of both economic interests and social or religious thought) to the development of early capitalism. Developing the connections between the theses of Williams and Davis would require more space than is appropriate here; therefore, I would like to turn briefly to Holt (whose work naturally and chronologically builds on his predecessors), and what he termed "the problem of freedom," for its compelling parallels to the apparent contradiction between freedom and power in Toussaint's Constitution.

Drawing on Davis's analysis of the ideological justification for both economic and moral opposition to slavery, Holt sets out to understand the forces that brought British legislators to abolish slavery. In his study of post-emancipation Jamaica, he argues that emancipation created the problem of compelling former slaves to return to work on the plantation. He makes a comparison between the creation of the white, British working class and the transformation of black slaves on Jamaica into wage laborers. For Holt, freedom is not a natural condition: it is a "historically particular and socially constructed phenomenon" (xxii). The argument is that the supposed liberal ideology of abolitionism was not based on altruism; rather, after the industrial revolution, it served to prepare the way for "free" markets, which required disciplined labor and came with their own forms of coercion. Holt looks closely at the "well-traveled, overlapping maps of evangelism and commerce" to contend that the humanitarian spirit of abolitionist movements competed with, and ultimately took a backseat to, outcomes that prioritized the governance of newly freed men and women, and to the ideology and policies that would transform them into a workforce (27).

Holt makes the case for a century of failure on the part of liberalism in its attempts to bring about substantive freedom for former slaves. Political change occurred in name only, he maintains, as the British government shifted from a regime of forced labor to one that "reformed" free workers in a voluntary system. No longer slaves, the workers were trained to think of themselves as participants in a "free market" with material aspirations that could be achieved through free labor. However, Holt demonstrates that when former slaves lived their freedom outside of, or in opposition to, the market, their refusal was met with assumptions concerning their aspirations and desires. This new conflict led to economic failures that, he argues, "fueled racist thinking and imperial ambition" (309). A host of stereotypical identifications comes to define British views on the black worker, culminating in the perceived necessity of a "beneficent despotism" over the "wayward children of the human family" (309).

What can a story about the British colonial government in Jamaica tell us about Toussaint's short-lived government? Despite enormous differences of time and place, of levels of violence, of colonial programs and ambitions, and certainly of the former slaves themselves, the two conflicts have much in common in the attempt to transform the "wayward children"—to recall, Toussaint used the same term to address the workers of Saint-Louis-du-Nord. Although Toussaint actively pursued international trade and opened the export market to bring in revenue in the effort to rebuild and protect Saint-Domingue, he conceived of economic responsibility less as a function of the marketplace than in terms of family, or the *oikos* of Saint-Domingue. This is not to say that Toussaint was not preparing for a greater share of the emerging Caribbean market. His immediate concern, however, was certainly not the creation of material aspirations. As evidenced in his many proclamations of general liberty, his thinking lay more in the abstract. It was very much about retelling a familial story, about instilling a sense of belonging to a society based on agricultural labor. In the *Précis historique*, Duboys cites a letter from Toussaint to "les cultivateurs," written after the departure of Hédouville. The central message of the letter laid the groundwork for the regulations contained in the Constitution:

> The freedom in which you glorify imposes upon you greater obligations than the slavery out of which you have come. It is to society, to the great family of which you are a part, to which you owe the work that you once sacrificed to the ambition of a master. It compels you to the law of work; it demands of you the practice of virtues that constitute a good citizen. (II:38)

Toussaint urged the laborers to understand that liberty comes with a "great obligation." Instead of celebrating freedom as the autonomy of an individual, he reshaped it as a sacrifice of belonging to a greater family. In and of itself, autonomy is not virtuous until it is given over to the communal well-being. Freedom, in other words, must lead to a shared commitment to work for one's country.

The reform of freedom that Toussaint laid out in the Constitution was tightly connected to the hierarchical confines of the family unit as a source of authority. The traditional narrative of family framed his exhortation to the former slaves to define their newfound citizenship in terms of the limited freedom he granted them. The understanding of family owed its development as an organizational unit to the discipline that Toussaint experienced in the military and to the structures of power of European administrations in the Caribbean in which he participated. The project of freedom that he institutionalized in the Constitution was profoundly influenced by its relationship to governmental power. In this manner his story differed significantly from the failure of British liberalism recounted in *The Problem of Freedom*. In Holt's telling, over the course of the nineteenth century the British put in place a series of "reforms" for an economic system that bore striking similarities to the beliefs in human nature and social order upon which the goals of its slaveholding regime were based. In contrast, Toussaint's constitutional narrative began with a firm conviction of the primal place of universal freedom. His story was not a failure of ideology; rather, it wrestled with the government's role in nurturing and restraining the freedom of its citizens. The articles of the Constitution narrated the thorny transition from the founding of universal freedom to the shaping of its limits. It became a tragic lesson of a profound political devolution that stifled the very people Toussaint set out to protect.

The Tragic Reach for Shared Sovereignty

Toussaint's time as the father of the family of Saint-Domingue came to an end less than a year after the proclamation of the Constitution. It is at once the story of an exhilarating overcoming and of a stark coming to terms with the relationship between freedom and government. Given what is known about the hardship of the former slaves and their continued exclusion from ownership of land, it is hard to imagine that they were able to enjoy freedom.[26] Likewise, given the restructuring of power between Saint-Domingue and France in the 1801 Constitution, it is not surprising that Bonaparte would seek to reassert French control. Despite the near crossing out of French power in the Constitution, Toussaint never proclaimed independence. It appears that he had his doubts, as evidenced in a second letter addressed to Bonaparte on 23 August, along with a duplicate of the Constitution.[27] Whereas Toussaint gave the first copy to Colonel Vincent, an otherwise trusted French officer, he dispatched Nogéré, a member of the Central Assembly, with the second. He did his best to persuade the First Consul but also betrayed his anger at those "enemies" who would slander his leadership:

He is charged with transmitting to you, along with the Constitution, the organic laws that develop from it, and to give you on this matter any necessary clarification. In particular, I charge him to give you any details you may desire, as well as to destroy in your mind any lies of my enemies, who, jealous of the calm that the colony enjoys and its rapid steps to prosperity under the administration of a black man, would like to incite the French government to measures that could bring about the disorganization of the order that I have established.[28]

Many have read this second constitutional missive as an obvious attempt to mitigate an unfavorable reaction from Bonaparte. In a defensive posture that predicts the *Mémoire*, Toussaint points to "organic laws," or the powers that his Constitution organized and that were, he argued, legal proof of his government; he also offers a corrective to French republicanism by elucidating how his reform of freedom on Saint-Domingue depends on a discourse of race. He defines his role as governor in opposition to Bonaparte, who subjugated the freedom of blacks to French sovereign plans. In the above letter Toussaint anticipates a negative reception in Paris, and in an emphatic first person warns Bonaparte against undoing the "order that I established."

Toussaint's warning was also a lesson. His word traveled from the oral (and mediated) space of public proclamation to its constitutional transcription as a legal foundation and to the deferential but timely art of persuasion in a letter to a superior. The series of emplotments was performative in that its political effects were rendered in literary and legal narratives that both transformed and repudiated Bonaparte's consular revision. By the time he wrote Bonaparte, Toussaint had Saint-Domingue functioning effectively, he argued, as a political entity to be reckoned with in the Caribbean. Because the Constitution took shape in the intermediary spaces that Toussaint had always occupied in relation to his rivals on Saint-Domingue, to Britain and the United States and, most important, to France, it led him to propose shared sovereignty. The Constitution blended the discourses of law, abolitionism, political theory, and international commerce in order to reconfigure republicanism by uprooting it from its nationalist and racist underpinnings. Toussaint narrated a complicated story: the necessity of containing freedom and directing it to produce disciplined citizens threatened to break up the family romance of general liberty. But these two internal narratives also delivered a powerful contestation of French and American discourses on freedom by strategically amending these antecedents with the inscription of the political and ontological rationalities of race. This rewriting of universal rights in the space of the Constitution will be a model for Haitian constitutions to come as well as for the future shaping of freedom in the Caribbean.

4 Toussaint Louverture at a Crossroads

The Mémoire of the "First Soldier of the Republic of Saint-Domingue"

8 October 1802, "Je vous prie au nom de dieu, au nom de l'humanité"
[I beg of you, in the name of God, in the name of humanity]

Vous me per me trai, premiere Consul, de vous dire avec tout le respec et la soumition que je vous doit. Le gouvernement a été trompé entièrement sur le conte de Toussaint Louverture, sur un de ce plus zéllé et couragé serviteur à St. Domingue.
[Allow me, First Consul, to tell you with all due respect and submission. The government has been utterly mistaken about the account of Toussaint Louverture, about one of its most zealous and courageous servants on St. Domingue.][1]

A LITTLE MORE THAN a year after publishing the Constitution, Toussaint was Bonaparte's prisoner. The transition from the Constitution to the writings in the Fort de Joux marked the final stage of his life, one that quickly passed from glory to misery. Bonaparte had neglected to heed Toussaint's warning and had gone ahead with an expedition to retake control of Saint-Domingue. Once on board *le Héros* Toussaint wrote the first of a series of letters to Bonaparte, in which he implored the First Consul for mercy but also justified his conduct. He acknowledged errors but also argued that Leclerc reneged on a word of honor by arresting him—a claim he will repeat in the *Mémoire*. Toussaint defended himself directly to the First Consul, even going so far as to equate his rise to power on Saint-Domingue with Bonaparte's Coup of 18 brumaire. He concludes by appealing to honor and justice: "I have too great an idea of the grandeur and of the justice of the First Magistrate of the French people to doubt for a moment his impartiality. I like to believe that in his hands the scale will not lean one way more than the other. I ask for his generosity."[2] A short while later, Toussaint had reason to doubt Bonaparte's sense of honor: "I am unfortunate, miserable, and a victim," he wrote on 8 October; nevertheless, he continued, "I am, all the same, continuously at the service of my country [*consécutivement au service de ma patrie*]."[3] The juxtaposition of victimization with a dogged nobility of spirit animated the letters to

Bonaparte. Some readers highlight the resignation in these letters as a sign of political failure, while still others, pointing out that Haiti will be an independent republic a short nine months after Toussaint's death, read the ultimate sacrifice for the future of his country. The varying interpretations find common ground, however, in the focus on Toussaint at a crossroads. In this chapter, I focus on the writings produced during his imprisonment, especially the *Mémoire du Général Toussaint Louverture*. Consistent with my approach thus far, I analyze these texts not in isolation but as the final chapter of the larger body of writing.

Scholars have dismissed the *Mémoire* and its importance for Toussaint's corpus.[4] In his study of eyewitness accounts of the Haitian Revolution, Popkin relegates the *Mémoire* to a note: "These memoirs, however, are a classic example of a politician's apology, and they are largely limited to an account of Toussaint Louverture's political and military actions in the four months following the landing of the French military expedition in 1802" (*Facing Racial Revolution* 368). As I will demonstrate, by writing "memoirs" in the plural, Popkin makes a subtle generic alteration to the kind of report that Toussaint wrote. At the outset, I suggest that the *Mémoire* is important for the manner in which it summarized key moments of Toussaint's leadership, including his priorities for the Constitution. Concluding with an appeal to justice and fairness, Toussaint offered a spirited defense, one that recognized setbacks and failures but also lashed out at the French, especially Leclerc. To appreciate the blend of regret and counterattack requires reading the Constitution and the *Mémoire* together as texts that reflect on the place of Saint-Domingue in a new geopolitical arrangement in the Caribbean and Atlantic worlds at the beginning of the nineteenth century.

At first glance, the Constitution is a forward-looking document, while the *Mémoire* is retrospective, as Toussaint looked back on what he had achieved in order to present his defense to Bonaparte. In the *Mémoire*, as de Cauna observes in his preface to the 2009 edition, Toussaint "reacts as a statesman and tightens his game with customary finesse" (34). The text is another maneuver that is consistent with and builds on earlier writings. Toussaint's skill at moving from one genre to another reveals the mediation that takes place between them: the links between the political context of the Constitution and the judicial and literary aspects of the *Mémoire* compel the reader to reconsider theses texts from multiple angles. Inasmuch as it leaves a record of activity that his successors could learn from, the *Mémoire* is also a prospective document in that it revises history for posterity's sake. As I argue in the second half of this book, Toussaint's political and dramatic artistry served as a blueprint for Césaire. The play between past and present in these final writings has great implications for our understanding of the intertwined histories of Haiti, France, and the United States.

The writing of the *Mémoire* was a complicated process that resulted in multiple copies. Following the archival trail cleared before me (by Sannon, Roussier, Boromé, de Cauna, and Desormeaux), I have located a total of four copies. However, there could be even more: in an intriguing letter he wrote to the minister of war, General Ménard, commander of the 6th Division in Besançon, noted that he confiscated nine "notebooks [*cahiers*]" that Toussaint "had wanted to conserve."[5] Of the four known copies in France, three are in Paris at the Archives Nationales, and a fourth is housed in Aix-en-Provence at the Archives Nationales d'Outre-Mer.[6] In his "Finding List," Boromé noted the sale of a copy at Sotheby's in London in 1957 as well as the existence of another copy that circulated in the mid-nineteenth century in Haiti's War Ministry.[7] It is difficult to follow Boromé's notes. It seems that he was unable to determine the precise chronological order in which the copies were produced, and, as evidenced by lines scratched out and marginalia, he revised his notes on several occasions. Of the three copies in Paris, the first is the shorter, original version, written entirely in Toussaint's hand in his phonetic French. This is the text that was found postmortem inside the handkerchief that Toussaint wore on his head. It has been integrated into the recent Girandole edition of the *Mémoire*. It is likely the manuscript that Toussaint attempted to give to General Caffarelli during one of their interviews: " I charge General Caffarelli, your aide-de-camp," he wrote to Bonaparte, "to give you my report."[8] In a letter to Bonaparte, Caffarelli reported that he could not read it and asked Toussaint to dictate it. As a result, the second and third copies are those that Toussaint dictated to Jeannin, a secretary at the Fort de Joux. The second copy is clearly a first draft, as nearly every page contains crossed-out sections and notes in the margins. It is written, de Cauna observes, with "correct orthography" and is signed by Toussaint.[9] The third copy is the revised version of the second but with an important addendum in Toussaint's hand, addressed to the "Premire consul." The copy in the colonial archives, written in standard French of a different secretary, is a "cleaner" version than the two dictated versions in Paris and also contains the same addendum written by Toussaint.

Generally speaking, the existence of multiple copies is not surprising, as it was not uncommon at the time to create duplicate texts. However, the difficulty of locating the existing copies of the *Mémoire*, and of determining the manner and order of composition of each one, speaks to the conditions of Toussaint's incarceration. The dispersal of this text and scores of others by Toussaint across public and private sites has impeded the reconstitution of his voice. As such, the *Mémoire* has not erased the doubts over Toussaint's literary authority; in fact, they have only been compounded by the misguided expectation that the text constitutes an autobiography, providing vital information on the period of his life leading up to the 1791 revolt. The *Mémoire* does not reveal undiscovered autobiographical details, but it does continue to reconfigure republicanism and colonialism. The emphasis on biography—and the concomitant search for the text that would provide a historical epiphany—leaves aside the rich narrative strategies that gained momentum in the course of Toussaint's conflict with Bonaparte. His argument to Bonaparte was consistent with the double rhetoric of "free and French" in the Constitution and "fidelity and probity" in the letter he wrote on 16 September: " I am of clear conscience [*for de ma consiance*] and, I dare say, truthfully, among all men of state, there is no one more upright nor more prudent than I, I am one of your soldiers, and the first soldier of the Republic of Saint-Domingue."[10] Toussaint signed off with "Salut et respec," a standard closing for much of his correspondence; he also opened the letter with a mark of esteem in "the respect and submission I owe to you . . . " But for whom did Toussaint soldier? The letter exhibits a "rebellious service," in that it contains an ambivalence that leads from "statesman" to "your soldier" and finally to "first soldier of the Republic of St. Domingue." Toussaint was at once in the service of Bonaparte and of Saint-Domingue.

Mémoire or Mémoires?

Toussaint's exposition of obligation and truth occupies a unique place in the genre of memoir writing. Two historians, Marc Fumaroli and Pierre Nora, provide helpful frameworks in which to examine the *Mémoire*. Fumaroli begins with the figure of the crossroads, "a place of meetings, exchanges, of mixing."[11] The metaphor is illuminating of the political and personal position in which Toussaint found himself as he engaged Bonaparte. The figurative meaning of "crossroads [*carrefour*]" in both English and French evokes a place where a crucial decision must be made, a middle ground from which the traveler/protagonist has a choice of a path to follow.[12] However, Toussaint moved from the crossroads of the Constitution, where he indeed had a choice, to a reverse "middle passage" that led to imprisonment in the Jura. At this juncture, choice was removed, and decisions were made under duress. In the analysis to follow, I propose to add to Fumaroli's definition the idea of a "meeting point of opposing elements and ideas," a place of adversity where all is not equal.

The tradition of memoir writing, which dates back to well before the nineteenth century, has always existed in an unequal relationship with the writing of History. In "Memoirs of Men of State," one of the essays he contributed to the monumental collection he edited, *Les Lieux de mémoire*, Nora argues that the memoir evolved out of a "particular kind of relationship of the individual to history. It is a relationship of lineage and identification, a block of crystallized beliefs in which one finds fused together . . . the epic poem, prose, and notions of nationhood and national destiny."[13] Nora's claim of a "fusion" of individual and collective memories—and the thesis of the connection between kinds of memorials and commemoration that holds together the *Lieux de mémoire*—depends on an understanding of the genre as central to the writing of History. "Memoirs are history personified," Nora writes, "the embodiment of a multiple, multiform France" (413). He brings the genre out of the margins of prose writing to bridge individual and national memory, making it a defining œuvre of "French" identity. He locates three kinds of memoirs in three historical periods: *mémoires d'épée* (military memoirs), *mémoires de cour* (aristocratic memoirs), and *mémoires d'état* (the modern memoirs of state). The schematic approach to the genre is consistent with the structure of the *Lieux de mémoire*, in which "memory" is conceived and categorized as a set of institutional "loci": *mémoire-royale*, *mémoire-état*, *mémoire-nation*, and *mémoire-citoyen*. Although certain memoirs overlap in this classification, Nora does little to nuance the idea of "nationhood" beyond the allusion to a "multiform France," nor does he mention Toussaint's text, which is unsurprising given that *Lieux de mémoires* includes not a single reference to Saint-Domingue. In fact, in all seven volumes the *mémoire-colonial* finds space in only one essay, and it concerns the Colonial Exposition in Paris in 1931.[14] Despite Nora's contention that the *Lieux de mémoire* was intended to serve not as a "history of France" but rather as the "history that France needs today," the neglect of a *mémoire-colonial*, particularly in the truncated English translations, inscribes history inside hexagonal memories.[15]

In contrast to Nora, Fumaroli locates the genre at the margins of History. In the sixteenth and seventeenth centuries History, he reminds us, was a noble genre: historiography was the writing that was sanctioned by, and usually about, the King or the State.[16] Fumaroli states that the classical aesthetic was "animated by the spirit of hierarchy, of distinction, of the separation of genres" (183). "Official genres," he continues, were "imprisoned in their definitions and doctrinal difficulties" (183). It is important to keep in mind that, for the most part, memoir writing was an aristocratic tradition: military officers, clergy members, and landowners inscribed their perspectives of events to add to, and to contest, official versions of royal historiographers. The memoir offered a form of resistance that, according to Fumaroli, was particular to France: "In the seventeenth century, in France, land of civil wars, conflicts, and quarrels, History is a trial for which posterity alone will be able to give a definitive conclusion" (188).[17] In this reading, "History is a trial," one in which the writer, as defendant, counters the "rigged accounts" of royal "prosecutors" by reminding the King of debts contracted (191–93). Fumaroli here joins Nora, who traces the general contours of the military memoir as "indictments against the ingratitude of fate and of the Court, whose royal propagandists lay claim to the official version" (414–15). If the soldier owed his social status to the king, then the king, too, must honor military service.

The notion that the memoir had been a long-standing element of a juridical process, one that weighed a system of twofold debts, is key to my analysis. For my purposes, the connection between historiography and memoir lies in the relationship between the First Consul as head of state and Toussaint as the general who, in the course of his service, was wronged by a superior. Discharged from an official role, Toussaint represented the tragic hero whose voice intersected the writing of History. He asserted his contribution to history, in which the official version of events met the will of the hero, who ensured his renown by appealing to a higher law.[18] By writing a memoir to Bonaparte, Toussaint inscribed his refutation of the government's official stance on him. At the beginning of this chapter, I placed in epigraph a passage from the 8 October letter, penned right after the *Mémoire*, that inaugurated this point of view: "Allow me, First Consul, to tell you with all due respect and submission. The government has been utterly mistaken about the account of Toussaint Louverture, about one of its most zealous and courageous servants on St. Domingue." The expression of submission is a façade, an epistolary and military formality. As Desormeaux notes, the dialectic between History and memoir is one in which Toussaint's protest rings out as a "principle of truth" (134). The deference to the chain of command does little to contain the spirit and language of protest that runs through the *Mémoire*. We recall that, while on board *le Héros*, Toussaint had already begun his defense by inculpating General Leclerc for having broken his word of honor. The accusation against Leclerc was also an implicit charge against Bonaparte, and thus Toussaint laid the groundwork for a seemingly respectful challenge to his status as hero-cum-criminal. The general had to observe proper form: Toussaint expressed obligation in the impersonal first sentence of the *Mémoire*: "It is my duty to give to the French government an exact account of my conduct."[19] He then writes emphatically, "So I will tell the truth, even if it goes against me." The dishonored hero's word escapes the boundaries of obligatory form because it is grounded in the "truth," one that may also hold him accountable.

In order to bring out the interaction between form and content, it is necessary to follow this incursion into matters of generic tradition with a brief turn to the etymology of *mémoire*. Antoine Furetière's *Dictionnaire Universel*, Emile Littré's *Dictionnaire de la langue française*, and the *Trésor de la langue française* all include several definitions.[20] The meanings of *mémoire* vary depending on its masculine and feminine forms. In the feminine, "memory" refers both to the cognitive power of remembering and the reputation that one leaves after death; as we have seen, it also has a juridical sense in the attestation of said reputation. The masculine form contains an important distinction between the singular and plural. In the singular, one finds a range of possibilities in academic, legal, and commercial contexts. Most of these refer to a summary or report that is to be judged and/or filed as a record of service. According to the *Trésor*, it is an academic thesis, as well as an "account," or a "petition" that a litigant would bring forward to defend himself in court. In Littré's *Dictionnaire*, we read also, "summary [*factum*], handwritten or printed, containing the facts and means of a case that must be adjudicated." In the plural, it generally signifies an account of one's life, such as a chronicle written to describe the events in which one participated or that one witnessed. Furetière's initial entry in the masculine singular is simply "a summary report that one gives to someone to remind them of something." He then makes a careful distinction between a lowercase *mémoires*, such as an affidavit presented via a lawyer, and an uppercase *Mémoires*, which "refers to history books, written by those who took part in events or who were eyewitnesses to them, or which contain their life or their principal actions, which corresponds to what the Latins called *Commentaires*." According to Furetière, *mémoire* is related to the Latin *monumenta*, "a memorial erected to preserve the memory of some person."[21] As a monument, the *mémoire* withstands the passage of time, and preserves, like a tomb, the reputation of its subject.

The lexical complexity has resulted in divergent readings of Toussaint's *Mémoire*, which fits more than one of the above meanings. To begin with, the differences between the singular and the plural have led to historical confusion over the correct title of the text, which clearly reads in the singular in the archives: *Mémoire du Général Toussaint*

Figure 4.1. *Mémoire du Général Toussaint Louverture*. AN, AF 1213, Dossier 1. The first page of the copy of Toussaint's *Mémoire* in his own hand.

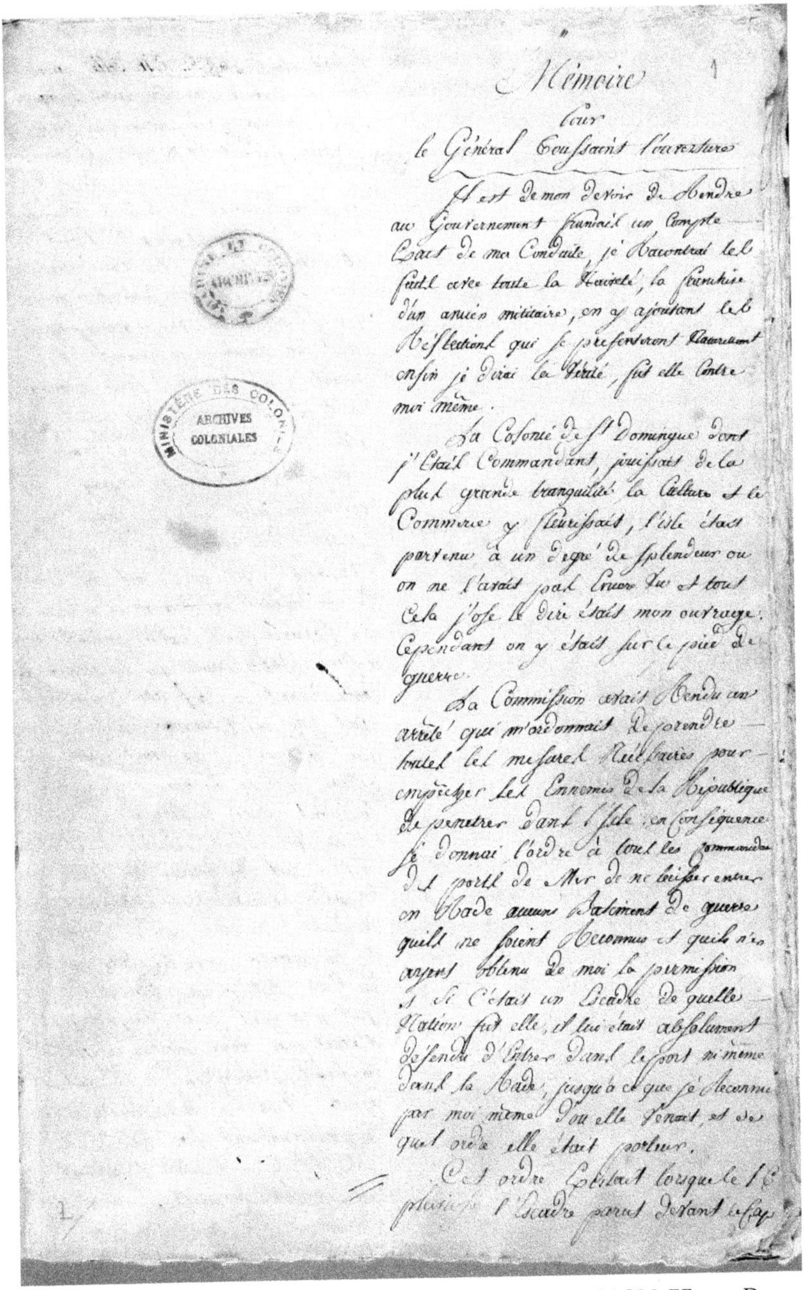
Mémoire
pour
le Général Toussaint Louverture

Il est de mon devoir de rendre au Gouvernement français un compte exact de ma conduite, je raconterai les faits avec toute la naïveté, la franchise d'un ancien militaire, en y ajoutant les réflexions qui se présenteront naturellement enfin je dirai la vérité, fut elle contre moi même.

La Colonie de St Domingue dont j'étais commandant, jouissait de la plus grande tranquillité, la culture et le commerce y fleurissaient, l'isle était parvenue à un degré de splendeur où on ne l'avait pas encore vu et tout cela j'ose le dire était mon ouvrage. Cependant on y était sur le pied de guerre.

La Commission avait rendu un arrêté qui m'ordonnait de prendre toutes les mesures nécessaires pour empêcher les ennemis de la République de pénétrer dans l'isle, en conséquence je donnai l'ordre à tous les commandants des ports de mer de ne laisser entrer en rade aucun batiment de guerre qu'ils ne soient reconnus et qu'ils n'en ayent obtenu de moi la permission et si c'était une escadre de quelle nation fut elle, il lui était absolument défendu d'entrer dans le port ni même dans la rade, jusqu'à ce que je reconnu par moi même d'où elle venait, et de quel ordre elle était porteur.

Cet ordre existait lorsque le 1er pluviôse l'escadre parut devant le Cap

Figure 4.2. *Mémoire pour le Général Toussaint Louverture*. CAOM, EE 1743, Dossier Toussaint Louverture, Dossier 02—Général de Division. The first page of the dictated copy of the *Mémoire*.

Louverture.²² Nevertheless, following Saint-Rémy, most critics have used (and continue to use) the plural form, creating a subtle misreading, and thereby potentially misleading their own readers.²³ When scholars and editors change the title to the plural, they burden the text with expectations of autobiography. Perhaps because the *Mémoire* provides scant information concerning the "profound mystery" of these early years, many have neglected or expressed disappointment in the text.²⁴ The desire to read in the plural is understandable, considering the widespread practice of those who penned *Mémoires pour Servir à l'Histoire*, particularly military officers who served on Saint-Domingue.²⁵ And yet to approach it through the more precise definition provided by Furetière brings the reader squarely back to a report meant specifically for Bonaparte.

Mémoire: "Défense et Illustration" of Toussaint

The digression to generic and etymological history refocuses the reader on a specific kind of memoir, certainly not the modern, autobiographical text. Nor does Toussaint's *Mémoire* fit neatly into Nora's classification, existing as it does in a gap between the *mémoire d'épée* of the ancien régime and the political memoir of the modern state. Desormeaux locates it in both the juridical and military worlds of the ancien régime, in which an officer acknowledged a debt of service to the state and sought redress for such service. By definition, the *mémoire* cuts both ways as recognition of debt and as an expression of protest, a powerful gesture that declares the nature of the debt to be reciprocal.²⁶ In his claim, Toussaint blurred the line between seeking justice for a public cause and memorializing his image for posterity. After the expression of obligation, the language reflects this tension in a shift from third to first person: "the island had reached a degree of splendor that had not been seen before, and all of this, I dare say, was wrought by me." The argument is straightforward: with order having been reestablished, commerce flourished. The statement is also self-aggrandizing and inflects the "facts" of the report with an emphatic first person seeking to repair his reputation. *Factum*, one might say, meets *monumentum*.

A close reading of the *Mémoire* reveals its component parts: the obligation to give an account of his role in the face of the French expedition, the indictment of Leclerc and attendant request to bring the matter before a military tribunal, and the final plea for mercy. To be sure, much of the text is less literary than administrative; Toussaint plods along for pages recounting the minutiae of military communication and strategy during the Leclerc expedition. This detailed approach does not empty out the value of what remains a narrative of many layers, which runs from summary account [*compte rendu*] to indictment to closing argument/plea for mercy. Toussaint alternately reminds Bonaparte of his service to Saint-Domingue, of his exploits that, he argued, ultimately benefited the French government, and of the injustice that took him away "like a criminal." The tripartite structure itself is another testament to the organization of Toussaint's writing. The opening of the *Mémoire* is remarkable for its attention to form and its exposition of a seemingly paradoxical state of affairs: if Saint-Domingue was flourishing under his rule, it was also, he admitted, "on the brink of war." The pattern of affirmation and contradiction runs through the *Mémoire*, both strengthening and weakening the argument.

More broadly, the *Mémoire* was a response to the greater contradiction between the ideals of universal freedom and the threat of reenslavement sailing once again toward Saint-Domingue in the expedition of 1801 to 1802. The conflict between French sovereignty and the freedom for which Toussaint and the former slaves had to fight boils over in the communication between Toussaint and Bonaparte. It was a struggle both constitutional and personal. Upon closer inspection, Toussaint's 1801 Constitution founded a republic based on universal liberty but also imposed troubling limits on this freedom. In a subsequent address to the "Inhabitants of Saint-Domingue," Bonaparte proclaimed, "whatever your origin or color, you are all French; you are all free and equal before God and the Republic" (*Napoléon* VII:315). As he had done previously, Bonaparte tied the freedom of the people of Saint-Domingue to French sovereignty, and this time he also invoked a higher authority. Also consistent with previous rhetoric, he undermined the recognition of their freedom with yet another menacing conclusion: "Rally around him [Leclerc]. Whoever dares to break away from him will be a traitor to his country, and the anger of the Republic will devour him, like the fire that devours your dried out cane fields." Bonaparte's warning contrasted sharply with Toussaint's understanding of freedom. Whereas the latter instructed the former slaves to continue to work for their freedom, one that would unfold over time, the First Consul conceived of freedom as a violent force. Furthermore, it could quickly turn against them, like a wildfire. The reference to cane fields was an intentional (and quite ironic) allusion to the 1791 revolt on the northern plain. The statement is further evidence that Bonaparte was prepared to take the revolutionary power away from Toussaint and his people.

In a string of correspondence from late 1801 to early 1802 Bonaparte epitomized the French contradiction, going back and forth between statements that championed liberty and those that exhorted his officers to reestablish order. In a letter to Toussaint on 18 November, he wrote, "The Constitution that you have made, while it contains many good things, holds others that are contrary to the dignity and sovereignty of the French people, of which Saint-Domingue forms but one part."[27] As I noted earlier, the 1801 Constitution paid lip service to French sovereignty, and Bonaparte made this point in many voices and to multiple audiences. First, there was the paternalistic proclamation to the people of Saint-Domingue, followed by the admonishment to Toussaint; the very next day, he sent a hopeful letter to Leclerc, in which he wrote, "I cannot wait to learn that you have rendered the greatest service to the Republic . . . and that we can proclaim you restorer of our great colony."[28] Finally, three days later, in the more measured tone required of the *Exposé de la situation de la République*—a sort of "State of the Republic" address—Bonaparte continued to speak of liberty for all, even affirming succinctly, "there are no more slaves" on Saint-Domingue; in the next paragraph, however, he acknowledged, "there will be different principles" elsewhere, and so slavery would remain on Martinique.[29] Toussaint had been fighting these "different principles" throughout his tenure, and the reasoning and passion in the *Mémoire* are intertwined with a profound distrust of French authority.

The *Mémoire* combines the emotional reaction to a new situation—he is a prisoner of war in the mountains of France—with a skillful retort to French Republican ideology in the Caribbean. After all, in communication to Leclerc leading up to and following Toussaint's arrest and eventual death, Bonaparte revealed his ultimate plan to defeat the "gilded Africans."[30] This notorious statement did not come out of the blue; it followed a series of objectives laid out to his subordinates throughout the late winter and early spring of 1802.[31] Toussaint had been on guard in the face of such duplicity for years; nevertheless, many readers of his final writings focus on the anger and defensive posture that Toussaint brings to his prosecution of the French. As a result of this reading, which downplays the underhanded way in which successive French governments and colonial assemblies treated him, it is Toussaint who is often described as deceptive and scheming, even by those who have celebrated him. While we should not discount Toussaint's willingness to deceive, we should also appreciate the political savvy that was a necessary means of survival. In this light, the meticulous prose of the *Mémoire* is an exertion of control in the face of horrendous odds. To this point, the sacrificial character of the text becomes clear in its retelling of the encounter with his sons and their tutor, Coisnon, at Ennery. The account of an otherwise emotionally charged scene hews instead to military decorum. Toussaint writes of learning of Leclerc's identity as leader of the French expedition and of feeling slighted by the lack of proper communication and respect. Despite the entreaties of his sons, he holds firm to his obligation and responds:

> Je leur representai que da pres la conduite de ce general je ne pouvois avoire en lui aucune confiance, quil etoit debarque comme ennemis que mal gré cela javois creu de mon de voire daller au devant de lui pour empechè le progrès dumal, que lors il mavoit fait tirer dessus, et que javois couru les plus grande danger, quen fin si ses intentions étoient pure comme celle du gouvernement qui lenvoiait, il aurait pris la peine de mecrire pour minstruire de sa mision, que meme il auroit du avant darrivé a la rade men voier un aviso avec vous comme se la pratique ordinairement pour me faire part de ses pouvoire et minformer de son arrivée.

> [I told them that after the conduct of this General, I could have no confidence in him; that he debarked as an enemy; that, in spite of this, I had understood my duty to appear before him in order to prevent further harm; that he had me fired upon, and that I had run the greatest dangers; that, in the end, if his intentions were pure like those of the government that sent him, he should have taken the trouble to write me to inform me of his mission; that even before arriving in the harbor, he should have sent me a dispatch boat with you, as is customary, to apprise me of his authority and to inform me of his arrival.]

It is certainly possible that Toussaint spun the event to his advantage. Yet the insistence on Leclerc's failure to follow protocol (including proper narrative form) is evidence of Toussaint's sense of discipline and his adherence to military hierarchy. The force of the argument lies in its flexibility: he crafts a scene of military subordination out of what could have been a family drama.

In making the case for his loyalty to the French government, Toussaint arrives at a crucial narrative transition, in which he declares Leclerc an enemy. The initial gesture of submission becomes, once again, a bold maneuver that sought to expose the weakness of a divided French authority. He writes, "These new hostilities brought me to new reflection. I found the conduct of General Leclerc so contrary to the intentions of the government, since the First Consul, in his letter, promised peace, while he [Leclerc] made war." Toussaint seizes upon the apparent divide between words and actions to bring Leclerc to order for the greater goal of saving the colony. Gradually, in the juxtaposition of peace to war and destruction to conservation, the *Mémoire* feels less detailed oriented, overtaken as it is by a series of logical steps that Toussaint is careful to elaborate. If the first few pages could be taken out of a general's field report, the second and longer section relies on rhetorical moves designed to convince Bonaparte of his innocence.

The accusation of Leclerc thinly veils the more powerful charge against metropolitan France. Leclerc is guilty, according to Toussaint, primarily because he did not respect the chain of command; the next logical move is to hold Leclerc and the entire French government responsible for pursuing a path of treachery and devastation. A series of rhetorical questions begins some twenty pages in, at a moment when Toussaint deflects an accusation that he allowed prisoners to be executed. Although he does not deny the assassinations, he asks, "But am I responsible for the wrong that occurs in my absence?" As many have argued, this may be an instance of characteristic misdirection, and it certainly opens the door to question Toussaint's role in the violence that surrounded him.[32] The use of rhetorical questions gains momentum two-thirds of the way through the narrative. In pointing out how Leclerc dishonored him, Toussaint makes an accusation of racism that goes beyond an individual general: "He treated me in ways that have never been used, even with respect to the greatest criminals. Surely I owe this scorn to my color. Yet has my color prevented me from serving my country with zeal and loyalty? Does the color of my skin detract from my honor and courage?" For Toussaint, service to country is beyond reproach. To deny him this honor on the basis of race is to bring shame to the Republican experiment. Like a skilled prosecutor, Toussaint cross-examines the French and demands them to reflect on their own crimes.

The conclusion of the report, delivered in a crescendo of provocative questions, moves from the accusation of racism to the justification of the 1801 Constitution. The argument is tightly constructed, treating the actions of Leclerc as symptomatic of a greater injustice, the calumny and atrocity of which he can only refute from the "depths of a cell." This wrenching passage, which I have cited in the previous chapter, is a plaintive denunciation of the dehumanization of French colonialism, an evil that "buries a man alive." In the next paragraph, Toussaint clinches the argument by making the obvious connection to racism as the scourge that "annihilates" the enlightened project of republicanism:

> Tout ce la a été bien conbiné a ma perte pour ment ne antire, et me détruire parce que je sui noire et in gnorant et je ne doit pas conte an nombre des soldat de la république ni avoir de merite, et point de justice pour moi, et ci je ne pas dant ce monde jorré dant lautre, jai cé con va cherché et paijer dans toute les diapasons de la colonie et par tous pour trouver ou faire des mensonge compte moi, mais l'homme propose et Dieu an dispose.
>
> [All this combined to my downfall to ruin me, and to destroy me because I am black and ignorant and because I must neither count among the soldiers of the Republic nor have merit, nor any justice, and if I have none in this world I will have it in the next, I know that one will seek and pay in all the diapasons of the colony, and everywhere, in order to find and make falsehoods against me, but man proposes and God disposes].

These are the words of a defeated man, who nonetheless leaves a "memory" of a just reputation and of the inherent unfairness of the French Republic. Toussaint briefly departs from a juridical frame to appeal to the proverbial wisdom of divine arbitration. Despite the violence of his past, including a civil war with Rigaud and a despotic work regime, he argues that everything was done with the permission of the people of Saint-Domingue. Resting on his faith, he continues, "And if I were I white man, after having served as I have served, all these misfortunes would never have happened to me." In an important way, Toussaint is vindicated by the colonial virulence of French generals, including Hédouville, Kerverseau, and Rochambeau, who assumed command of the French expedition upon the death of Leclerc.

This simplistic reasoning sets up the defense of the 1801 Constitution. Toussaint once again stresses the legality of his rule which, combined with the accusation of the imperial and racist strain of republicanism, defines the foundation of the document. He will protect the people from racial discrimination and the reestablishment of slavery. In proclaiming the Constitution before submitting it for approval, Toussaint bypassed proper channels, a move that both disrespected Bonaparte—which was ironic given his condemnation of Leclerc—and invalidated the authority of the metropole. In doing so, he reinforced the precedence of universal freedom against French sovereignty. He shores up the foundation of the Constitution in a final series of rhetorical questions: "Why, therefore, does one wish today to impute to me a crime which cannot be so? Why does one wish the truth to be a lie, and for lies to become truth? Why does one wish that shadows be light, and that light be shadows?" Binary metaphors are recurring figures in Toussaint's rhetoric, going back to his early communication with the former slaves. They convey the simple truth of the argument: the

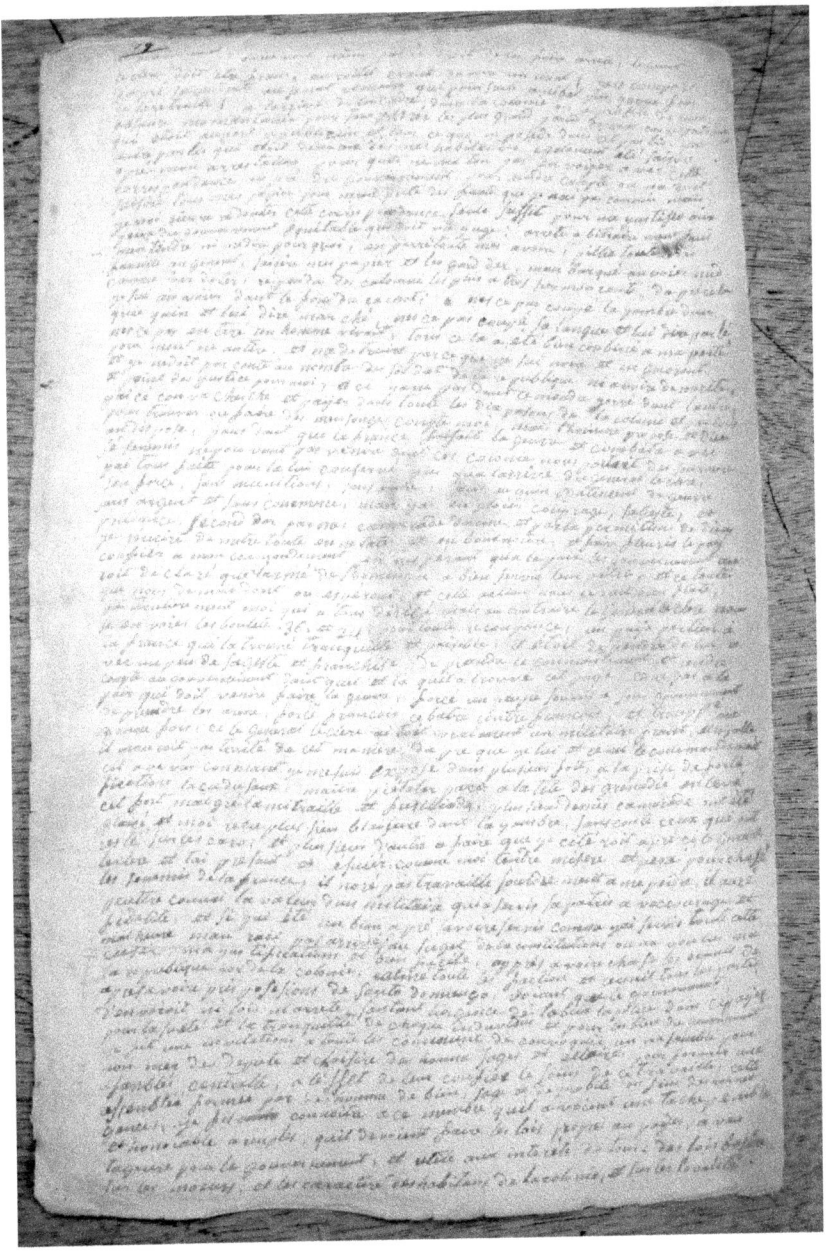

Figure 4.3. The page of Toussaint's handwritten *Mémoire* containing the block quotation cited.

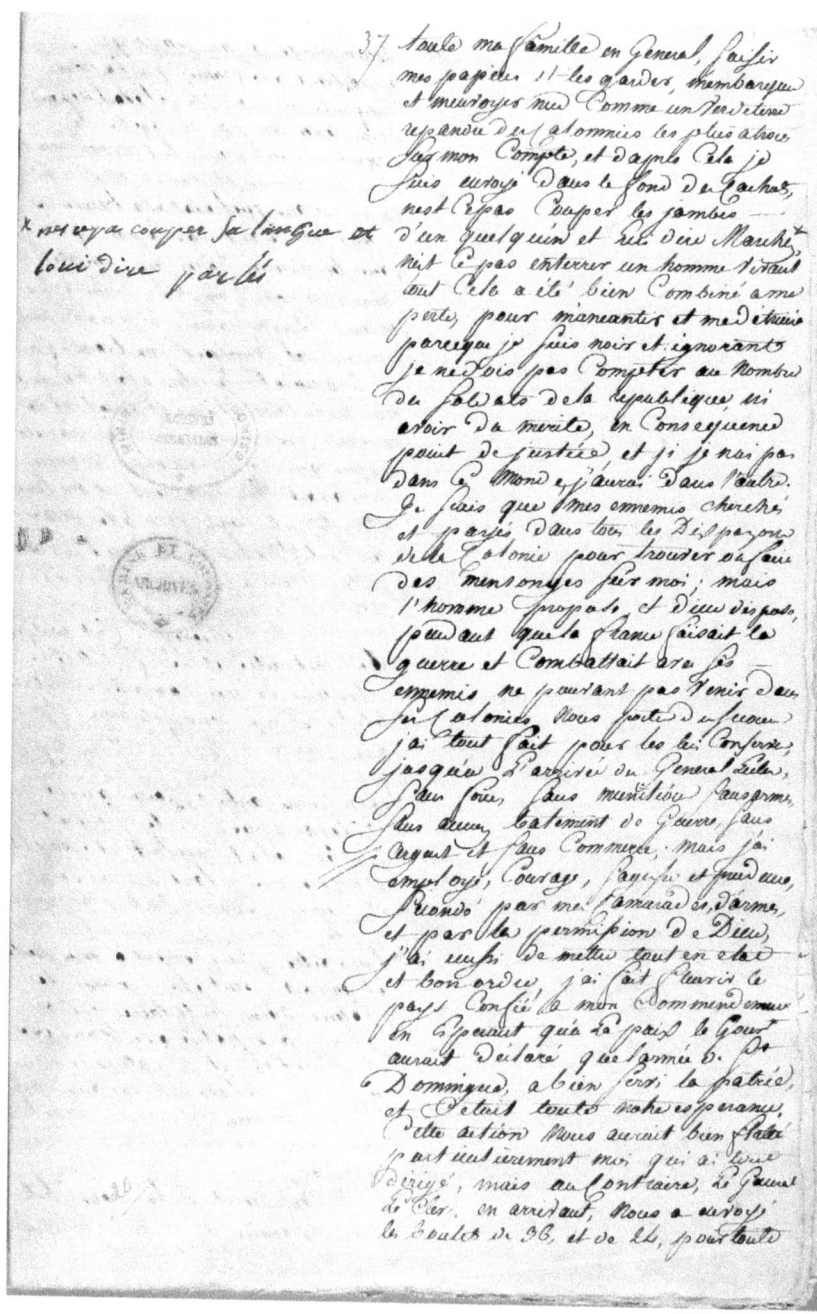

Figure 4.4. The dictated copy of the *Mémoire* at the CAOM.

French Republic committed a crime against Toussaint and the project of universal freedom on Saint-Domingue.

Translating Saint-Domingue as *Lieu de mémoire*

When the shadows brought darkness to his cell, Toussaint rested his case. The pattern of narrative emplotments followed the form of the *mémoire justificatif*: a general falsely incriminated called out his superior by establishing a record of service, cross-examining his accuser, and closing with a plea for mercy. As I have argued, it is a report that came to embody the fateful position of Toussaint, France's highest-ranking officer on its most prized colonial possession. The embodiment of Toussaint transformed the report into a memorial left for posterity. Though written on French soil, in a prison from which there would be no escape, this act of commemoration would, ironically, find no place in the troubling history of republicanism and colonialism. If Nora's *Lieux de mémoire*, those "principal loci, material or immaterial, in which [this] memory had become embodied and which, through the actions of men or the work of centuries, remained their most specific representations and most dazzling symbols," then how do we understand the extraordinary absence of the French *mémoire-colonial* of Saint-Domingue? In her trenchant essay on the aphasia at work in the most important French historiographical project of the twentieth century, Stoler asks, "Why was there such ample room to remember the partage de l'espace-temps (division of space-time) that separated Paris from its provinces but no reference to that pervasive political distinction that still divides archival storage, history writing, and popular memory between what was "outre-mer" (overseas) and what was France?" (147).[33] In her account of Nora's willful dissociation—"There is nothing that Nora "forgot" (147)—Stoler distinguishes between amnesia and aphasia by pointing out that the former is a form of forgetting that is passive. "In aphasia," she writes, "occlusion of knowledge is the issue. It is not a matter of ignorance or absence" (125). After a lengthy study of the term, in which she draws on multiple disciplinary perspectives, Stoler arrives at a succinct definition: "Colonial aphasia is a political disorder and a troubled psychic space" (153). This understanding serves us well, I think, in the attempt to make sense of the compartmentalization made possible by Nora's concept "memory sites" and their capacity to store away a shameful past; by extension, we can begin to grasp the willful, historic split between French republicanism and the violent spaces of its colonial base. In his introduction to the English translation of *Lieux de mémoire*, Nora attempts to explain the "inevitably gallocentric character" of the concept of memory sites, even acknowledging the French title as an "untranslatable neologism" (xx). It is telling that Nora brings us back to the place of the crossroads, this time in the space between languages, between memories, but with a decidedly national bent.[34]

Toussaint also had an untranslatable problem. He personified the triumph of the Haitian Revolution as well as its tragic demise. In the attempt to repair his reputation, he went so far as to demand the right to a military tribunal: "I demand to be brought before [*traduit*] a tribunal or a war council, where General Leclerc would also be made to appear; and that we be judged, after having heard each of us; fairness, reason, laws, all assure me that I cannot be refused this justice." Even though Toussaint remained confident in the rule of law until the very end, Bonaparte failed to honor any such pact with him. In lieu of what could have been one of the greatest trials in the history of the French Caribbean, Bonaparte ordered silence.

In asserting his right to a trial, which would have been a military sequel to the *Mémoire*, Toussaint asked to be "traduit," or brought before a tribunal. The French *traduire* has its roots in the Latin verb *traducere* (lead across, transport). The same verb also leads to the French verbs *traiter* (treat, trade) and *traire* (draw out, extract). Toussaint's word resonated with multiple linguistic ambiguities that cannot be ignored in the context of Saint-Domingue and the greater colonial Caribbean and Atlantic. Reading "traduit," one hears and sees both "traite" and "trade." *Traducere* can also mean "to pass one language into another," and so we might also plumb Bonaparte's silence as a failure to translate. Bonaparte purportedly admitted his mistake in *Le Mémorial de Sainte-Hélène*: "It was a great error to have wanted to bring to heel by force; I should have contented myself by governing Saint-Domingue through the intermediary of Toussaint" (769). If Bonaparte had been able to put Toussaint's constitutional proposal into terms he could understand, he would have been able to mediate rule of Saint-Domingue. Such was the logic of Bonaparte in hindsight during his own imprisonment. The irony is rich and not a little unsettling, but it serves little purpose if the Toussaint-Bonaparte relationship remains understood as a historical tragedy with no bearing beyond the early nineteenth century.

I close Part I with Toussaint's demand to be brought before a just hearing. His faith in Bonaparte and in the rule of law proved to be his tragic downfall; but we, readers of French and Haitian history, can still bring him forward. This is, I would argue, the invaluable legacy of the *Mémoire*. It is an intricate text, both prosecution and defense, one that was not meant to be lost in a locus of memory, frozen in time, but rather to be translated by future leaders. Instead of memorializing the site of Toussaint's political project, it is imperative to reexamine the *Mémoire* and to reactivate the ideas that Bonaparte and metropolitan France chose to ignore. Their failed *traduction* not only killed Toussaint, but would also have grave implications for the future crossroads of the French Caribbean.

PART II
Aimé Césaire

5 Césaire Reads Toussaint

The Haitian Revolution and the Problem of Departmentalization

THE CENTRAL CLAIM of Part I is that Toussaint transformed the relationship between Saint-Domingue and France, especially in the consolidation of his agency, understood both in terms of literacy and political skill. The core argument that I develop in Part II is that his vision for the future for Saint-Domingue was passed on to Césaire, who, shuttling between Martinique and France, contemplated the interstices of colonial past and departmental future. In the space of the French Caribbean, both men, though separated by some 150 years, battled the obdurate forces of French colonialism and the specter of slavery. Educated in the school of French republicanism, both men were apprenticed to the language of liberty, equality, and fraternity; in return, both men inscribed lessons that erstwhile masters failed to translate. While Toussaint and Césaire share the mantle of anticolonial struggle, their stances, and the ambiguities of these positions, differed significantly. Toussaint was a leader of rebel slaves, a supreme military tactician who defeated European armies, and a skilled administrator, yet some of his policies, particularly those related to agriculture, were a continuation of French colonial methods. Césaire's anticolonial voice first rang out in the pages of *L'Étudiant noir* and in the epic *Cahier d'un retour au pays natal*, but his subsequent political decisions, most notably the project of departmentalization, compromised his anticolonial legend.

Throughout Part I, I argued that Toussaint walked a fine line between autonomy and assimilation, and read in his writings a less binary history of the Haitian Revolution. Similarly, Césaire's texts defy the more simplistic understanding of

99

departmentalization as wholesale integration within France. And as it was with Toussaint, Césaire's multipronged approach to writing about a political act—to reflect, educate, criticize, or justify—was often more revolutionary than the course of action itself. In this sense, the tension between autonomy and assimilation is mirrored by the conflict between discourse and political action. The writer, who enjoyed a great deal of freedom to experiment, frequently opposed the politician, who conceded much to necessity. Before analyzing this paradox, I want to return to the theoretical questions raised in the introduction, those concerning the filiation set up between Toussaint and Césaire and their expression of "free and French," in order to develop them more fully for the historical-literary approach that continues in this section. These are the issues of temporality and narrative: how did Césaire sort through the past of Toussaint for the present and future of departmentalization, and how might his responses be read today? Furthermore, to what extent does the manifestation of a political (and existential) conundrum turn on the genres that delivered his responses?

In the analysis of historical writings and events, my work attempts to build on important antecedents. I would like to return to the discussion of C. L. R. James (and particularly David Scott's reading of *The Black Jacobins*) and Hayden White in order to draw out the implications of narrative form for historiography. In the prefaces to both the 1938 and 1963 editions of *The Black Jacobins*, James reflected on the history he presented and its relevance for the momentous time in which it was written. In 1938, he wrote, "The violent conflicts of our age enable our practised vision to see into the very bones of previous revolutions more easily than heretofore" (xi). With characteristic flourish, James observed that the experiences of the present inflect the writing of the past, such that the kinds of questions asked about the choices made by Toussaint necessarily took into account the revolutionary conditions that surrounded him (James) in the years leading up to 1938. This temporal web, in which events of the late eighteenth century and the early to mid-twentieth century intermingled, opened a critical space concerning narrative form. Thus the last sentence of the 1938 preface: "The book is the history of a revolution and written under different circumstances it would have been a *different* but not necessarily a better book" (xi; emphasis mine). And it is twenty-five years later, under changed circumstances, when James was able to elaborate on the "different" book he published in 1963. In the short preface to the second edition, James looked back on the first, in which he had imagined Toussaint as the heroic if flawed revolutionary leader who overcame enormous odds and prepared the way for his successors. Reflecting on a new Appendix, "From Toussaint L'Ouverture to Fidel Castro," he wrote that it "attempts for the future of the West Indies, all of them, what was done for Africa in 1938. Writers on the West Indies always relate them to their approximation to Britain, France, Spain and America, that is to say, to Western civilization, never in relation to their own history. This is here attempted for the first time" (viii). The prefatory statements (and especially the interaction between them) can be read as discursive interventions in which James attempted to make sense of a historical problem through the exigencies of the present. The mythmaking story of a rising up that he tells in 1938 depended on the geopolitical landscapes to which he was a witness. As the ideological ground shifted during the time of war and revolution that reshaped the world from 1938 to 1963, James felt compelled to revise story lines of resistance and overcoming to those of tragedy.

Scott reads this reflection as a lesson: "James seems to offer us a provocative challenge, one that we, from where we are today, would do well to consider with care and focus" (29). After describing in some detail the events that altered the focus of James's writing—in broad strokes, the Spanish Civil War, the rise of Stalin, and British imperialism in Africa—Scott argues that we cannot read his accounts of Toussaint and "the San Domingo Revolution" without considering the "age of *The Black Jacobins*" (28). Were this the essence of Scott's argument, there would be little if anything to question. However, his larger point is about the relevance of the dual temporality of James's "world-historical moment":

> That moment of social, political, and ideological upheaval framed by the Spanish Civil War, the Moscow trials, and the emerging revolutionary anti-Stalinist and anticolonial movements defined for James, in a distinctive cognitive-political vocabulary and through a range of institutional and organizational alternatives, a horizon of possible futures that are not, any longer, ours to imagine, let alone seek after and inhabit. (29)

The passage treats several overlapping time periods, including the 1930s and its foreseeable future, and "ours," which Scott defines as the "disappearing present," effaced by the inexorable pull of the future (29). The temporal confusion is compounded by the loss of a critical mandate to explain constituent events. Just *when* this decline occurs, however, is not clear, despite the fact that Scott traces a transition from "possible" to "not, any longer." In this view, to accept the impossibility of a future is a sign of an awareness of ineluctability; it is also evidence of a paradoxical openness not possessed by those who insist on possible futures. Several questions arise: When and how does one horizon (the possible) recede and another (the impossible) begin? Why does Scott separate these romantic and tragic visions for the future? Finally, as I questioned in the introduction, just who makes up the community of readers identified by Scott as "we" and "ours"?

This book considers these questions not through a close reading of *The Black Jacobins* but by comparing the circumstances of James's revision to those of Césaire and his historical work on Toussaint. For James, the future of 1963 was a time that foreclosed the activism that had enabled the "horizon of possible futures" still visible in 1938. James can no longer see this horizon, Scott contends, because he recognized that anticolonial calls for nationalist sovereignty had faded into a landscape of African and Caribbean independences under neocolonial supervision and into an international communism under the yoke of the Cold War and totalitarian regimes. It was in this harsh light that James revised *The Black Jacobins*, specifically the last chapter, "The War of Independence," in which he reconceived Toussaint's heroism as a tragic flaw, not necessarily of his own making, but of his "attempting the impossible" (291). This interpretive adjustment allowed James to account for Toussaint's "total miscalculations of the constituent events," which, he took pains to state, was not a "moral weakness" (291). For Scott, this was a belated recognition on the part of James, who would have seen the will to freedom as an illusion. The removal of Toussaint's ability to act of his own volition enables Scott to judge Toussaint in terms of a tragic impossibility: "Toussaint is a tragic subject of a colonial modernity to which he was, by force, conscripted" (168). Read this way, James's historical revision goes to the question of agency, in that Toussaint sought freedom by way of the very conceptual language of French discourse that had previously enslaved him. Toussaint could be a historical actor, so goes the logic of *Conscripts of Modernity*, only insofar as his choices are limited to, and contained within, the very "colonial modernity" from which he cannot escape.

I have attempted to respond to this questioning of Toussaint's agency in Part I, but I would like to extend the dialogue with Scott by drawing out the connection between historical crises and the ensuing narrative tension that responds to such turmoil. As I mention above, James's second thoughts on the narrative of heroic resistance would derive from the rupture between anticolonial and Marxist/Socialist movements that developed with the onset of the Cold War. Perhaps the most stunning example of disillusionment came from Césaire himself, who famously resigned from the French Communist Party (Parti Communiste Français, PCF) in 1956 in a letter to the head of the party, Maurice Thorez. Césaire delivered the letter, which displays an essayistic flair that anticipates *Toussaint Louverture*, as one horizon receded (his participation in the PCF) and a new one arose (his founding of the PPM). Like James, Césaire reconsidered the narrative of Haiti's beginnings, going from the essay on Toussaint to the play on Christophe. The narrative transformation at work in *The Black Jacobins* occurs in parallel with Césaire (*Christophe* is published in 1963) and is illuminating of the analyses below. For James, the choice of narrative form for a history of Saint-Domingue on the verge of postcoloniality calls out, and responds to, the demands of both anticolonial fervor (1938) and postcolonial melancholy (1963).

The reframing of the final chapter of *The Black Jacobins* is a metacommentary on the connection between the form a narrative takes and the consequences for the outcome of the story the historian wishes to tell. In setting up his observation in the 1938 preface that "it could have been a different book," James directly addressed the art of writing history. The problem he put forward in the debate over history as art of representation and as science of demonstration was played out in the poetic flair of his handling of archival material. Yet it is better understood in the interaction between Toussaint the "whole man" and the persona that he constructs in the pages of *The Black Jacobins*. James was careful to distinguish between the real-life decisions faced by Toussaint and the "factual statements and the judgments" that retroactively attempt to bring him to a dramatic textual stage. For James, writing the history of Toussaint was much more than organizing data and judging people and events; it was a matter of finding a narrative frame and voice that rose to the occasion of Toussaint as historical actor and to the "historical actuality of his dilemma" (291). As I have argued above, James's annotation on tragedy resonates with Césaire's depiction of the final days of Toussaint on Saint-Domingue. In his essay Césaire rendered the scene of Toussaint's capture by General Brunet as one of surrender, the ultimate sacrifice for the future of Saint-Domingue. However, what draws my attention is not so much that two leading anticolonial thinkers produced similar portraits of Toussaint at nearly the same historical moment—the second edition of *The Black Jacobins* arrived two years after Présence Africaine published *Toussaint Louverture*—than their mutual awareness of the relationship between narrative and the events and characters that go into the process of historical representation.

Both James and Césaire tread with care at the juncture of history and metahistory, as did Hayden White, another interlocutor for my imagined dialogue between Toussaint and Césaire. In *Metahistory*, White lays out an overarching theory of the literary structures that govern historiography. A historical work, he argues, "explains" data and connects events through a narrative that contains a "deep structural content which is generally poetic, and specifically linguistic, in nature, and which serves as a precritically accepted paradigm of what a distinctively 'historical' explanation should be" (ix). Following Northrop Frye, he contends that to provide recognizable meaning for a story, historians structure plot in one of four possible modes: romance, tragedy, comedy, and satire.[1] To identify a story—and as I demonstrated through James above, this also turns on the historian's ideological positioning between past and present—the historian "emplots" events according to a chosen modality. I will not go into the plot structures traditionally required of each mode; in the case of James's 1963 revision, we recognize the elements of tragedy in the portrayal of Toussaint as a flawed character caught in an impossible dilemma. Once he establishes the literariness of history writing, White's next critical move is tropological: he identifies four tropes (metaphor, metonymy, synecdoche, and irony) that the historian mobilizes to articulate the particular mode of emplotment. Thinking historically, for White, is to access a "deep level of consciousness . . . by which to explain or represent his data" (x). He posits a gap between observable data in a given field and the ability of the historian's "structures of consciousness"—which are, White reminds his reader, poetic and linguistic—to grasp and *speak of* the data. As he writes in the opening paragraph of *Tropics of Discourse*, "the data always resist the coherency of the image which we are trying to fashion to them" (1). Recalling my reading of Aravamudan, as slippages, or "turns" in discourse, tropes help make sense of the space between objects and the adequacy of language to analyze them. Therefore, White argues, tropes are key to historical thinking as vehicles that mediate between the form of a text and its contents. As we have seen, the trope of family (indeed, two families) was the key to Toussaint's negotiation with French metropolitan and colonial representatives, as well as with the laborers over whom he governed. The role of mediation is a central function of the narrative art of historical discourse.

In my reading of White, I am particularly interested in the mediating role played by the story mode and its attendant tropes and the content to which it gives shape. In the effort to open up different ways of thinking about the future, White, like James before him, sought a methodological and stylistic way out of the middle ground between art and science. The mediation that he describes is limited to the workings of one text alone; it is an internal exchange between its mode of emplotment and the resulting story. In "The Burden of History" White argues that the governing metaphor of a mode of emplotment does not allow the historian to provide the definitive perspective on "all the data in the entire phenomenal field" (*Tropics of Discourse* 46). One story of the Haitian Revolution, for example, plotted in a particular mode, would not be privileged over another story because, for White, there is no one epistemological authority. It follows, then, that there is no History but Histories, "no *single* correct view of any object under study but . . . *many* correct views " ("Burden" 47; original emphasis). Many have critiqued the apparent relativism of this position, despite the fact that he had tried to deflect such an accusation in the same essay by asking the historian to "show some tact" in the use and limits of the metaphors that carry the analysis (47). As Scott has pointed out, White later attempted to reemphasize the precaution he took in "The Burden of History" by elucidating limits on the kinds of histories that a historian can write on a given topic.[2] Therefore, he also contended that "we are indentured to a *choice* among contending interpretative strategies in any effort to reflect on history-in-general" (*Metahistory* xii; original emphasis). The resulting quandary, which is signaled in the paradoxical tension that runs through "indentured" and "choice," is that it is impossible to interpret data and events through one archetypal mode alone, especially if one denies any interpretive authority (whether moral, political, aesthetic, or epistemological) to the narrative frame constructed by the historian.

I wish to hold the tension in White's theory between the possible modes of historical representation and the responsibility that ambiguously attaches to it. The idea that the historian should be restricted to one mode tends to fix the subject under analysis to a more limiting time and space. In the case of Toussaint, who occupied several spaces at once—and who wrote from each of these positions in an array of voices and genres—multiple modes would seem to be required to write a more complete story of his tenure on Saint-Domingue and his imprisonment in France. What I am suggesting is that the focus on *which* mode to employ, as well as the "tactfulness" of this approach, is unproductive because incomplete. Coming at Toussaint from multiple perspectives is more revealing of the breadth of his agency and of the diversity of his responses to the French. Moreover, allowing these different modes (be it the romanticism of the anticolonial struggle or the tragic frame to which Scott subscribes) to interact with and mediate each other would render a more complex historical figure. The letters to Laveaux and the addresses to the laborers, read alongside and against each other, speak to Toussaint's dual conception of family; the 1801 Constitution and the *Mémoire* approach the problem of "free and French" in terms both loyal and oppositional. In this manner, it is possible to extend the limits of White's theory of mediation from an internal mechanism (within a text) to an interactive filiation (between multiple texts). Instead of focusing on the hero, it then becomes possible to open up the histories of Toussaint, be it as military correspondent, administrator, prosecutor, teacher, or father, all of which mediate each other.

This more expansive idea of mediation owes much to the desire to open up ways of thinking about the past that energizes White's interrogation. History writing long suffered, according to White, from the "burden of history," which he describes as the undignified, disciplinary limbo that engendered a great deal of hostility. In turn, such reproach created a concomitant *burden*, or an obligation to "transform historical studies . . . to a liberation of the present" in which history would also serve to prepare the future.[3] White urges his readers to contemplate not only the possibilities created by the historian who "plunder[s]" multiple narrative perspectives but also the "present-ness" of History; or as he writes concerning history's "golden age" of the early to mid-nineteenth century, "history was less an end in itself than a preparation for a more perfect understanding and acceptance of the individual's responsibility in the fashioning of the common humanity of the future" (*Tropics* 48–49). White rethought the notion of responsibility as a sort of moral-critical imperative, which, presumably, the historian must take to a community of scholars and readers in the attempt to document the past.[4]

It has been almost fifty years since James reevaluated *The Black Jacobins*. His lesson on the larger significance of Toussaint's story—that it would be "a mistake to see him merely as a political figure in a remote West Indian island" (291)—coupled with the challenge White offers in focusing on the deeper, literary dimension of history writing, contains an awareness of the implications of "past-ness" for present and future that I have pursued in my analyses of Toussaint. Just as I have considered a range of Toussaint's textual positions, and their relationship to each other, I now move to examine Césaire's writings as he confronted departmentalization. In Part II, specifically the passage from this chapter to chapter 6 (the migration from the essay to the theater), I develop more fully the idea of intertextual mediation that I have begun to sketch out here.

In this chapter I examine the genealogy explored by Césaire in his longest essay, *Toussaint Louverture: La Révolution française et le problème colonial*. By "genealogy," I mean two interrelated concepts. In a historical sense, it acknowledges the trope of family so dear to Toussaint and to French Republican ideology; as a theoretical structure, it refers to a chain of thought that remains active from the past through to the present. As Françoise Vergès proposed in the introduction to her interview of Césaire, "rereading Césaire in light of the present gives today's debates a history, a genealogy that grounds them."[5] In a 1987 speech on negritude, Césaire had defined his historiographical method as a "reactivation of the past with a view to its own *dépassement*."[6] Such a poetic turn of phrase plays on the idea that the past always *surpasses* any understanding of it as fixed in time. Césaire's desire to renew the past was consistent with Glissant, who wrote in the preface to *Monsieur Toussaint* of the "prophetic vision of the past" (7). "To get back in touch with [*renouer*] one's history," he continued, "is to devote oneself to the savors of the present" (8). Glissant stated that such an approach to the past is a "poetic ambition" (8); it is one whose dynamic temporality offers a way to rethink the passage from colony to overseas department by looking back to the first postcolonial moment in the Caribbean.

These genealogical approaches to thinking historically added to the dramatic portrait of Toussaint in *The Black Jacobins*. James followed Victor Schœlcher's grandiose archival study, *Vie de Toussaint Louverture*, by reinvigorating the model of writing the Haitian Revolution through the story of Toussaint. Césaire's depiction is similar to the heroic account found in James, with an important difference that had implications for his view of departmentalization: where James moved from the story of overcoming to one of a tragic flaw, Césaire portrayed a heroic sacrifice for the future of Haiti. With some exception, Césaire validated the historiographical paradigms established by Schœlcher and James. Later historian-biographers, notably Pierre Pluchon and, most recently, Madison Smartt Bell, reaffirmed the centrality of Toussaint to the history of Saint-Domingue. Where the latter relied heavily on the person of Toussaint, Césaire reestablished the relevance of debates in the late-eighteenth-century French legislature over the status of its colonies. It was a moment, he was well aware, when the idea of departmentalization developed from a triangular genealogy, one that moved along European, African, and Caribbean routes.

This context is critical to understanding the place of Césaire's essay in the historiographical traditions of the Haitian Revolution. It will be equally important to delve into the place of Haiti in his literary and political writings, and the impact it had on his vision for negritude. A trip to Haiti in 1944 portends the productive if volatile mix of literature and politics in his long life. Up until the lectures given in Haiti and, following soon after, conferences at the Sorbonne and speeches in the National Assembly, the expression of what it meant to be a black Martinican found an outlet through poetry, beginning with the *Cahier d'un retour au pays natal*. His turn to historiography flew under the radar until the past five years.[7] This is a curious omission, considering that *Toussaint Louverture* was not written in isolation. The visit to Haiti and subsequent entry into politics engendered a flurry of essays, including the first edition of the *Discours sur le colonialisme* in 1950 and the *Lettre à Maurice Thorez*, both of which are key to making sense of Césaire's changing views on departmentalization.[8] By way of a detour through a crucial time in his life, I examine *Toussaint Louverture* as an attempt to walk through a long history of France's "colonial problem" in Saint-Domingue.

A Haitian Itinerary and a Turn to Political Life

In the spring of 1944 Césaire embarked on his first visit to Haiti. The Allied blockade of Martinique and Guadeloupe had ended only nine months earlier, allowing him to accept an invitation from Pierre Mabille, then Free French cultural attaché in Haiti, to give a series of lectures.[9] The centerpiece of the tour was the Congrès International de Philosophie in Port-au-Prince, organized by the Société haïtienne d'études scientifiques and Camille Lhérisson, on 20–24 September 1944.[10] René Depestre, the celebrated Haitian poet, recalled Mabille's generosity and commented that Césaire's lecture tour was "a major event in our life." Depestre also remembered that "intellectuals such as Carpentier [the Cuban playwright who visited in 1942] . . . opened windows in the oppressive system of Lescot, in the obscurantism of his men."[11] This reminiscence offered a unique perspective on a stifling political climate, one under which a group of students struggled mightily. According to Gérald Bloncourt, a prominent activist, as the end of the war approached "things were heating up."[12] Having become increasingly dictatorial since his presidency began in 1941, Élie Lescot was granted a mandate to extend his term from five to seven years. The new term began just as Césaire arrived in May. Jacques Roumain, also a writer, politician, and communist activist, had recently returned from Mexico City, where Lescot had appointed him chargé d'affaires. Roumain had just finished the manuscript of his masterpiece, *Les Gouverneurs de la rosée*, when he died in August, a short three months into Césaire's trip.[13] The return of the gravely ill Roumain, who was already an icon in Haiti, may have emboldened student and artist communities to demonstrate more actively against the repressive policies of the Lescot administration.[14]

Over a period of seven months, Césaire charmed his audiences and, according to Bloncourt, "paved the way for Wifredo Lam and André Breton" (Bloncourt and Löwy, 97). The Cuban painter and the French surrealist poet were major intellectual figures who alighted on Haiti, following not only in the footsteps of Césaire but also writers of the Harlem Renaissance, including Langston Hughes and Zora Neale Hurston. According to Depestre, it was Breton who, a year after Césaire's visit, sparked the circle of activists, including Jacques Stephen Alexis and his cohorts at the journal *La Ruche*. Mabille invited Breton to give five conferences, including a famous speech on 20 December 1945 at the Rex Theater in Port-au-Prince, where Lescot sat in the front row along with several members of his administration and the military.[15] In his lively account of the speech, Depestre wrote of Breton's "contagious lyricism": "the scandalous and subversive atmosphere that had characterized surrealism in the heroic period of its Parisian era was created at the Rex. From the moment André Breton began to speak, we knew that the time was ripe in Haiti to unleash, before the event and *mutatis mutandis*, a terrific May '68 in the tropics!"[16] The Haitian government seized the January 1946 edition of *La Ruche* (which published Breton's speech), imprisoned Alexis and Depestre, and forced Bloncourt into exile. What began as student unrest led to larger demonstrations that brought about Lescot's departure in the "January Revolution."

Césaire had returned to Martinique well before Breton incited the young activists at *La Ruche*. His recollection of the trip contrasted sharply with what Haiti inspired in Breton. Whereas, according to Depestre, Breton spoke of the "inalienable enthusiasm for liberty" and the "lyrical element . . . [that] comes from the aspirations of an entire people," Césaire encountered a vast divide between intellectuals and the people. He had witnessed peasants "working often like chained animals." "They were real [*d'une grande vérité*] but pathetic," he remembered (*Nègre je suis* 52). "In Haiti," he continued, "I saw above all what should not be done! A country that had supposedly conquered its liberty, that had conquered independence, and what I saw was more miserable than Martinique, a French colony! The intellectuals intellectualized, they wrote poems, they took positions on this or that issue, but with no connection to the people themselves. It was tragic, and it could have also happened to us Martinicans" (56). The two poets developed widely disparate visions of what Haiti represented to them. While Breton celebrated the lyrical and cultural potential of the masses—and thus was more in tune with the indigenous, cultural revolution sought by the activists of *La Ruche*, many of whom had been inspired by Roumain and Price-Mars—Césaire was more concerned with the revolutionary origins of Haiti's founding, an epic that could explain the cohabitation of general liberty and continued servitude. Césaire revealed that the experience of this tragic dichotomy led directly to his research on Toussaint, the Haitian Revolution, and the kingdom of Christophe.[17]

The turbulence in Haiti occurred as Césaire's political career was taking shape. Colin Dayan suggests a cause-and-effect scenario: "Césaire arrived in Haiti in 1944 a poet and returned home later that year a politician."[18] Upon returning to Martinique, Césaire was asked to run on the Communist Party ticket for mayor of Fort-de-France and won easily in May 1945; in October he was elected deputy to the First National Constituent Assembly and went to Paris to work on the new constitution of the Fourth Republic. It is hard to imagine his turn to politics without taking into account his time in Haiti. In numerous interviews Césaire spoke of Haiti with reverence, and it is undeniable that he had an almost spiritual attachment. The question rarely asked, however, is what critical reflection gave intellectual weight to the emotional bond? Henock Trouillot's recollection of Césaire's visit is atypical in that he begins by acknowledging Césaire's study of Haitian history before playing up the emotional attachment.[19] After testifying to the popularity of Césaire—"The young professor, then thirty-one, filled the Haitian youth with enthusiasm by his warm and vibrant eloquence" (405)—Trouillot states that Césaire "looked into [*s'est penché*] periods of the history of Haiti with interest. First, his *Toussaint Louverture*, written from numerous and unpublished documents. Without a doubt, it is based on documents from the National and Constituent Assemblies, the Convention, and the Directory. The poet accomplished the work of a historian" (408). At this point, however, Trouillot downplays the scholarly side: "If he considered closely certain historical circumstances, he also had a sort of nostalgia for Haiti, barely kept in check. He followed his heart, if it can be said, to arrive at our history" (409). The emphasis on nostalgia makes more sense in conjunction with an earlier monograph, *L'Itinéraire d'Aimé Césaire*, in which Trouillot had contextualized the 1944 visit by way of comparison to the dilapidation and misery of wartime Martinique: "This wealth of facts and meanings attracts Aimé Césaire more than most aspects of the history of his own country, this Martinique whose flatness he stigmatized" (133). In this way, Trouillot grounds Césaire's emotional attachment to Haiti in the lament in the *Cahier* of the "flat, spread out city [*ville plate-étalée*]" of Fort-de-France. In the end, what interests Trouillot is the camaraderie that, he argues, most Haitians felt toward Césaire. Because Césaire's lived experience had so much in common with "us Haitians, the semi-colonized," Trouillot wrote, it was as if the author of *Le Discours sur le colonialisme* was writing about, and to, us (410).

Trouillot lends support to the idea of a shared Caribbean history between Martinique, Guadeloupe, Saint-Domingue, and Haiti. His attention to the affective dimension of Césaire's study of Haiti can be explained away, in part, by the fact that as a personal remembrance, it is not necessarily meant to serve as a critical analysis. That being said, over the years some of the most prominent scholars have given priority to the emotional charge of Césaire's Haitian itinerary. In his intellectual biography, M. a M. Ngal referred to the trip by highlighting its supposed curative powers: "The timidity that came out in a stutter would only go away during the trip to Haiti in 1944" (32).[20] To be fair, Ngal brings out Césaire's formative experiences by way of thorough if mainly thematic readings of his works. His summary of the trip to Haiti occupies but one paragraph that focuses on the "pilgrimage to the country where 'Négritude stood up for the first time'" (117). Moreover, while Ngal discusses the importance of Toussaint as an iconic Césairean hero, he spends virtually no ink on *Toussaint Louverture*. For Ngal, it is enough to state that the trip to the *pays natal* was transformative. Likewise, in their biography, *Aimé Césaire: Le Nègre inconsolé*, Toumson and Henry-Valmore reinforce the emotional draw of Haiti, from where Césaire returned "shaken, his awareness mature and broad: 'Haiti, where Négritude stood up for the first time'" (79). The idea that the journey served as a turning point is neither new nor an end unto itself.

The link between Haiti and the oft-cited passage in the *Cahier* informs the well-worn criticism of Césaire's vision of *négritude*. In part, the argument is that in the attempt to undo the Eurocentric hold on universal rights and cultural superiority, Césaire replaced it with a nostalgic, essentialist conception of Africa. Following this logic, the readings of Ngal and, to a lesser extent, Trouillot are but a short step from substituting Haiti for Africa. In fact, in *Aimé Césaire: Une Traversée paradoxale du siècle*, another (less charitable) biography, Raphaël Confiant claims that Haiti is just such a substitute (89). In defense of Césaire, Christopher Miller states, "Confiant gets around the problem of Césaire's considerable emphasis on Haiti—the birthplace of Negritude according to the *Cahier*—by claiming that Haiti ... is simply 'a substitute for Africa.' One wonders who is doing the substituting" (*The French Atlantic Triangle*

507). Earlier, in an overview of Césaire's contribution to negritude, Miller devotes considerable space to the *Cahier*, including a synthesis of criticism on the epic poem. He then calls attention to the strategic place that Haiti occupied in Césaire's thought and to the poem's larger "Atlantic substitution" (325). He contends that Confiant's criticism is predicated on a false substitution, one that ignores the positioning of the Caribbean in the writings on negritude. It is precisely this French Atlantic/Caribbean dimension that Césaire develops in his extensive study of the history of Saint-Domingue. Césaire refers to the "Haitian optic" in *Toussaint Louverture* at a critical juncture, when Toussaint outmaneuvered the French Directory's agent, Hédouville. Césaire understood Toussaint's political moves as uniquely "Haitian": "Toussaint very much planned on remaining in charge, using the white colonists and not serving them" (257). For Césaire, the fight over the persistent discrimination of French republicanism is something that Toussaint and future Haitians mastered. Nowhere in the essay do we read the story of an African triumph. Nevertheless, critical attention to Césaire's vision of negritude has rarely considered *Toussaint Louverture*, choosing instead to substitute an uncritical, nostalgic view of Haiti for an even more idealistic vision of Africa.

In retracing Césaire's itinerary, I have focused less on the "false" framework of Haiti/Africa than on the place of Saint-Domingue/Haiti in the Caribbean. As Toumson and Valmore point out, Césaire's encounter with Haïti was an "intellectual and affective shock," one that resulted in a decade of writing "that Aimé Césaire will devote ... to the country of the 'Black Jacobins,' to the heroes of the anti-slavery revolution" (79). Césaire remained in Haiti from May to December 1944, during which time he elaborated on his treatise on poetry, "Poésie et Connaissance," extracts of which were published in the January 1945 volume of *Tropiques*. He also lectured on Mallarmé, Lautréamont, Baudelaire, and Rimbaud;[21] upon his return to Martinique, along with his wife, Suzanne, and René Ménil, he devoted most of this final edition of *Tropiques* to Haiti. In addition to "Poésie et Connaissance," the volume contains contributions by Mabille on the Cuban painter Wifredo Lam and by Menil on humor. The essays in *Tropiques* represent a variety of cultural, artistic, and ethnographic perspectives on Haiti.[22]

Between the figuration of the revolutionary process in the *Cahier* and its dramatization in *Christophe*, *Toussaint Louverture* is a pivotal work that scholars have only recently analyzed in depth. In *Modernism and Negritude: The Poetry and Poetics of Aimé Césaire*, A. James Arnold initially described the essay as a "serious historical work" but refers to it only once in the entire study, and indirectly at that (13). In the context of an analysis of Césaire's poem, "Mémoriel à Louis Delgrès," Arnold comments on the description of Delgrès in *Toussaint Louverture*, where the memory of the hero of Mount Matouba finds "four pages of rather dry, matter-of-fact prose" (275). Furthermore, the passing reference becomes problematic in the incomplete assessment of it as "a black history of the Caribbean" (275). Arnold hints at its importance in Césaire's corpus by highlighting the "implications of poetics and politics." The essay's "historical subject," he continues, "guarantees a high degree of continuity in Césaire's poetic vision in that it incarnates in a real hero of the Caribbean World the drama of the agonistic hero that Césaire had previously treated as an atemporal, mythic topos" (275).[23] Years later, in his contribution to *Césaire à l'œuvre*, Arnold reevaluated his initial assessment of the essay and concluded that it is a "literary work" ("Devenir Aimé Césaire" 214). This revision is more in step with Gloria Nne Onyeoziri's essay, "Le *Toussaint* d'Aimé Césaire," which is a rare close reading of the "literary optic that Césaire adopts" in the presentation of historic events (89). Onyeoziri described the methodology as lyrical, journalistic, rhetorical, and theatrical and underscored "the manner in which Césaire conceives of historical developments" (94).

Césaire's conception of history was key to the connection he made between the legacy of Toussaint and the problem of departmentalization. In the *Discours sur la Négritude*, delivered in Miami in 1987, Césaire stated, "*Négritude* is a way of living history in history" (82). It would perhaps be enough to interpret this as a nod to the cyclical nature of history, that the colonial always remains part of the "postcolonial." Césaire's connection to the historical event of the Haitian Revolution is something archetypal in its relationship to modern conceptions of race, citizenship, and national power. He continued in Miami:

> But, you will tell me, a revolt that is only a revolt constitutes nothing else but a historic impasse. If Negritude was only an impasse, that is because it was leading us somewhere. Where was it leading us? It was leading us to ourselves[,] . . . but the essential point is that with us had begun a process of rehabilitation of our values by ourselves, a deepening of our past by ourselves, a re-rooting of ourselves in a history, a geography, and in a culture, the whole translated not by an archaic [*archaïsant*] attachment to the past, but by a reactivation of the past with a view to its own surpassing [*dépassement*]. (85–86)

In this speech, Césaire reflects specifically on negritude as a catalyst of African independence movements. More broadly, he emphasizes the temporality of history: the past contains within it a potential that must be reactivated in the future. Toussaint's fight to eradicate slavery was part and parcel of a revolutionary process that brought, in Nesbitt's words, "contingent, local, historical events into relation with their foundation, the eternity of a singular truth, in the attempt precisely to make that eternity realize itself *in time*, that is to say, historically" ("A Singular Revolution" 40; original emphasis). For Nesbitt, the "singularity" of the Haitian Revolution lies in the liberating truth that "escapes" linear temporality to anticipate futures problems between liberty and colonizing forces (40). In 1987 Césaire continued to articulate the future of the historical process of the Haitian Revolution and its relation to negritude and the question of universal rights: the past is something to "reactivate in order to go beyond."

As I move now to a close reading of the essay, it is imperative to reconsider the fluid temporality of a *dépassement*, or the idea of "going beyond," that, because of its inherent incompleteness, became an obstacle for Césaire. In a real sense, the backward and forward movement implied by this act, which carries with it the burden of detaching oneself from an "archaic attachment to the past," meant that Césaire inhabited multiple eras. It is from these different temporal zones that he mobilized the Haitian Revolution as a way to confront the refractory problems still at work in the Caribbean.

Toussaint Louverture: Reading Césaire's Essay

Césaire's study is, first and foremost, an *essayistic* activity, one in which, to use a common trope, he "walks" through the archives on Saint-Domingue. In his contribution to *The Modern French Essay: Movement, Instability, Performance,* Charles Forsdick elaborates on the essay as a "peripatetic genre" ("De la plume comme des pieds" 50). Picking up on the theme of the essay-as-walk, Forsdick leads us through a number of poetic and prose genres and their thematic connection to the activity of walking. In contrast to the linear movement associated with the "closed structure of the individual *walk,*" Forsdick goes back to the French tradition that originated with Montaigne, for whom "reflection depends on motion" (50; original emphasis). The peripatetic is the "unbounded practice of *walking*" in which one meanders across different and "uneven terrain" before arriving at a destination (50; original emphasis). Metaphors of walking as observation and reflection, and of the concomitant challenge of processing space and time, are endless. Anyone who has spent time in the archives, sifting through folders in box after box (the road to a digital archive is a long one!), can appreciate the unevenness of the documentation; as a result, the knowledge that accumulates makes for an itinerant journey. The analysis that comes out of this process is, more often than not, a work in progress. It is illuminating to read Césaire's essay in medias res, as it were, a peripatetic activity that might be explored differently, or reenacted, on another "walk." Read this way, the essay reflects a search for *how* Toussaint rewrote French colonial-republicanism and *where* the accumulating power of this revision might have taken Haiti.

The form of the essay deserves attention for its engagement with the Hegelian dialectic.[24] It is divided into the predictable three parts of this method: "La Fronde des Grands Blancs, la Révolte Mulâtre, et la Révolution Nègre," in which the thesis of the white planters' role leads to the antithesis of the Mulatto Revolt and finally to the synthesis in which the former slaves accomplish the unthinkable revolution. Before analyzing its structure, a summary is helpful. The first section analyzes an array of archival materials and an impressive range of nineteenth- and twentieth-century French, British, and Haitian historiography.[25] Césaire pours over speeches in metropolitan and colonial assemblies, documenting the planters' quest for autonomy in the wake of the French Revolution and the inconsistent responses of legislators in France. He draws out the attempts of French politicians to reconfigure colonial governance and to navigate their complicated relationship with mercantile interests in the colonial and slave-trading lobbies. The second section traces the struggle of the *gens de couleur* to be included in debates over governance and autonomy by asserting their rights under several decrees passed by the National Assembly.

The frame of Césaire's historical narrative betrays the linearity of the dialectic. The essay contains an analysis that is more than straightforward cause-and-effect sequence, and it thus disrupts the anticipated, distinct phases of its tripartite structure. As Césaire demonstrates, conflict and negotiation occurred repeatedly between and within all three populations (white, black, and *gens de couleur*). One battle or treaty did not lead to the next; it often came back to an antecedent, revised it, and presaged a future complication rather than clear-cut truce. Although the traditional structure appears to give order to an unstable event, it redirects the expected flow in a series of internal oppositions. The chapter titles themselves telescope this tension into a narrative economy that often reads against the titles of the three sections. "La Révolte Mulâtre" opens with a chapter titled "Crétinisme Parlementaire," which we soon learn speaks not only to the mulatto negotiation with the duplicitous colonialist lobby but also to the compromised standing of the mulattoes with various black rebel groups in the wake of such collaboration.

The reading of the materials in the first two parts brings out the contradiction in the subtitle of the essay. Both Figueroa and Hurley note the jarring absence of "Haitian" in the title, and it is worth pausing here to reflect on the apparent lapsus. For that matter, a similar argument could be made of James's *The Black Jacobins*, in which "Black" would function as an adjective for the nominal focus on the (French) Jacobins. Césaire set out to expose the fault lines of the French Revolution before championing the revolutionary actions of the slaves on Saint-Domingue. The third section, "La Révolution nègre," begins with the chapter "Les Limites de la Révolution Française" and is thus consistent with the doubled structure of the entire essay, in which chapter titles often require a reorientation of the expected analytic sequence. Here, Césaire buttresses an earlier claim, concerning the internally flawed logic of the French Revolution—"at the moment of the colonial question, the French Revolution had started to come up against itself . . . , to split, and thus to define itself" (110)—by pointing out the historical limits of universal rights under the control of the French bourgeoisie:

> To wait for the abolition of slavery in a spontaneous gesture of the French bourgeoisie, under the pretext that this abolition was in the logic of the Revolution and more precisely in the Declaration of the Rights of Man, was, taking everything into account, not to know that its own historical task, the bourgeois revolution itself, the bourgeoisie had only accomplished it because they were harassed by the people. (171)

Césaire locates a troubling connection between republicanism and the power of the bourgeoisie; specifically, the latter was forced to accommodate the rights espoused by the former. In a rehearsal of the same argument, Césaire wants abolition to be the logical result of revolution but, once again, must acknowledge that violence was necessary to bring about a resolution between universal rights and sovereign interest: "the abolition of slavery was in the logic of the Revolution, of course; but it was necessary to brutalize seriously the historical protagonist so that it would consent to play its role to the end" (215–16). Césaire argues that the Haitian Revolution confronted the colonial question head on by exposing a French republicanism that could not disentangle itself from its imperial needs.

In Césaire's logic, the insistence on the priority of universal rights over sovereign particularities would enable Toussaint to decolonize Saint-Domingue. He read the 1801 Constitution as a precursor to twentieth-century autonomy: "Brilliant intuition. The idea of a French Commonwealth starts here. Louverture made only one mistake: to be ahead of his time, and by a good century and a half" (283). *Toussaint Louverture* ends before the final war of independence, or precisely when the revolution would become a national story. By this reasoning, Toussaint was both a man of his time and one who could be deployed at future moments. The opening paragraph of the essay, "Une Colonie exemplaire," reflects a cartographic consciousness that also marks the transition from past to future: "Reaching out to the west, the mouth of an enormous gulf, with, to the south, the outsized prognathism of a jawbone. Its back to the Spanish side, this is the French part of Saint-Domingue, today the Republic of Haiti, a thin ribbon of highlands, surrounded on its three sides by the clearest blue of the Caribbean Sea" (21). In a poetic evocation of the passage from colony (Saint-Domingue) to republic (Haiti), Césaire signals an attention to language and wastes no time to arrive at the heart of the matter: the exemplariness of Saint-Domingue was not its wealth but its modern system of exploitation, a triangular trade that pitted the French Revolution against its own colonial underpinnings. In an incisive response to the taxonomy of race that came out of the *Code Noir* Césaire brings out the defining flaw of the French Revolution:

> The thinking of the eighteenth-century legislator appears uniquely theological. When one has fallen into "color," one can never come back. As there is original sin, so there is, in colonial society, something close to it: the original mark. And the black mark that the mulatto carries, indelible as it must be, marks his place. Forevermore. (35)

The collusion of racial conflict and colonial interest conspired against the negotiations that took place among all three populations on Saint-Domingue.

Césaire does not so much analyze the three-pronged movement he lays out as orchestrate the archival material to speak for itself. Although the poetic language of the introduction gives way to prolific citation of letters and reports, the dramatic feel of the text is no less palpable. In her reading, Onyeoziri points to the "forme de didascalie" that operates in the text, directing the flow of letters, reports, and decrees, and revealing contradictions and theatrical surprise. "By removing himself this way," she contends, "Césaire, in the role of playwright, does not always assume the responsibility of making links between texts and documents; he often lets them create these links or allows them to show the relations themselves in the form of a dialogue" (89). Whether giving way to the abbé Grégoire in a long citation of the denunciation of the colonialist lobby in the National Assembly or, much later, when presenting Toussaint's capture by the French as a sacrifice, Césaire moves in and out of the narrative scene. The effect is to cede interpretation to the reader, despite the fact that he constructs these linkages in the first place. The restaging of the archival material also creates a pattern of paratactic construction, and the gaps left to fill in give the essay a more poetic texture. Because the logic of Césaire's analysis is implicit, the parataxis focuses our attention on the language of the citations themselves and builds layers of meaning without being didactic. Following Onyeoziri, the reader is witness to a "literary optic" that poetically elaborates through the metaphor of parataxis the problem-space of a revolution of many layers.

Toussaint Louverture is a historical essay that in its lyrical attention to language and rhetoric is also a work of literature. The literary mode is a response to the political theater that Césaire read in the archives. After meticulously analyzing the deeper historical, international, and political layers of Saint-Domingue, he allows Toussaint to take center stage in the third and climactic act. The scene of the sacrifice is evidence of Toussaint's principal role as the one person who, according to Césaire, was able to synthesize the stakes of the revolution. The passage describing his capture by the French is indicative of Césaire's overall strategy and deserves to be cited at length:

> This role of martyr, Toussaint accepted it, even better, anticipated it, because he believed it to be indispensable. I will not go so far as to say that the surrender of Toussaint was a sort of classic *devotio*: the relinquishment of a life, his own, that of a leader, in an act of faith, for the salvation of the people. I see more than a mystical act: a political act. Yes, this journey that led him to captivity and death, he conceived of it as his last political act and, without a doubt, one of the most fruitful. On what followed, it is better to give him the last word. (313; original emphasis)

Many have found fault with the hagiographic tendencies of this language (martyr, *devotio*), and this is a fair criticism. As I have shown, Césaire is hardly the first to focus on Toussaint at the expense of what Carolyn E. Fick has called the "making of Haiti from below." In the passage above, Césaire reads surrender as a sign of prescience: Toussaint surmised that as a political act his surrender would bring the rebels together to defeat Bonaparte's army. Like James, he argued for a tragic hero who transformed the consciousness of the former slaves. He continued with even more dramatic language: "He had been given gangs, he turned them into an army. He had been left a peasant revolt, he brought about a Revolution; a population, he transformed it into a people. A colony, he created a state; better still, a nation" (331). Césaire revises the thesis of the creation of a commonwealth to argue that Toussaint brought the former slaves to the cusp of a new nation.

The focus on Toussaint in the final section makes for a forceful conclusion. Césaire was careful to pay attention to the heterogeneity of archival material, and so it is ultimately a more balanced conclusion in that it rests less on his protagonist than on what the Haitian Revolution meant for the discourses of emancipation and French colonial interests. Reflection on the "colonial problem" leads to a questioning of the departmental problem. In a passage on Toussaint's "essential contribution" to the doctrine of universal rights, one finds a revealing conflation of past and present: "The false universalism has accustomed *us* to so much deception, the rights of man have shrunk often enough to be but the rights of the European, that the issue is not superfluous" (343; emphasis mine). The insertion of the pronoun *nous* brings the eighteenth century into contact with the twentieth, launching the reader into Césaire's negotiation with the French following World War II.

Working through the Future of Departmentalization

Césaire cosponsored the project of a law for the constitution of the new French government that would transform the status of the colonies of Martinique, Guadeloupe, French Guyana, and the Île de la Réunion into overseas departments.[26] As I have shown, the idea of departmentalization was not new; attempts to define the connection between the *mère-patrie* and her colonies go back to the nascent stages of the First Republic, and precisely to the momentous summer of 1795, when the National Convention ratified a new constitution.

As we recall, Title I, Article VI, of the Constitution declared that the colonies "are integral parts of the Republic, and are subject to the same constitutional law." In theory, the clause eliminated any administrative difference between the metropole and the colony. Bernard Gainot refers to this period as a "new colonization" and argues that scholars have dismissed the significance of this constitutional reform. He singles out Césaire's *Toussaint Louverture* as a "vulgate," a source of "reductive approaches" that assume the "duplicity of metropolitan legislators" with regard to their colonial policies ("La Naissance des départements d'Outre-Mer" 52). In the effort to rehabilitate the more reform-minded wing of French republicanism, Gainot reminds us of the first proposal for departmentalization, which became the Law on the Constitutional Organization of the Colonies on 1 January 1798 under the "post-fructidor" Directory.[27] The resistance to the proposed law was as familiar as it was durable: a wise and steadfast nation was required to govern the people of color who labored in the tropical climate. According to Gainot, the most well known advocate of "tropical particularism" was the former *conventionnel*, Boissy d'Anglas, who had actually been one of the principal authors of the constitutional reforms for the colonies. The equation of departmentalization with assimilation goes back to a speech he made as the National Convention debated the new Constitution. Gainot laments that the speech was a "tableau filled with all the clichés put forward by the adherents of climatic determinism" (72). In this logic, liberty was a heavy burden for the black laborers, who needed the tutelage of the metropole. By "assimilation," Boissy d'Anglas referred to the administrative supervision of the colony, a custodial relationship that concerned the governance of a people who, though rightfully granted freedom, were unfit for full citizenship.

The theory of assimilation proposed by Boissy d'Anglas was blatantly paternalistic and racist. Before citing a lengthy passage, Césaire wrote, "Never had French assimilationism been given such free rein" (245). Gainot concedes as much; however, he argues that it was unfair for Césaire to define assimilation on the basis of Boissy d'Anglas alone. He points out that the *ex-conventionnel* was banished from the legislature following the Coup of Fructidor and goes on to state that those who supported the 1798 law of departmentalization—including Laveaux, who was essentially Toussaint's representative in Paris—had flatly rejected the continued subjugation of blacks and had aimed to redefine assimilation as a full extension of rights. For Gainot, the post-fructidor Directory has been lost in a historiographical blind spot, in which departmentalization as assimilation has been understood, in Césaire's terms, as "the mask of subjection" (246).

The debates surrounding the 1798 law reveal more ambiguity than resolution concerning the meaning of assimilation. While Gainot is right to highlight the more progressive elements behind the law, he fails to mention that the "reformed" Directory approved the appointment of Hédouville as its agent on Saint-Domingue a short six months into the new law. The former "pacifier of the Vendée" had a mandate to restore order and to control Toussaint's growing power. It could be argued that Césaire honed in on Boissy d'Anglas at the expense of those legislators for whom assimilation meant full integration into the Republic. It is clear, however, that the extensive debates that gave rise to the first law of departmentalization were well known to Césaire. The question of assimilation was left unresolved in 1798, and the citizenship of the people of the French Caribbean remained tenuous despite the abolition of slavery in 1848. Césaire's view of assimilation had also been shaped by the political engagement of his predecessors, who had wrangled with a discriminatory Republican tradition.[28] It is also true that the French Caribbean was further isolated from France during World War II. The Law of Departmentalization passed on 19 March 1946, yet it would take the French government, then under the Second Constituent National Assembly, almost two years to enact it. This administrative delay aggravated Césaire, who was well versed in the historic deferral of rights during and after the Haitian Revolution.

Césaire's stance on assimilation, and the distinction he made between political and cultural assimilation, has been one of the most misunderstood aspects in the evolution of his political thought.[29] As we have seen, he rejected Boissy d'Anglas's articulation of departmentalization as colonization by another name. To appreciate the rush of political essays in the 1950s, it is imperative to go back to the two written before the *Cahier*. These are the essays in *L'Étudiant Noir*, the journal of the student association in Paris of which Césaire was elected president in 1934. Until recently, Césaire was known to have written only one piece for the journal, "Nègreries: Jeunesse noire et assimilation," in which he lashed out against cultural assimilation because, anticipating Fanon, it "always ends in contempt and hatred and it carries within itself the seeds of the struggle of people against their own kind [*lutte de même contre le même*]."[30] "Nègreries" was a raw essay, framed by a Marxist discourse that still resonated with Césaire. Even at this early stage, he infused the class-based revolution of Marxism with the language of race. It is clear that Césaire was developing the political and racial dimensions of negritude that would contrast with the more irrational component that finds space in the *Cahier*. For years it was thought that he coined the term *negritude* in his seminal poem, despite the fact that both Senghor and Damas recalled its first deployment in the pages of *L'Étudiant Noir*. In 2008, in *Negritude Agonistes: Assimilation against Nationalism in the French-Speaking Caribbean and Guyane*, Christian Filostrat reproduced the lost, second essay published in the May–June edition of *L'Étudiant Noir*.[31] The discovery of the essay, "Conscience raciale et révolution sociale," necessitates a rethinking of Césaire's views on assimilation, specifically in terms of his long-standing if tumultuous relationship with Marxism and the French Communist Party.[32]

"Conscience raciale" is a call to an awareness of an "exploited race." Before taking part in revolution, Césaire argues, the black man must know "it is fine [*beau*] and good and legitimate to be a Negro [*nègre*]." In "The (Revised) Birth of Negritude" Miller declares that this passage should "leap off the page to the readers of the *Cahier*" because the call to the "beauty" of racial awareness precedes the nearly identical passage in the poem, "And mine my dances / ... / The it-is-fine-and-good-and-legitimate-to-be-a-Negro dance" (746).[33] As Miller observes, the essay then takes a literary turn to recall Occide, the Communist character of "Le Tzar noir," a story by Paul Morand, to make an example of Occide as a "sterile, imitative monkey." Instead of being able to take his place in the Communist struggle, Occide has been segregated by the very political force through which he seeks liberation. This rereading begins to put Césaire at odds with the priorities of Marxist thought as early as 1935, as he introduces negritude only once near the end of the short essay as the new growth of racial consciousness: "Plant our negritude like a beautiful tree until it bears its most authentic fruits." For the reader-spectator of *La tragédie du roi Christophe*, the organic metaphor that carries this political birth should also leap out from the page because it reappears as the lesson on nation building that the British abolitionist, Wilberforce, delivers to Christophe: "One does not invent a tree, one plants it. One does not extract its fruit, one lets it carry them." In Wilberforce's cautionary tale, the founding of a nation takes time ("ring by ring") that the new king did not have, and so Christophe rejected the advice, without entirely seeking a rupture with the model of British monarchy (Christophe establishes a court, distributes royal titles, and so on). Césaire's essay could also be read as a warning to his fellow colonized Antilleans: the upstart militant does not necessarily create a new foundation, but he does rationalize the *replanting* of Marxist thought in the particular, racialized terrain of Europe's colonial possessions. Therefore, Césaire does not wish to raze the revolutionary field of Marxism; instead, negritude is a revision, one that should be a partner to the larger revolution. Césaire attempts to bring negritude and Marxism together at the end of the essay, but the result is less than clear. Miller reads this early articulation as an ambiguous dichotomy in that "the ostensible subordination of negritude" occurred in a more utilitarian approach to Marxism, which Miller aptly phrases in the French as "marxisant" (747–48). The present participle places Césaire in between the two, working through the first iteration of a politicized negritude and preparing for both its poetic amplification in the *Cahier* and its more robust activation in the looming confrontation with the French Communist Party.

Twenty-one years after this essay, ten years after passage of the Law of Departmentalization, and five years after the first publication of *Le Discours sur le colonialisme*, the tree of a *marxisant* negritude bears fruit, not of a harmonious, shared struggle between European, African, and Caribbean peoples, but of discord. During his initial association, Césaire had fully expected negritude to take root in the French Communist Party. Shortly after becoming a member, he contributed the following to *Pourquoi je suis communiste*, a pamphlet put out by the party in 1946:

> I joined the Communist Party because, in a world not yet cured of racism, where the fierce exploitation of colonial populations still persists, the Communist Party embodies the will to work effectively for the coming of the only social and political order we can accept—because it will be founded on the right of all men to dignity without regard to origin, religion, or color.[34]

Although both the interview with Ngal and the above brochure are evidence of Césaire's political optimism during this time, they also evince a note of reserve. For much of the decade to come Césaire stayed in line, even going so far as to publish a poem, "Maurice Thorez parle," on the occasion of the secretary general's fiftieth birthday, in which he praised Thorez as "the thunderbird [*l'oiseau tonnerre*] in the capitalist sky all drab [*tout terne*]."[35] However, as Brent Hayes Edwards has recently written, "Clearly much had changed by fall 1956" ("Introduction" 116). In an open letter published in *Présence Africaine* on 24 October 1956, Césaire grounded the "thunderbird" and announced his resignation.

Before treating the letter to Thorez, it is necessary to discuss the writings that led up to it and that parallel the disappointment with departmentalization. Beginning with the *Discours sur le colonialisme*, the denunciation of French humanism that opened the decade, these can be read as a sequence that led to the publication of *Toussaint Louverture*. Preparing the deeper, historical work to come, the *Discours* accused Europe of celebrating its own liberation in willful ignorance of the genesis of the colonial problem in the late eighteenth century. Césaire argued that Europe and the United States had conflated republicanism with universal rights: "The great reproach that I address to pseudo-humanism: to have diminished for too long the rights of man, to have had of them, to have still a conception of rights that is narrow and fragmented, partial and biased, and, when all is said and done, sordidly racist" (14).[36] Arnold states that the fiery essay was one that Césaire would have liked to give as a speech on the floor of the National Assembly. The revolutionary prose reads more like a performance, yet its hortatory power (especially to his *camarades*) was not matched by an equally persuasive act.

Césaire first had to understand the failure of departmentalization before seeking a more autonomous direction. Wilder's study of the inherent contradictions of the "French imperial nation-state" is particularly relevant. He finds that the strategies of the negritude poets, including Césaire, was to "reconfigure rather than reject interwar colonial rationality, to excavate and exploit political possibilities that were immanent to an internally contradictory imperial order in order to imagine an alternative political formation organized around integration, circulation, reciprocity, and federation" (*French Imperial Nation-State* 252). The preface to Daniel Guérin's *Les Antilles décolonisées*, a short essay that followed the second edition of the *Discours*, reflects this strategy of working in and through a French Imperial-Republican system that imposed a series of restraints on its colonial subjects and simultaneously offered to include them as citizens.[37] Looking back on a brief ten years that probably felt like much more, Césaire clears the air on the decision to pursue departmentalization:

> Of men recognized for centuries as formal citizens of a state, but a marginal citizenship, how should one not understand that their first collective step would be not to reject the empty form of their citizenship but to make sure to transform it to full citizenship and to go from a mutilated citizenship to citizenship period? That is all that is necessary to understand the law of 19 March 1946. . . . But, I would add that it is very true to say that the law did not have only positive aspects. It made up for a contradiction but it created another. Equality was from then on complete by law; in point of fact, inequality worsened each day. (10)

He pleads for the importance of legal rights but laments growing social inequality. Furthermore, he recognized that the "terrible contradiction" of departmentalization "could only be resolved by [its] negation" and would lead to "an inevitable national awareness" (10–11). Césaire here returns to ideas first developed in "Conscience raciale," both to reactivate the condemnation of Eurocentrism and to acknowledge the belated awareness of the impossible position in which he found himself. Nevertheless, he remained convinced that departmentalization was fundamental to political progress, from which would come "a demand of a nationalist kind" (11). He justified the law despite "being swallowed in the dreary universalism of an empire" (10).

The critique of assimilation, in both its cultural and political forms, takes a crucial turn in the late summer and early fall of 1956. Invited to speak at the First International Congress of Negro Writers and Artists, hosted by *Présence Africaine* in September 1956 at the Sorbonne, Césaire delivers "Culture et colonisation," in which he broadened the scope of his critique of colonialism to include the African and African American diaspora. Edwards has given more attention to the speech and the response of the African American delegation in attendance than to the *Lettre à Maurice Thorez*; therefore, at the risk of eliding the importance of "Culture et colonisation," I would like to move to the letter, both in the interest of space and in the desire to return to the question of the cohabitation of autonomy and assimilation. Moreover, scholars have generally focused on the political significance of Césaire's resignation but have neglected to comment on the narrative form that delivered such stunning news.[38] Even though he addressed it to Thorez, Césaire published it in the open. From the start, the more personal confines of the letter straddle the line with a very public declaration: it is an official correspondance *and* a manifesto that attempts to justify a political act. The generic flexibility that Césaire gives to the letter can be read in the pronominal slippage that occurs at a crucial transition of his argument. He begins the letter in the first person but switches to the plural of the communal "we" to decry the French Communist Party's continued subjugation of its colonial members: "It is to say that we are convinced that our issues, or, if you will, the colonial question, cannot be treated as a part of a more important whole" (8). From this point on, Césaire weaves the singular with the plural, speaking to Thorez but also to the greater audience of an international communism. He speaks for himself (as the departmental representative of his fellow Martinicans and, it could be argued, as a disciple of Thorez) *and* for "black peoples." The genre of the letter allows for this movement from the (more intimate) singular to the (more public) plural. Much like Toussaint, Césaire layered his correspondence so that it fit within the traditional frame but also transformed it.

It would not be too much of a stretch to read the *Lettre à Maurice Thorez* alongside several of Toussaint's letters and reports. Metropolitan authorities such as Laveaux and Sonthonax were, like Thorez, father figures for their Caribbean protégés. Toussaint and Césaire cultivated these relationships in the language of family. In fact, Césaire explains that his decision was the result of a "fraternalism ... imbued with its own superiority and sure of its experience, [it] takes you by the hand (a hand, alas! sometimes rough) in order to lead you on the road where it knows how to find Reason and Progress" (11).[39] Césaire also negotiated with two families, Europeans convinced of their superior universalism and Martinicans desiring to assert their own solutions. He recognized a debt to the revolutionary ideals of Marxism but refused its "inveterate" subordination of the questions of race and colonialism: "This is not a desire to fight alone and disdainful of all alliance. This is a desire not to confuse alliance and subordination. Solidarity and resignation [*démission*]" (10). The staging of pairs of opposites, and the pragmatism that conveys them, harks back to the language and tone of Toussaint's prison letters. In this sense, the "loyal opposition" that Césaire presented to Thorez is similar to Toussaint's *Mémoire*. The 1956 letter is a final report to a superior from a member (and, by extension, an overseas community) wronged by the Party.

The expression of redress sought by Césaire was at once political and literary. Unlike the *Discours*, which was a rhetorical tour de force not supported by a specific political act, the *Lettre à Maurice Thorez* was the rare, committed text. Yet Césaire insisted that the letter was not an outright denunciation, and so it is essential to reflect on the rhetoric that delivers the political act. On the surface, the resignation he submitted in 1956 was no more a rejection of communism and Marxism than what he had printed in *L'Étudiant Noir* in 1935. Still willing to be patient in the fall of 1956, Césaire declares, "And then? Then we will need the patience to resume our work; the force to redo what has been undone; the force to invent instead of follow; the force to 'invent' our route and to rid it of pre-made [*toutes faites*] forms, petrified forms that obstruct it" (15–16). Initially, he writes of building but also, perhaps having learned from the past, of "ridding" the land of "petrified forms." It appears that the tree he had planted as the hopeful, central metaphor of "Conscience raciale" must now grow in a new place.

The growing disappointment with departmentalization, the resignation from the French Communist Party, the founding of the Parti Progressiste Martiniquais, and the concomitant desire to create a more autonomous Caribbean federation all point to an evolving treatment of assimilation. The academic tone of the preface to Guérin and the assertiveness of the letter to Thorez lead to the confident rejection of assimilation that he located in Toussaint: "Toussaint was too intelligent, too intuitive as well not to feel that what was hiding behind the liberalism of the form, was dependence, depersonalization, constriction of local freedoms. Assimilation, as always in history, has only been the mask of subjection, and he well understood this" (246). The final pages of *Toussaint Louverture* are tinged with both melancholy and hopefulness, leaving Césaire in an uncomfortable position. In the end he finds that Toussaint was both "operator and intercessor" (344): he intervened in the struggle between the universal and the particular, fully aware that universal rights had derived from French sovereignty. His role, according to Césaire, was to liberate rights from a national imperative to a truly universal setting: "Toussaint Louverture's fight was the fight for the transformation of formal rights into real rights, the fight for the *recognition* of man" (344; original emphasis). Césaire also recognized that the times in which Toussaint lived would not permit such liberty, thus the "Intercessor" becomes the "Precursor" (345). This last word of the essay, set apart as a nominal sentence, propels the reader to the present of departmentalization and beyond in order to reactivate both Toussaint's and Césaire's responses to colonialism.

Césaire's writing at this time ought to be situated within narratives of the 1950s and 1960s that resonated with calls for a national awareness at the same time that they recognized the complex of the (formerly) colonized and the masks required to live in neocolonial societies. In this light, Césaire's reading of the Haitian Revolution as a means to reflect on the problem of departmentalization makes sense. He looks back to the past to learn from Toussaint's attempt to decolonize in order to look forward to the possibility of a future Caribbean that would include equal rights, social benefits, and political autonomy, all existing in a new partnership with a transformed French Republic. Much later, Césaire remarked that he believed in independence, though "it would be necessary that Martinicans really want it" (*Nègre je suis* 43). "For me," he continued, "neither independence nor assimilation, but autonomy, that is, to have one's specificity, institutional forms, one's own ideal, all the while belonging to a greater ensemble" (43–44). Césaire walked a fine line, seeming to propose a sort of shared sovereignty. The emphasis on Caribbean specificity recalls the colonial design of the Constitution of 1791 and the tropical determinism of Boissy d'Anglas, without, of course, the underlying racism. The focus on Martinican institutions and ideals was less a questioning of departmentalization than it was a rejection of assimilation into an oppressive and homogeneous French citizenry that would then conveniently elide the colonial past of slavery. One way to read the conclusion of *Toussaint Louverture* is that it provides direct access to a profound, imaginative reflection on a way out of the seemingly intractable problem of departmentalization. Given the long-standing criticism of his role in the 1946 law and the adulation following his recent passing, we might follow his reading of Toussaint to see departmentalization as a necessary sacrifice for the benefit of future generations.

Another way to interpret it would stay close to the assessment provided by Césaire, who wrote that the essay was an "insufficient synthesis" (345). With the benefit of another fifty-two years, the unease of such self-evaluation is understandable. If Césaire read Toussaint as the story of a necessarily "brutal" revision of the French Revolution, as a rupture of now-mythic proportions, then how do we read Césaire's own predicament with what Wilder has called "the devolution of departmentalization" ("Untimely" 23)? Reading the text of the interview with Vergès, one gets the sense that he remained caught between resignation and hope. Of course, this is a feeling similar to that which he expressed in the *Lettre à Maurice Thorez*. But it is important to recall how the literary reimagines the political: the act of resignation was not delivered by a language and tone of resignation. Moreover, the transformation of the guiding metaphor (from the planting of a tree to the removal of petrified forms) demonstrates that the literary art of Césaire's political writings moved between, and beyond, historical moments. However, the political move represented by the letter, followed by the research into a historical hero at a crossroads, elevated Césaire to a status quite out of reach of the people he represented. The essays of the last half of the 1950s, including "L'Homme de culture et ses responsabilités," the speech he gave at the Second Conference of Negro Writers and Artists in 1959, and, later that same year, "La pensée politique de Sékou Touré," are direct evidence of attempts to understand the solitude of power.[40]

What *Toussaint Louverture* lacks is a conclusion. The title of the last chapter, "By Way of [*En guise de*] Conclusion," compels the reader to anticipate the next step of this peripatetic genre. Therefore, by way of conclusion to this chapter, I would like to look forward to the next, and to the sequel of Césaire's study of Haiti's beginnings. Like James, Césaire changed the narrative frame, albeit in a much shorter interval: where James needed a quarter of a century, Césaire required but three years. Leaving Toussaint alone in a dungeon, he departed from the essay to stage the tragedy of Christophe, Toussaint's former lieutenant and autocratic successor. As one scholarly horizon recedes, another, more dramatic one rises, and this change in form will have consequences for Césaire's thinking on the past and future of departmentalization.

6 Haitian Building
La tragédie du roi Christophe

In the previous chapter, I argued that Césaire looks back to Toussaint and to the legislative debates of the First French Republic, particularly those leading up to the first law of departmentalization in 1798, in order to deliver a profound critique of the aftermath of a similar law passed by the Fourth French Republic. Like Toussaint, Césaire authored (and legislated) a delicate balance between France and the Caribbean. He adamantly defended departmentalization for its extension of administrative rights and economic protection but clearly lamented the failure to improve racial and social inequality. Following James, Césaire risked a near hagiographic portrait of Toussaint inside a larger historiographical account of the links between French republicanism and its colonial mission. I now shift from Césaire's essays to his playwriting. This is pivotal because it reflects the choice to go beyond Toussaint without leaving behind Haiti's beginnings. It is a transition from Toussaint's revolution to Christophe's kingdom.

In a book that brings together Toussaint and Césaire, it may appear odd to conclude with Christophe. I would like to suggest, however, that it is essential to the core argument: As a revision of the foundational problems of the French Caribbean, *La tragédie du roi Christophe* mediates *Toussaint Louverture*. Toussaint was not the only voice of dissent, nor was he *only* a voice of dissent. Césaire's research and travels led him to examine additional historical figures, and to experiment with another genre. The transition to Christophe—and, as we will see, the central role of the king in the tragedy—invites criticism for its insistence on the figure of the hero. Be that as it may, the play balances the rebuke of French colonialism that drove *Toussaint Louverture* with a critique of the authoritarianism of Christophe's regime. The turn to theater opens up another way to approach the Haitian Revolution and its aftermath, including the fault lines on which the new kingdom was founded. The mise-en-scène of Christophe's tragic struggle to build Haiti allows for a rereading of the more scholarly analysis of Toussaint's dilemma.

The interaction between genres is illuminating of Césaire's representation of the historical Caribbean hero. The staging of *Christophe* revised not only the essay but also his first tragedy, *Et les chiens se taisaient*, which, until recently, was thought to have been first composed as a long, lyric poem. Initially published in 1946 in *Les Armes miraculeuses*, it was then adapted for the stage in 1956.[1] However, Alex Gil has revealed the discovery of a typed text that suggests that Césaire had originally created *Et les chiens* as a historical drama in three acts.[2] Referring to a number of documents written during the early 1940s (including correspondence between Césaire and Breton that few scholars have seen), Gil compares this "Ur-text" to the version in *Les Armes miraculeuses*. As Gil shows, this copy casts Toussaint and other historical characters, and differs considerably from subsequent versions. Analysis of this newly discovered text would necessitate some readjustment of Rodney Harris's classic study, *L'Humanisme dans le théâtre d'Aimé Césaire*, which analyzed the later version.[3] According to Harris, the character of the Rebel was largely a reprise of the dramatic poet-narrator of the *Cahier*. As the name makes clear, he incarnates revolt and represents a coming to awareness of race and of his dehumanization by the colonizer. Although this version of *Et les chiens* was not set in a specific historical moment, its hero, who also died in a jail cell, was evidently modeled on Toussaint.

Unlike the timeless Rebel, Césaire's Christophe was fully drawn for the stage, and there is no doubt that Césaire went back to the genre of tragedy in a more expansive way than he had in *Et les chiens*. The proximity between Toussaint and Christophe, the historical actors, mirrors the continuity between *Toussaint Louverture* and *Christophe*. In the interview with Ngal, Césaire himself confirmed this progression:

> Christophe is a logical suite [to my work].... King Christophe incarnates negritude confronted with three problems: the metaphysical problem of race itself; the political problem, which is that of the charge of having a state to build; and the human problem, which is the people's adaptation to the new state, going from dependence to independence and responsibility. (247)

It is important to stay with the positioning of the play as a *suite*, part of the effort to historicize a series of interrelated "problems." To paraphrase the 1987 speech on negritude, *Christophe* was the aestheticizing of a political process that "was leading somewhere." Furthermore, the reference to a "logical suite" means that to watch/read the play without having read *Toussaint Louverture* or *Et les chiens* is to neglect the process of adaptation that leads from one version of the character to the next.

As I suggested in the previous chapter, the ending of *Toussaint Louverture* prepares for the possibility of a sequel. The idea that Toussaint was a martyr who sacrificed himself in the cause of universal liberty is called into question by the 1801 Constitution, which could be read as an authoritative blueprint left for Christophe. The transition is announced in the final chapter, "By way of conclusion," a title that leaves the essay open-ended and implies a movement to another topic. The reader senses a change in Césaire's direction when, after citing Toussaint for pages, he silences him in the final four chapters. The tone of the essay takes on a quiet that, Césaire imagines, Toussaint must have felt on the road to Ennery. The silence is broken shortly before Toussaint boards the *Héros* and gives the famous "tree of liberty" speech. This proclamation of the rootedness of resistance is uncomplicated, as Césaire does not contrast it with the texts produced during Toussaint's imprisonment in France. It is disconcerting that Césaire elided the prison letters and, save for a passing reference, the *Mémoire*. The final writings allow for a more sympathetic view but are also a justification of service to Saint-Domingue; as such they could have nuanced Césaire's interpretation. Given the tragic circumstances, these letters could also be read to fortify the myth of Toussaint. Near the end of the essay, we read a detailed description of the Fort de Joux but no longer hear Toussaint's voice. Instead, we read the reports of Caffarelli and the regular updates of the jailer, Baille, a "Cerberus" (326) who is eventually replaced by Amiot. These guards of Bonaparte's icy Underworld have the honor of reporting Toussaint's death to the minister of the marine and colonies.

In an ending fit for the model of the surrender-sacrifice, Césaire leaves Toussaint in an underground dungeon. The narrative stillness stops the flow of citations, or the didascalic movement of the text. The silence marks the end of Toussaint, and it is a death that is necessary to his place in the pantheon of the revolution. As if paving the way for the playwriting to come, Césaire writes the scene in the language of myth: "Of course the historical situation of Toussaint is difficult to grasp [*malaisée*], as with all men of transition. But it was great, irreplaceable: like no other, this man constituted a historical articulation" (331). The argument that Toussaint was a "man of transition" is consistent with Césaire's dynamic conception of History; it also allows him to conclude somewhat simplistically, despite the fact that the last stage of the revolution was far more complex. Toussaint becomes the legendary "center of Haitian history, without a doubt the center of Caribbean history" (331). He died nine months before the founding of the Republic of Haiti, yet the centripetal force of the essay collapses time and space: "Truth be told, with him went Saint-Domingue. But then Haiti had been born as well" (331). The use of the past perfect marks Toussaint's death as an early founding moment of Haiti. This is the strongest case for the Precursor, an honorific that also signals a transition to the future.

From a fixed political perspective, the near future is the founding of the first postcolonial state on 1 January 1804. Césaire compels the reader to reconsider the date in more fluid terms. The graphic tension is held in the conjunctive phrasing of "went

Saint-Domingue. *But . . .* " and then released in its forward momentum. In this analogy, Toussaint's death means the end of Saint-Domingue but obtains greater meaning in postrevolution Haiti. Admittedly, the idea of finding meaning in death as a rebirth risks cliché; however, Césaire's pursuit of this meaning across genres strengthens the analogy. The connection between the essay and the play is a shifting ground. I will come back to the fault lines that move beneath Christophe's kingdom later in this chapter; for now, I would like to follow the unstable generic movement, from the itinerant form of the essay to the shift to the stage.

Toussaint and Césaire faced crises of representation that were at once political and textual. Or, to return to the idea of intertextual mediation that I raised in the previous chapter, their writings mediated the political goals they promoted as statesmen. Theories of mediation are at the center of two recent works in Haitian Studies, Chris Bongie's *Friends and Enemies: The Scribal Politics of Post/Colonial Literature* and Deborah Jenson's *Beyond the Slave Narrative*.[4] Both works examine the discursive methods by which the Haitian revolutionaries and early nationalists expressed their freedom and the right to establish an independent republic, or, as Jenson frames it, the right of "unbecoming slaves" (3). In her analysis of a body of texts that emerged *in the middle of* a revolution, Jenson focuses on this process of "un-becoming." The growing discursive power of former slaves on Saint-Domingue changed dramatically, from nonexistence to a new kind of authorship. Jenson points out that her "focus on mediation is somewhat different [than Bongie's]" in that the latter separates the new state's power and the scribes whose role was to represent, or mediate, this power (6). A brief review of these subtle differences sharpens my own focus on the mediation *between* narrative forms and the political crises in which they intervened.

Bongie and Jenson begin with the Latin root, *mediare*, "to be in the middle." From there, however, the English has both transitive and intransitive meanings. In both uses, the focus is on the action of an intermediary. Transitively, the emphasis is on conveying, in the sense of carrying some idea or action *across* from one point to another. To mediate is to "bring accord out of"; "to effect by action as an intermediary"; "to bring, effect, or communicate"; or "to transmit as intermediate mechanism or agency." The intransitive use of the verb is most often found in a legal context, or *in the middle of* two disputing parties: it is a coming to terms, or an attempt to reconcile differences. There is an important distinction to make between the transitive ("to convey") and the intransitive ("to reconcile"). To reconcile, or to settle, is not necessarily to erase difference; it can also mean to accept, or to account for, them.

The theories of mediation in *Beyond the Slave Narrative* and *Friends and Enemies* derive chiefly from the idea of meaning conveyed through an intermediary. Jenson sets her sights on the intermediary as "mechanism" or "service" (39); the processes of mediation in her analysis (which parallels the understanding of Toussaint's authorship on which she elaborates and which I took up in chapter 2) include both the concrete work of transcription, editing, and publication and the more abstract influence of prevailing discourses (for example, of abolitionism or the ancien régime tradition of the *mémoire*). In this manner, mediation is about the composite production or informed development of the narratives in question. Jenson is more concerned with the process of "the coming to writing" that was the logical next step to "un-becoming a slave" than she is with the possibility that the *Mémoire* might be read as a mediation, or reconciliation, of the terms of the Constitution. At the very least, she gives priority to mediation as a kind of authorship that gave voice to former slaves, and that was also a near-universal practice at the time. Moreover, secretarial assistance was not the only form of mediation. Jenson underscores that Toussaint was an early "spin doctor" quite skilled at using newspapers to advance a cause. The text of "mediatic persuasion," in which Toussaint filtered his voice, was an indispensable part of his political repertoire (13).

The mediation of political power through ideologically motivated writers is at the center of Bongie's notion of "scribal politics." This understanding of mediation, which posits a separation of "political leaders [and] those writers who represent their interests," is informed by the historical circumstances of the founding of Haiti (32). Bongie examines the literature of early Haitian writers, who praised political patrons and cast aspersions on rivals. This war of words is but one iteration of the "friends and enemies" in his title. The analysis of the literature of these spokespersons brings Bongie to declare that "the birth of the post-colonial state (like that of any state) is inseparable from the emergence of an intellectual elite charged with *mediating* the state's power" (32; original emphasis). The use of "mediating" here is strictly about the scribe's role in conveying the political power represented by the leader. At first glance, the meaning is straightforward because the scribe and political leader are kept apart. As Jenson observes, the study of Toussaint and Dessalines (or just before the period under analysis by Bongie) does not allow for such discrete roles. "Toussaint himself," she argues, "must be seen as a 'scribe' as well as a politician, and Dessalines ... was too deeply involved in the invention of scribal processes to be assigned securely to the 'power' side of what Bongie calls the 'scribal relation to power'" (13). Bongie's location of "scribal politics" in the quarrel of the publicists of Christophe and Pétion disentangles the intertwining of literature and politics that gives Jenson's theory of mediation a more woven texture. However, the separation of literature and politics into two camps at the end of his introduction is somewhat artificial. It is part of a deliberate "middle of the road" strategy deployed throughout the book to tease out more fully the imbrication of these two spheres of postcolonial studies. Just prior to the analysis of the scribe as mediator, or one who conveys the state's power, Bongie brings up the role of memory as a powerful if problematic intermediary of both literature and politics.

Bongie's analysis of scribal politics is in the service of a larger discussion concerning the split in postcolonial studies between literature and politics. The polarizing debate concerns the place of textual analysis in the pursuit of social and political justice for communities formerly subject to colonial rule. *Friends and Enemies* participates in the debate through three richly layered and overlapping "incursions." While it is not within the purview of this book to engage them more fully, I would like to highlight the introductory reflection on memory, and more specifically, the notion of the "doubled memory of post-independence Haiti" (25). Bongie asserts that memory—and particularly the imperative of the *devoir de mémoire*—occupies a pivotal place in postcolonial studies. Practitioners on both sides, he contends, work through this obligation. It is not surprising to read that *Friends and Enemies* is anchored in one of the seminal postcolonial moments: "of all the 'memories of resistance' invoked, and interrogated in this book, none is more prominent than that of the Haitian Revolution and its immediate aftermath" (24). Memories of this event, animated by all manner of writers in a patchwork of competing interpretations, are far from cohesive. The most common story of the colonized overthrowing the colonizers is called into question by its divisive aftermath. One narrative of "friends and enemies," Bongie argues in a passage that deserves to be cited in its entirety, "doubles" another:

> By contrast, the period following upon Haiti's declaration of independence on 1 January 1804 puts that singular memory into question by doubling it, with the formal division of the country into the republic of Haiti to the south, led by the 'mulatto' Alexandre Pétion, and the kingdom of Hayti to the north, ruled over by the 'black' Henry Christophe. The existence of these two rival Haitis troublingly replicates the binary division between friends (the colonized) and enemies (the colonizers) upon which the world-historical outcome of the Haitian Revolution depended, and it is for precisely this reason that I am drawn to (the disconcerting memory of) it. (25)

In "contrast" to the world historical slave rebellion, the division of the nascent republic constitutes a subsequent narrative that "troublingly replicates" the binary structure of its precedent. For Bongie, this process is a "doubled memory": Haiti/Hayti doubles, or puts into question, the "world-historical outcome" of the "singular" revolution. The warring leaders of newly independent Haiti dishonored the memory of their Precursor. These competing memories are a problem for political power and the narratives that mediate it. On the one hand, the fractured leadership of postcolonial Haiti cast doubt on the legitimacy of the revolution, especially since those at the helm of the republic/kingdom were also leaders of the revolution. On the other hand, the binary logic of "friends and enemies" struggles to mediate a power that always exceeded its limits. The theory of doubled memory, then, calls for another look at the mediation of political power.

Bongie writes that he is "drawn to (the disconcerting) memory of *it*," and the object of his attention is both the representation of the Haitian Revolution as world historical and the dependence of this outcome on a simple, binary narrative of "friends and enemies." This is troubling, he suggests, because such a limiting narrative forces a taking of sides, a political move that Bongie takes pains to avoid throughout his readings (even though it could be argued that occupying a middle ground is still taking a position). Nevertheless, the process of replication also means that the narrative of the revolution conveys meaning for a political future that, in turn, looks back to reconcile itself with, or to account for, an antecedent. The two events mediate each other, and this mutual dependency binds narrative to the political power it represents. In other words, we should not be drawn simply to the representation by the scribe who mediates the state's power but rather to the power of the representation itself. For Bongie, who draws on Régis Debray, the doubling of this relation to power between scribe and leader makes them "frères ennemis," or antagonistic partners.[5] The inherent conflict in power sharing and the reinforced ties between representer and represented provoke a great many questions, particularly with respect to the seemingly endless representations that can be made of memory. Indeed, of great concern is the susceptibility of memory to political manipulation. With this in mind, I would like to return to the textual dimension of the intersection of literature and politics, one that has been especially antagonistic in the history of the French Caribbean but one whose "doubled memory" proved so critical to Césaire's own conflicted identity as scribal politician.

This intersection is one where a crisis of politics leads to the promise of the text; it could also be the other way around, a textual crisis leads to political promise. Either way, it is essential to the series of filiations that structure this book. It is where Césaire first locates Toussaint, his ancestral scribal politician, followed by Christophe, who represents the doubled memory of the codependence of liberty and power. It is also where Césaire narrates his own political trials. What is more, the effect of the intersection is that one reading must yield to the other; one heroic figure and the genre that animates him can be reassessed by another. The representation of the singularity of universal emancipation is then understood to have papered over stories of rivalry and conflict, and the continued suffering of the black laborers, both of which come to a head in *La tragédie du roi Christophe*. Christophe's demise is also the tragedy of peasants who died during the construction of the Citadel. Césaire's play carries out a damaging, if truthful, revision of the logic of "friends and enemies." The dramatized suffering of the peasants *mediates* another way to read their plight (and periodic revolt) under Toussaint. These episodes reveal the distance between two fathers and their rebellious children; put another way, Toussaint and Christophe are *pères-ennemis*.

Closing with the analysis of doubled memory brings me to Césaire's reenactment of Christophe. It also opens to the larger reactivation of Haitian history as well as the implications for his mediating role in departmentalization and African independence movements. These multiple connections expose the weakness of the binary logic of "friends and enemies," which struggles to mediate the complicated relationships between members of the family of Saint-Domingue and their legacy for the greater Caribbean. The idea of a doubled memory allows for a more robust theoretical analysis of several key problems that structure this book, from Toussaint's family romance to the colonial pedagogy of the Louverture boys to the multiple meanings of *mémoire* to the changing conceptions of assimilation and, now, to the rereading of the problem of freedom from revolution to kingdom.

> Christophe has been presented as a ridiculous man, a character who spent his time aping the French. This aspect, very real, has been emphasized, but I, too, am a black man [*nègre*], and this black man, did not just have an ape to him. In this ape, there was also a profound thought, a real angst; I wanted to pierce through the ridicule [*grotesque*] to find the tragic. (*Nègre je suis*, 57)

In an interview that took place in 2004, Françoise Vergès asked Césaire about the place that Haiti occupies in his œuvre. In response, Césaire commented on his travels to Haiti and on the research that led to the essay on Toussaint, followed by the play on Christophe. As I have shown, the interview is illuminating of his approach to these historical figures and, more generally, to his dynamic conception of History. What draws my attention here is how he answered a follow-up question concerning the "solitude of power" as a "recurring theme" of his work (55). In recollection of a trip to Cap-Haitien he pondered the historical treatment of Christophe as a "ridiculous man, a character who spent his time aping the French" (57). As the passage cited above indicates, Césaire took control of the racist double entendre to state that "in this ape, there was also a profound thought, a real angst; I wanted to pierce through the ridicule [*grotesque*] to find the tragic" (57). At this moment, just as he begins to expound on the "profound questions about the encounter of civilizations," Césaire interrupts himself to reenact a key passage of the play, in which Christophe receives a letter from an ally, the British abolitionist, Wilberforce.[6] I will come back to this scene of *Christophe* later; for now, I would like to stay with the scene of the interview and the insight provided by Césaire, however inadvertently, on the historical reenactment of a tragic figure.

Over the years, Césaire granted numerous interviews during which he discussed a wide range of issues pertaining to *Christophe*, including the relationship between history and drama, his intentions for bringing his art to the stage, the presentation of characters, as well as differing interpretations of the play. In the analysis to follow, I do not wish to overstate these interventions; however, the brief recitation during the interview with Vergès, taken together with the response to the question as a whole, is revealing of his role at the forefront of an anticolonial movement and of his diverse attempts to explore the unique problems of the solitary leader-poet. In this respect, it is tempting to see Césaire's theatrical interview as a sort of *mise-en-abime* of the historical process to which he subscribed. In 2004 he restaged a pivotal scene from the 1963 play, itself a dramatization of the early nineteenth century, all in contemplation of the "solitude of power."

Once he declaimed his lines, Césaire explained the choice of the theater as a venue more accessible to the people: "Senghor and I thought that it was necessary to speak to the people, but how to address them?" (63). To be sure, the idea that theater is better suited to communicate to the masses than (esoteric) poetry is not new. Even though he regularly advocated for the theater as a popular aesthetic medium, Césaire rejected the idea that the people could not understand his poetry. In the spring of 1966 the play had its first showing in Africa, at the Festival of Negro Arts in Dakar, Senegal.[7] At a time when several African and Caribbean nations had recently gained independence, the choice to "leave traditional history," which, Césaire argued, "had always been written by whites," for the political potential of the stage should not be understated (Vergès 63). The aesthetic object of the play (its African and Caribbean actors, the music and dialogue, both of which included Haitian Creole, and the setting of Haiti) doubled as a medium for a political practice and a historical process. John Conteh-Morgan wrote of the play's overwhelming success: "It marked the advent on the French stage of the Third World, both in its post-1960 political pre-occupations, which constitute the subject of the play, and in its cultural forms" (85). Conteh-Morgan emphasized the dynamic space of the theater, specifically the temporal movement of the staging of nineteenth-century Haiti for the 1960s. It is a conception that recalls the double meaning evoked by Pamphile Lacroix to refer to Toussaint's "theater" as both dramatic awareness of words and actions and the place of Saint-Domingue as the staging ground on which colonial desire was enacted. For my purposes, it is additional evidence of the fundamental place of narrative and of the way historical actors and events are represented. The play is a historicized drama that is also, in theory, a politicized staging for a larger public.

Césaire's 2004 reenactment distilled the central conflict of the play: "We have to liberate the black man, but also liberate the liberator" (Vergès 63). This affirmation could be read primarily as a political problem surrounding the "solitude of power" that beset leaders of colonial emancipation, those charged with fighting for universal freedom and having the simultaneous responsibility of setting limits. In *Toussaint Louverture*, we recall that Césaire largely explained away the despotic power of Toussaint by finding the 1801 Constitution a necessary evil. The irony is that the document led Bonaparte to launch the French expedition against him. As Césaire famously hedged, Toussaint presided over a "work of circumstance" and left a "precious contribution to political science by giving shape, he the first one, to the theory of 'dominion'" (279). Drastic measures, it appears, were required to achieve revolution. Two years later, the dramatization of the dual embodiment of liberty and power in Christophe reflected a shift in Césaire's thinking. In the world of the play, once he is proclaimed king, Christophe is no longer a revolutionary liberator. Césaire had turned away from a political analysis in the closing chapters of the essay to focus on a tragic persona; in *Christophe*, he gave even greater attention to the conundrum of the liberator-cum-tyrant.

The essay culminated in a legendary Toussaint who sacrificed himself for the greater good of freedom for the people. As historian, Césaire chose to focus on the power of Toussaint as a revolutionary force that overcame great odds. He did not so much ignore the latent contradiction of the people's suffering under Toussaint as leave it to the playwright to put the spotlight on the struggle of a nation to give meaning to its newfound freedom. The play takes place in a different time (postrevolution), a different, divided space (Haiti/Hayti), and with a different power (the monarch, Henry Christophe). The transition means that the playwright must imagine a new scene and the questions and responsibilities that come with it. How does Christophe rule over a free people? What does freedom mean for his people, the majority of whom had known only slavery and war? These questions are similar to those I took up in chapter 3, especially concerning Toussaint's Constitution. There, I discerned two narrative threads, one that granted freedom and another that severely limited it. By stifling the very family of Saint-Domingue that he brought to the cusp of independence, Toussaint undermined his legacy. The tragedy of Toussaint was just as much the death of an innovative political project as it was the agony of a man buried alive in the Jura. The playwright cast the burden of Christophe in a similar light, yet the magnitude of the tragedy was tied more intimately to the persona of the king. To quote Nietzsche, the philosopher of tragedy who deeply influenced Césaire—and to whom I return later in this chapter—it is through the persona of the dying hero, who is witness to the suffering he has wrought in an otherwise noble cause, that the spectator has a "glance into the secret and terrible things of nature, as it were shining spots to heal the eye which dire night has seared."[8] Christophe's tragedy is the burden of nation building.

Built by the People, Built for the People: Christophe and the Problem of Freedom

First, a few remarks about the two versions of the text, followed by a summary. According to Harris, as it was first written the 1963 edition was never performed on stage due to logistical and artistic modifications. The director, Jean-Marie Serreau, stated, "Each performance was a rehearsal for the next performance, which was different.... This is why I am in complete agreement with [Césaire], that he considered that there was never a definitive version of a performance" (cited in Harris, 109). Harris states that the 1970 publication of the play represents the "continuous creation of which Serreau speaks" (109). In his scene-by-scene analysis, Harris follows the first version; however, most commentators after Harris refer to the 1970 edition, which revised not only some of the language and characters but also the structure.[9] In the analyses to follow, I refer to the 1970 edition.

La tragédie du roi Christophe is a historicized re-creation of Christophe, the former slave who, after rising through the ranks to general, became king of the northern part of a divided Haiti from 1811 to 1820. In three acts and two intermissions, the play follows the king from the beginning of his reign to its tragic conclusion. The first act stages the historical rift that occurred in 1807 between Christophe and Pétion, and then telescopes the events that took place during the establishment of the kingdom. The opening act ends with the hallucinatory vision of the Citadel, the monument constructed at the top of a mountain in northern Haiti. The second act plays out the concurrent dramas of building the Citadel and Christophe's efforts to shape the people into productive participants of the nation. The act comes to a terrifying close with a thunderous storm, which punctuates the suffering that went into the monument and foreshadows the tragedy to come. The final act depicts Christophe's demise amidst a body that betrays him, a people in growing rebellion, and a strengthening of the Republican forces to the south in the historical transition from Pétion to Boyer.

My focus is on the problem of freedom as it plays out in Césaire's conception of tragedy. I remain chiefly interested in a historicized literary analysis that also examines Césaire's revision of the historical record for the political problems of his own day. Because it treats but one play, the present chapter is a limited examination of Césaire's theater. My point of departure, through Vergès, is on the solitude of power as the thematic center of the play; the reflection on the antinomies of freedom and subjugation that begins in *Toussaint Louverture* is expanded upon in *Christophe*. In this first section, I examine the depiction of the gulf between the monarch and his people. Through a series of metaphors inspired by a turbulent natural world, Césaire portrays a spatio-temporal divide that is defined by fundamentally different conceptions of freedom and labor. In the second section, I study the structures of history and myth that Césaire develops to contemplate the unfolding tragedy. These elements depend on different concepts of time and space, which allow Césaire to contemplate the relevance of Haitian past for the political drama of the 1960s.

A central feature of Christophe's distance from the people is the perception that his "Haitian building" is tied to the enduring pedagogical relationship between colonizer and (formerly) colonized. To illustrate the problem, I would like to fast-forward to the end of Act I (I, 7), and precisely the pivotal scene recited by Césaire in the interview with Vergès. Christophe celebrates the anniversary of his coronation with a banquet. He is surrounded by his "familiars," who include Hugonin (described as a "blend of parasite, buffoon, and political agent"—he is in many ways a double of Christophe), the Master of Ceremonies, the Bishop, Chanlatte (the state poet), Prézeau ("confidant and jack of all trades"), and Madame Christophe. Consistent with the directions for the entire first act—"in a parodic and jester style, where the serious and the tragic emerge abruptly in flashes of lightning"—the scene is a parody of Christophe's attempts to bring his court up to the royal standards of the former colonizers while at the same time make heard the "national genius." The satire moves in the gestures of every character and is heard in their speech. The Master of Ceremonies instructs in a manner that is "doctoral"; nearly all of Christophe's lines are exclamations; Chanlatte sings an ode to the glory of rum, the "national drink" of Haiti; and Hugonin has a quip for everything, frequently in song. There is seriousness behind the ridicule that, following Césaire, the spectator-reader is expected to "pierce through." The parody masks the real sense of pride that Christophe announces: "Rest assured, gentlemen, you will not serve, you will be served." The constant doubling of language and voice (*servir/être servi*; *tranchant/tranchera*) as well as the juxtaposition of formal and popular linguistic modes, of French and Haitian and of different styles of song, reflect Césaire's attempt to get to the crux of the matter through a mixture of playfulness and gravity. In this manner, Christophe's desire to raise national awareness is unsettling, and leads the spectator-reader to appreciate the enormity of the task of "elevating this people to civilization" as well as to see the risk of imitating the civilizing mission of the French.

One aspect of Césairean tragedy is the conflict inherent to the aspiration to civilize a people who are still "climbing out of the ditch" of slavery (I, 7). The turning point of the scene occurs as Christophe receives a letter from Wilberforce. Delivered as a sign of goodwilll, it also offers a lesson that Christophe ultimately rejects. The letter deploys a key metaphor to teach the new monarch about nation building: "One does not invent a tree, one plants it. One does not extract its fruit, one lets it carry them. A nation is not a creation, but a ripening, a slowness, year by year, ring by ring." Christophe mocks Wilberforce's metaphor-filled guidance—"he's got some good ones!" At this point, Madame Christophe interjects and uproots the Englishman's metaphor only to supplant it with another. She fears that the king, "As a result of taking on everything, of accounting for everything," has become the "the great fig tree that takes all the surrounding vegetation and suffocates it!" Christophe immediately offers a corrective—"This tree is called a 'cursed fig tree'"—to redirect her concern to his larger goal. If he is the cursed fig tree, he suggests, it is because he (and by extension the kingdom) does not bear the fruit of the people's labor. Christophe mobilizes the parable of the fig tree to replace metaphors of natural growth with something more concrete.

Ruling over a suddenly emancipated people who had been dehumanized, Christophe chooses to re-create life by refusing the organic metaphor of his erstwhile mentor. He thinks on a grander scale, and his speech is laden with the vocabulary of building and of work. In Césaire's revision, Toussaint and Christophe understood that a sustainable freedom must be productive, yet they differed significantly on *how* the people would produce it. Whereas Toussaint reestablished the agricultural system of the colonizer, Christophe aimed to bring forth a new state not *out of* but *onto* nature through edification. In the search for something more "solid," such as the "cement" of a "cornerstone," he conceived of the people as construction material in a national enterprise. This direction is set up in the first scene of Act I, which reimagines the historical dispute between Christophe and Pétion. The latter affirms that the Senate has unanimously voted Christophe president of the republic, largely due to his "status as former comrade-in-arms of Toussaint." Christophe sees it as an empty gesture that would make him a mere figurehead. Showing no desire to return to past glory, he takes a stand against Pétion:

> The greatest need of this country, of this people that must be protected, that must be corrected, that must be educated, is . . . liberty, without a doubt, but not simple liberty! And, therefore, it is to have a State. Yes, Philosopher Sir, something thanks to which this transplanted people can become rooted . . . something that, if need be, by force, obligates them to be born to themselves and to go beyond themselves. (I, 1)

The rebuke is nevertheless pedagogical, both to Pétion (his would-be philosophical master) and to the people over whom they govern. Conquering liberty during revolution is easy, Christophe asserts, maintaining it after independence is the hard part. According to Christophe, the people won the former but "need" the latter. In his language, which predicts Sarkozy's address to the people of Guadeloupe, to gain this new liberty the people must have a state to "protect, correct, and educate" them. He will develop it, and, "*if need be by force.*" And while Christophe uses an organic metaphor to refer to the people's need to "take root," he later discards it in his response to his wife, when he rejects the role of arborist, which requires time that his people do not have, for that of architect.[10]

In an important way, the choice to become an architect-king, one whose goal is to reinforce the people's freedom, was a necessity, as international forces still threatened Haiti's sovereignty. The play magnifies the impossibility of Christophe's historical position, which would be a more logical explanation of tragedy than his dictatorial tendencies. In his mind, the people must also be forced to do "something impossible": "Against Fate, against History, against Nature" (I, 7). Just as Haiti was brought into being against all odds, so the people must attempt to define their freedom in similar terms. The force of this vision leads Christophe to imagine the Citadel, "built by the people . . . built for the people." Built as a towering symbol of hard-won freedom, built to protect against threats to that very freedom, not yet firmly rooted in Haitian soil. The moral of the parable of the fig tree is transformed by the hallucination of the monument to come: it is only through labor that the people will realize their freedom.

That the parable ends in a hallucination does not bode well for Christophe and his subjects. The vision of the Citadel that floats to the monarch and "lights up" his dream actually does more to announce the greater tragedy to come than hail the "destruction [*annulation*] of the slave ship" (I, 7). The specter of the slave ship continues to haunt the scene as a foreboding symbol of Christophe's patrimony.[11] The Citadel is a powerful doubled memory: an edifice that was meant to bring the slaves out from the bowels of the slave ship to the haven of its prow, was built on the backs of thousands of laborers, scores of whom died during its construction. It is an enduring monument to the problem of freedom. According to the stage direction for the final moments of Act I, Christophe's "vision of the Citadel moves to the distance, lit up in the night on a row of mountains." The image of the mountains rising up in the background contrasts not only with the cursed fig tree but also with the tree of Wilberforce's lesson on nation building. Where the latter requires time and patience, mountains erupt suddenly from shifting ground. As Christophe's dreamlike vision recedes to a row of mountains, the spectator's line of sight focuses explicitly on Haiti (the Taino word meaning "mountainous land").[12] The rise of the mountains evokes the force of the natural world and is a reminder of the revolution that destroyed the French colonial regime of Saint-Domingue and gave birth to Haiti. The vision of the hero takes over the stage as a dream that will become a monumental reality for the entire kingdom. The grandeur of his vision creates an illusion that masks the toil and death that also make the Citadel a slave ship on land.

The organic power of the natural world, transformed into metaphors of destruction and rebirth, disrupts Christophe's national construction. According to Keith L. Walker, "The phenomenological dramas of the meteorological and telluric forces, including the dramas of the flora, fauna, hurricanes, and volcanic eruptions in the Caribbean and Africa, are mimed and staged in Césaire's theatre" (Walker 181). Nature comes alive in Césaire's writing; in the first intermission Haiti is animated as "a strong jaw . . . [in which] the tongue of Haiti . . . fables an inextinguishable name: the Artibonite." The description is similar to the one that opens *Toussaint Louverture*: "Let us imagine, reaching out to the west, the mouth of an enormous gulf, with, to the south, the outsized prognathism of a jawbone" (21). Haiti opens its jaw to the west, where, in the Gulf of Gonâve, just south of Grande Saline, the Artibonite River flows out of its mouth. The longest and most important river in Haiti, the Artibonite is the *"papa-fleuve* of Haiti, as King Christophe says" (65). It is both a life-giving and destructive force, one that carries "the hope and hopelessness of a people, the angst of the high plateaus and the savannah, the violence and tenderness of a people." Once the Artibonite is set up as part of Haitian consciousness, two raftsmen, a captain and his apprentice, take over the scene in a proverbial dialogue that contrasts sharply with Christophe's speech at the close of Act I. Like the king, the senior raftsman has a lesson, although instead of preaching about monuments, he moves at a much slower pace: "The truest of true is not to go as if one knows where to go." The raftsmen travel up the river, "No sail. No rudder," transporting trunks of trees tied together. The work is vital to the Haitian economy, yet the raftsmen are less concerned with the end result than with taking the time "to sing, to tell stories, and to philosophize" (66).

Act II continues to explore the dichotomy between nature and the place of the peasants within it, and the distant rule of the architect-king. The first scene, which opens on two peasants at rest in a field, is important for the way it speaks to the peasants' concepts of freedom, time and work.[13] The men appear to discuss nothing in particular—the river, rum, weather—when the second peasant remarks, "Yes brother. I'm not saying no. The country is good, sure, but not the time, the time we're living in" (II, 1). When the first man downplays this observation, he continues, "Brother, believe me: there are those who don't let you take the time. They stick it in the back of your throat like medicine. . . . I say to myself that if we have thrown the Whites to the sea, it was to have it for ourselves, this land, not to suffer on the land of others, even blacks, to have it for ourselves like one has a woman!" Set in the historical framework of friends and enemies, the exchange also gives voice to the idiomatic language of the peasants. Instead of toiling and being forced to take off-tasting medicine, the second peasant would rather *take the time* to enjoy the land. The first peasant, playing the foil, suggests that Christophe is just being a good, if strict, father: "But the father is the father, and the hard stuff that he does, it's for the good of the son." Césaire returns to the colonial family romance, which suggests that Christophe's forward-thinking vision as architect remains linked to the regime of his Precursor. In illustration of this bond, two royal guards ride in on horseback to read a proclamation of the king. The decree, which is punctuated by two drumbeats, orders the peasants to fulfill their duty as farmers. The proclamation closes with a warning: "*liberty cannot subsist without work*" (II, 1; original emphasis). The articles of these agricultural regulations are strikingly similar to those promulgated by Toussaint, and thus Christophe was not just an architect: this *père-ennemi* was also the overseer of the countryside.

The second act develops the conflict between the linear speed of Christophe's rule and the peasant experience of a cyclical history. While Christophe rejoiced in the glow of his coronation in Act I, and assured his court that Haitians would no longer serve, the tables have turned by Act II, as the *Code Henry* is enacted to oversee the construction of the Citadel. In one of several moments when Césaire constructs a "play within the play," two bourgeois ladies discuss the ominous new law intended to bring the workers up to speed. The second lady recounts to the first a frightful story, in which the king, "from the top of the Citadel, through his spyglass [*lorgnette*]," sees a worker asleep. Soldiers aim the cannon, and "you can guess what happened next!" Not only is the spectator-reader called on to complete the scene, he also sees it in a "flash-back" on the corner of the stage. Vastey enters the scene and attempts to persuade the women to see the large workforce as "the fine, rare spectacle" (II, 2). The women can only understand the spectacle as a force that crushes the workers; it appears to them as a déjà vu. The technical (and almost cinematic) sleight of hand employed by Césaire brings the spectator into the play not only to see *with* the king (through his spyglass) but also to assume and experience the violence of the law.

Set inside the doubled stage (at once narrative and visual), the collision between the time demanded by the *Code Henry* and that given by the dormant worker is an explosive critique of Christophe's nation building. The two ladies take Vastey's image of the "spectacle" only to turn it around on him by suggesting that they have seen it before. Under their direction, the stage moves to another (unscripted) flashback of the revolution, in which Vastey fought against colonial violence. In this multilayered scene, the two ladies critique the cyclical, neocolonial violence of the *Code Henry* and accuse the king of perpetuating slavery. The second lady punctuates the scene: "The charming paradox! In sum, King Christophe would serve liberty by means of servitude!" In Act I, Césaire sets up the thesis of Christophe's vision, which is to educate and nurture the people, to instill in them the need to work for their freedom. By calling out the king's scribe for the "charming paradox" under way in the construction of the thesis-Citadel, the second lady brings out its antithesis.

For Césaire, however, the scene holds a second paradox, one that takes the spectator out to a critical distance and leads to another possible interpretation of the irony of Christophe's role. The ladies quickly turn their attention to other matters, as the first lady declares a pause in this "politics" and asks her daughter to play the harp and to sing about Ourika. Vastey inquires about this "charming child, Ourika," and the lady informs him that she is the "heroine of a novel that has all of Paris in tears." By evoking *Ourika*, the famous novel by Claire de Duras, Césaire changes the narrative lens of the scene to a cross-cultural parody of two salons, the Haitian one in the play and the French one of the novel. A locus of discussion of politics and the arts, the historical salon of the Duchess of Duras was where *Ourika* began, first as a story told by the duchess to her friends, then written and published as a novella. The history of the novella's production and reception, both in the nineteenth century and late twentieth is well known.[14] While I do not wish to stray from the analysis of *Christophe*, the interruption of this popular historical text deserves some explanation for the connection Césaire makes to his tragic hero. Duras adapted *Ourika* from real events: the Chevalier de Boufflers, governor of Senegal, "rescued" a Senegalese girl—de Boufflers called her a "little captive"—from a slave trader and brought her back to France in 1786, where the young girl was raised by the Chevalier's aunt, fictionalized by Duras as the *Maréchale de B.* (*French Atlantic Triangle* 23, 159). The novella, which is written in the first person from the point of view of Ourika, depicts her benefactor's generosity and the salon as a meeting place for like-minded abolitionists. The climax of the story occurs as Ourika, seated behind a screen, overhears a visiting marquise exclaim to the Maréchale, "Who will ever want to marry a Negress?"[15] In this tragic instant, Ourika looks in the mirror and becomes aware that she is black. Distraught, she eventually retreats to a convent, where she tells her story to a doctor.

    Until recently, readers of *Ourika* had lauded it as a profound psychological portrait and allegory of racial prejudice. The action of the novella, which runs from the French Revolution through the Bourbon Restoration, parallels the historical time of *Christophe*. Although personally linked to slavery and the slave trade through her family's property in Martinique, Duras belonged to the second abolitionist movement under the Restoration. The story of Ourika told in the salon was part and parcel of the moral and political cause of French abolitionism.[16] Yet, as Miller has demonstrated at length, the Atlantic dimension of the novella calls into question the more enlightened support of abolition that many have taken from the story: "The realities of the Atlantic triangle frame the tale, while remaining *almost* completed removed from the main narrative" (165; original emphasis). At a pivotal moment in the novella, Ourika is distressed over her new identity and imagines another life with "people like [her]." The memory of the violence of Saint-Domingue interrupts her dream, and she is "ashamed of belonging to a race of barbarians and assassins" (20). The sympathy that Duras creates for the plight of Ourika would seem to lend support for abolition and for an end to racism. However, in the evocation of Saint-Domingue, it appears that Duras's abolitionist leanings only went so far.

    The ambiguous pity of the salon women grabs the spectator-reader's attention in *Christophe*. In their denunciation of the violence of Christophe, the ladies of the Haitian salon mimic the ironic sentiment expressed by Ourika, who cannot ally herself to the revolutionary cause despite the patent racism she suffers in the Marquise's question. By way of this intertextuality, Césaire unsettles an otherwise obvious tragedy with parody. The bourgeois accusation of Christophe has its limits, especially since the two ladies pass over the murder of the laborer to return to the comfortable safety of the salon. The king's scribe, Vastey, recognizes the superficial interpretation given by the ladies and redirects it through a narrative of liberty and work: "I think of Christophe, Madame. Do you know why he works day and night? . . . So that from now on there will no longer be a young black girl throughout the world who is ashamed of her skin" (II, 2). Following Vastey's rereading, the spectator-reader is likewise compelled to reconsider Christophe's cause in a more favorable light.

The stage displays competing narratives of Christophe's reign, even if the parody does not replace the ultimate tragedy. The end of the second act sees dark clouds arise once again. The construction site of the Citadel has taken on "pharaonic proportions" (II, 8). As Christophe himself picks up a shovel and gets to work, rain, lightning, and thunder betray his effort to justify the project. The storm responds with a "crash of thunder and explosions"; nevertheless, Christophe implores the foreman to march on, to unleash violence against violence, until an aide-de-camp tells him that lightning has struck a powder keg, causing an explosion that destroyed the Treasury and buried several men. In the act's closing moments, Christophe raises his sword to the sky as if in battle with the elements. The image of the sword, brandished in grandiose fashion against nature, foreshadows the final tragedy.

The series of explosions also brings Christophe back to earlier battles and to a past that he cannot leave behind. Césaire deploys the upheavals of the natural world as a sign of what Walker has called "psychodramatic space" (185). The stage is the public venue on which Césaire works through the drama of a shared colonial lived experience through the persistent uprisings of the historical colonized. The king who adamantly pushes forward is irrevocably tied to revolts past. Métellus, a soldier with Christophe in Toussaint's army, rekindles this spirit to accuse his former comrade of tyranny. Instead of founding a country, Métellus argues defiantly, Christophe and Pétion are "procurators dividing the house" (I, 5). In this scene, a hero of the past rises up only to be executed for having challenged the king's identity as liberator. The death of Métellus is symbolic of Christophe's larger sin of turning his back on the revolution.

The dual signification of *soulèvement* (from Christophe to Métellus) creates a temporal space that enables Césaire to reactivate historical uprisings across generations, from revolution to kingdom and beyond. In the portrayal of a hero-statesman's attempt to bring a nation into existence from the aftershock of colonial rule, the spectator-reader takes in and away a vision of Caribbean history that resonated deeply with multiple audiences of the 1960s.[17] Nearly all analyses of the play point to the mobilization of Haitian past for the Caribbean and African present. Nesbitt offers an exemplary summary: "In writing *La tragédie du roi Christophe* in 1963, as commentators from Lilyan Kesteloot and Barthélémy Kotchy on have remarked, Aimé Césaire drew upon Caribbean history as a means of addressing the process of decolonization and the creation of African states occurring all around him." (*Voicing Memory* 127).[18] Nesbitt marshals additional evidence by citing Césaire's fellow Martinican and collaborator on *Tropiques*, René Menil, who, shortly after the play was first produced in 1964, wrote: "Paradoxically, it is not the past that [Césaire] invites us to witness in the historical reconstruction he undertakes, but rather our future" (127). In numerous interviews, Césaire discussed the play's impact on both the Afro-Antillean and African worlds. In *Magazine Littéraire* he stated:

> The black world is going through an extremely difficult phase. In particular, with the entry of African countries to independence, we have entered the moment of responsibility. From now on, black peoples must make their history. It seems rather natural to me that at the moment one enters into responsibility, on takes a look back, one interrogates oneself, one tries to understand, one tries to master his destiny. It seems to me that this calls out naturally to the theater.[19]

In these remarks, in addition to reinforcing the narrative and political importance of theater, Césaire makes the case that the historical coming to nationhood of the first generation of Haitians becomes a collective responsibility: "we have entered the moment of responsibility." This *"nous"*—which interrupts in similar fashion at the conclusion of *Toussaint Louverture*—could either be fellow leaders or the people, or both. In his status as a departmental deputy, Césaire had an obligation to speak as a representative of his fellow Martinicans; as poet and playwright, he created aesthetic objects that raised consciousness of the experience of colonialism. Both roles (politician and poet), however, placed him at a distance from the people he represented. As Nesbitt states, rather than deny this reality, "[Césaire] repeatedly searched for ways to mediate the antinomy between his bond with the 'people' and the movement away from them implied by his creation and occupation of an isolated space for the intellectual/poet" (*Voicing Memory* 142). In this view, the retrieval of Christophe is an exploration of a personal-public dilemma for Césaire. The tragedy of Christophe speaks to the decolonization of Africa and the Caribbean in the twentieth century, as well as to Césaire's position as intermediary of these movements. I now turn my attention to two remaining questions: How did Césaire reinterpret Christophe's construction of a nation for the 1960s? And what lessons does he take away from this solitary leader?

A Tragedy between History and Myth

In this section, I take a closer look at the overlapping structures of history, myth, and tragedy that govern the play. Thus far, I have argued for the importance of the move from essay to theater, and have demonstrated the political possibilities and the spatiotemporal movement of the stage. I have also rehearsed in some detail the defining aspects of Césaire's tragedy in the impossible position in which Christophe found himself between revolution and kingdom. The tragic pathos that surrounds the hero is due to the paradoxical movement of freedom after the revolution. In the push to complete the Citadel, Christophe leaves much suffering in his wake. Yet Césaire found something noble in him: after all, Christophe's dream at the end of Act I is that his people, after so many years of being on their knees, stand up.

Christophe was profoundly influenced by of a host of dramaturgic antecedents. While most critics have placed it at the forefront of a "theater of decolonization" (Conteh-Morgan, 85), they also see and hear in his plays a rich combination of the ancient Greeks (Sophocles and Aeschylus) and Shakespeare, as well as several twentieth-century playwrights, notably Claudel, Artaud, Ionesco, Brecht, Sartre, and Camus.[20] As such, there are a number of models of myth and of the hero at Césaire's disposal, but as Conteh-Morgan pointed out, "The exact mythical figure which Césaire's hero represents is a problem.... Many figures have been used to describe him, but none seem to fit perfectly his contradictory qualities" (97).[21] Many point to the particular importance of Nietzsche's *The Birth of Tragedy*.[22] Well known as a work of youth, the essay was second-guessed by Nietzsche in an introduction to a later edition. Césaire's portrait of Christophe bears the stamp of Nietzsche's study of ancient Greek theater and the tragic hero. Nietzsche conceived of a perpetual strife between Apollo and Dionysus, the two "art-deities of the Greeks," the former being "the art of the shaper" and the latter "the non-plastic art of music" (22). He argued that the spectator witnesses the union of Dionysian frenzied suffering and the intelligible, clear forms of Apollonian dialogue, an antagonism that gives birth to tragedy. This conception of antagonism bears similarity to the dual powers of creation and destruction that Césaire symbolizes in the natural forces that surround Christophe. Furthermore, Césaire's architectural mastery of the stage—particularly at the level of the "play within the play"—owed much to Nietzsche's conception of tragedy as the spectators' contemplation of their world represented in the vision presented to them onstage. "It is an indisputable tradition," Nietzsche wrote, "that Greek tragedy in its earliest forms had for its theme only the sufferings of Dionysus, and that for some time the only stage-hero therein was simply Dionysus himself" (81). Later on, the hero becomes the stage-figure who incarnates the sacred grandeur of this Apollonian/Dionysian antithesis.

In *Toussaint Louverture*, the hero's death and rebirth as mythic figure came about in the strife of two opposing, world historical forces in unimaginable freedom and dehumanizing subjugation; it was a thesis-antithesis that became a symbol for the birth of Haiti to come. As a mythico-historical articulation at the end of the essay, Toussaint (who had already served as a template of the Rebel in *Et les chiens*) was also a reference for the character of Christophe. Harris argues that Toussaint "represents ... an outdated stage" (75); Christophe is necessarily post-Toussaint, that is to say, beyond revolt, beyond colonization proper. "More concrete, more real than the Rebel," Harris continues, "the new hero of Césaire is placed at the center of a history that takes place at a precise moment" (75). To be sure, this observation is made in comparison with *Et les chiens*, yet it reveals to some extent a forced attempt to keep Toussaint and Christophe at a historical distance.[23] Making Toussaint a figure of the past allows Harris to project (Césaire's) Christophe forward to the "grand phenomenon of the twentieth century, [which] is decolonization" (75) I do not wish to make too much of the expediency of this line of reasoning, especially since the historical projects of both men elevated them to the realm of myth. It is true that Césaire created a sort of bifurcated myth of Toussaint: he recognized the principles of shared governance of Saint-Domingue as a model for twentieth-century commonwealth but left the man himself in a dungeon. It could be argued that the decision to ignore the defiant stance in the *Mémoire* colored Césaire's image of Toussaint with a hint of resignation. In his rendering of Christophe, the suffering is wrought just as much on the body of the king as it is on the desire to found a state in complete isolation. This is clear in the dialogue between Christophe and Pétion in the first scene of Act I, where Christophe states, "The change brought to the Constitution by the Senate constitutes a measure of defiance against me, against my person." Incredulous, Pétion replies, "I regret to have made myself unclear. I spoke of *principles* and you persist to speak of your person." (I, 1; original emphasis).

Christophe sees himself as the incarnation of the struggle for freedom; in Nietzschean terms, it is through his person that the spectator-reader begins to contemplate the suffering of the people. Toussaint's body deteriorated under French rule—on French soil no less—and so it is more difficult to represent his death as connected to the people, once they had conquered independence. In this light, Harris's observation of an "outdated Toussaint" makes sense. The failure of Christophe's body is intimately tied to the fate of the people. Although Césaire locates both heroes between the circumscribed drama of history and the atemporal symbolism proper to myth, he casts Christophe as a warning to newly independent African countries, and, I would argue, to Haiti, which, by the time the play was first published, was but one year away from "electing" François Duvalier president-for-life. In the experience of African, or even Caribbean, decolonization Christophe resonated more profoundly, perhaps, than Toussaint. Widening the historical gap between the two, and insisting that one is a more meaningful allegory for the twentieth century than the other, has consequences for the writing of history.[24] If one departs early-nineteenth-century Haiti to follow the allegory of African decolonization, then where does that leave the remnants of the struggling Haitian Republic, which, in the aftermath of the historical setting of the play, was in negotiation with France for recognition of its independence? While the revised ending of the play strengthens the allegorical reading—and I do not mean to downplay the allusive mode of the play, which Césaire himself acknowledged—it is important to ground the mythical elements in the historical context of Haiti. Returning to a few structural elements of the play helps to bring this problem into focus.

The Haitian optic of the Prologue zooms in on a cockfight, which is introduced as the "principal pastime of the Haitian people." This inaugural scene—whose circular pit represents another example of the "play within the play"—sets in opposition two cocks, "Christophe" and "Pétion," and their peasant handlers and partisans, thus recasting the historical leaders as ruffled combatants. The exuberance of the crowd and its familial language give voice to the popular pastime. The opening allegory showcases the popular wisdom that runs throughout the play in the form of seasoned proverbs in the mouths of cockfighters, raftsmen, farmers, and laborers. Christophe is indisputably the central character of the play, but his voice is challenged by a variety of secondary characters. The voice of the folk, which rings out in the cockpit, is archetypal and is juxtaposed with the archetype of the hero. Before Christophe can become the guarantor of freedom through his person, he must pass through the symbolism of the cockfight. Césaire pits one archetype (of the folk) against another (of the hero); one vision of Haiti is immediately followed by a rematch of sorts, this time between Christophe and Pétion as men. The agonistic tension of the cockfight parodies an otherwise heroic dialogue.

Before Christophe and Pétion take the stage as men, the speech of a "Presenter-Commentator" interrupts the cries emanating from the cockpit. By way of this brief exposition, Césaire prepares the spectator-reader with a historical sketch that goes from the fight for liberation under Toussaint to the founding of the Haitian empire under Dessalines to the split between Pétion's southern republic and Christophe's northern kingdom. Coming at the end of the Prologue, the summary grounds the play in a specific period but creates interpretive tension between allegory and history. The role of the presenter is to tether allegory and its political dimension to the historical situation of Haiti. The modes of the play are not necessarily in competition; in fact, they are a bridge to one another. Because he stands outside the narrative frame of the play, the Presenter, who returns to open the first intermission, relays historical information that is extradiegetic. According to Arnold, the Presenter learns something from the cockfight and, in turn, passes this understanding on to the spectators. Arnold downplays the significance of the historical dimension as a "didactic element" ("D'Haïti à l'Afrique" 143). In this reading, the "transparent political and ideological function" of the history lesson opens up the larger thematic structure that governs the play (144). Following Arnold, the Prologue opposes the modes of History and Myth, each one operating on a different conception of time. The timeless pace of the cockfight comes up against the political history of two leaders, who desire to build a new order. The rhythms of these temporal layers create a depth that allows Césaire to look ahead and outward.

The forward-looking dimension of the play depends on the complexity of its historical setting. To listen to the voice of the Presenter as satirical or didactic is to give less weight to the presence of history in the play, despite a plethora of references. In the interest of space, I will cite but two that deal with the constant international pressure on Haiti. Both scenes establish a historical problem, and each one retains the mix of buffoonery and gravitas that lead to the tragic effect sought by Césaire. The second scene of the play opens onto a public square in Le Cap, with a "view toward the bay. Boats on the horizon" (I, 2). The boat is an explicit reminder of the French blockade of Haiti, which was carried out to force the fledgling republic to pay reparations for the loss of property (both human and real estate). In response to a concerned Citizen, who wonders about the ominous presence of the vessel, Hugonin sings a playful tune: "It's the ship of the king of France! I'm telling you this for your information: if Monsieur needs a big stick to treat his lumbago, the ship's hold is full of them. . . . And if Monsieur's derrière wishes to be trimmed, we can do that too!" The Monsieur in question is Louis XVIII, who acceded to the throne under the Restoration, or three years into Christophe's historic reign. Despite his mocking tone, Hugonin takes an aggressive stand against the French, while the Citizen echoes Pétion's willingness to pay an indemnity in order to gain recognition of independence. Hugonin scoffs at such diplomacy and asserts proudly, "There are countries given to upheaval, convulsionary countries, and such is our lot." The plural form, *pays convulsionnaires*, is an obvious reference to several African countries making the transition to independence, as well as any number of countries struggling to come out from colonial rule. But Césaire also wants us to stay with Haiti, whose political (and financial) dilemma predicted troubled futures for postcolonial nations. Convulsion is essential to revolution but hugely problematic for nation building. This is the lesson that Césaire puts forward in the pairing of Hugonin and Christophe. Hugonin's initial playful chatter with the Citizen turns serious, almost pedagogical, and presages his master's reading of Wilberforce's letter. Where the jester accepts the reality of fate—that Haiti will always have to respond the French presence—the king looks inward to attack the "enemy of this people, . . . its indolence, its insolence, its hatred of discipline, the spirit of joy and torpor" (I, 2).

Christophe will also take a stand against the French. The return of the French king in Act II marks the persistent efforts of France to regain power on Saint-Domingue. In lieu of a show of force, Monsieur attempts to bribe Christophe. His secretary of foreign affairs, Franco de Médina, delivers a letter addressed to "General Christophe, Commander of the Northern Province of Saint-Domingue" (II, 5). What follows is a parody of the French denial of the existence of Haiti:

> Christophe: "Vastey, it must be a secretarial error. How do you say it, a lap..a laps . . . "
> Vastey: "A lapsus, Majesty. A slip of the pen [*lapsus calami*]."
> Christophe: "Yes, well, a lapsus escaped from the secretary of the Secretary of Foreign Affairs of my cousin, the King of France. Well then! For every sin, let there be mercy! Come now, this need not prevent us from getting to the bottom of what my good cousin calls 'the question of Saint-Domingue.'"

The scene mocks the French both at the level of the unconscious and the level of the political. What is more, the satire is doubled by Christophe's inability to complete the word "*lapsus*." Vastey's recognition of a *lapsus calami* speaks to the inherent problem of mediation, which is itself mocked in the comic repetition of "secretary." Césaire was well aware that historical French leaders and merchants considered the loss of Saint-Domingue temporary. For more than twenty years, until France finally recognized Haiti in 1825, the "question of Saint-Domingue" arose from the belief in the reassertion of French control.[25] In the ensuing exchange with the king's representative, Christophe dispenses with banter to resolve the "question" once and for all: "Make it known to France that, free by right and de facto independent, we will never renounce these rewards; no! never will we allow the edifice that we have raised with our hands and cemented with our blood to be toppled." The language of the architect-king returns to shore up the authority of Haiti; moreover, the correction of the French lapsus also reinforces the earlier justification of the renaming of his court (I, 3). The defense and illustration of new names and courtly titles had initially taken on a comic air under the tutelage of the Master of Ceremonies, but Christophe's intention of giving his people a "new birth" is serious, if, in the end, quite problematic.

These historical events are indispensable to the central themes of the play and to the mythical elements that allow it to speak to several audiences. The drama of political convulsion, the assertion of independence and sovereign pride, the renaming of the downtrodden, all of these seemingly timeless problems find common ground in early-nineteenth-century Haiti. The structural balance between History and Myth is a hallmark of *Christophe*. Arnold describes the interaction between the two as series of "constant interferences" ("D'Haïti à l'Afrique" 135). "Interference" here is not to be understood as "hindrance" but rather in the sense of "mutual effect": the two modes of the play meet, with one figuring more prominently only to decrease in amplitude at another moment. At times, Césaire depicts the slowness of peasant life in deliberate strokes; at others, he leaves them in the background of a grand political debate. But as interferences, these scenes regularly overlap in a rich weave of the lives of the people and the king. In the effort to take the measure of the distance between the two, Césaire also finds an intimacy, or inseparability. The result is a very Nietzschean perspective on tragedy in that he brings the spectator-reader into the play to understand the anguished noble leader and his suffering people. Nietzsche wrote, "A public of spectators, as known to us, was unknown to the Greeks. In their theatres the terraced structure of the spectators' space rising in concentric arcs enabled every one, in the strictest sense, to *overlook* the entire world of culture around him, and in surfeited contemplation to imagine himself a chorist" (65; original emphasis). Césaire's tragedy, too, is about looking into suffering in an almost introspective manner.

Before Christophe makes his entrance in the concluding act, the stage is set for a kingdom in decline. The tragedy is foreshadowed by metaphors of turbulent natural forces, which both create and destroy. Whereas Christophe brandishes his sword to defy nature, the people have the wisdom and patience to respect her. Mirroring the personification of the Artibonite in the first intermission, the second intermission (which precedes Act III) pays homage to the earth, as the scene opens onto a dialogue between two peasants cultivating the land. After not hearing the bell to announce the end of the workday, the first peasant wonders if "there is something wrong with the machinery of this kingdom." In opposition to the mechanistic approach of the king, the first peasant expresses "friendship" with the earth. It is not just the peasants who protest; members of Christophe's court and the army join the chorus of growing rebellion against the royal fantasy. Hugonin and Chanlatte discuss the news of the succession from Pétion to Boyer, which hints at the strengthening of republican forces to the south. Later on, Christophe is surprised to learn that Pétion's agents are going so far as to spread the news of plans to sell plots of state-owned land. No sooner is the Citadel finished than Christophe burdens his army of laborers with the construction of another palace. In response to the "Great Admiral's" desire to build a fleet, Magny, the officer who had carried out the execution of Métellus, now laments that Haiti herself has become a "big galley [*galère*]" (III, 1).

As the kingdom heads for the gallows, the spectator witnesses an alienated king who is no longer able to see the people as living beings but rather as abstract objects in the service of a future utopia. Losing touch with the people, Christophe turns to the Gods. The final act reveals a pronounced shift away from the politics of nation building to the search for absolution. Christophe is ushered onstage by a group of African pages, whom he introduces to the court as orphans he has saved, "My Mandingos! My Congolese!" Césaire's revisions of the play were intended to give a larger presence to Africa: "the images of Africa, the invocations to Africa are more prominent . . . [and] Haiti and Africa are more intimately linked," Harris explains (111). The proliferation of African images, especially of deities, parallels the deterioration of Christophe's body and of the humanity of his kingdom. During the Feast of the Assumption (which commemorates the corporeal ascension of the Virgin Mary into heaven) Christophe shows signs of coming undone as he interrupts the Mass with his own chanting in a mixture of French, Creole, and Latin. Suddenly, he has another hallucination, this time it is of Brelle, the former archbishop whom he had buried alive in the previous Act (II, 7). In the act of praying for Mary's body, the new archbishop, Juan de Dios, has instead summoned Brelle's ghost and condemned Christophe, who is paralyzed by a stroke (III, 2).

At first, the loss of the ability to move does not disable Christophe's vision for Haiti. His body weakened, he affirms, "my soul, rest assured, is erect, intact, solid, like our Citadel" (III, 3). His speech, which implores the people to take hold of their "opportunity," retains an ambiguity that will be heard another way, and so the ironic weight of the Citadel comes crashing down on him. When he receives reports of the defection of his generals to Boyer, Christophe is paralyzed by doubt and retreats to the palace. From the veranda, the king scans the horizon with a pair of binoculars to behold the ruins of his national edifice. In the final movement of the "play within the play" the spectator-reader, too, contemplates the fallibility of man. A dialogue ensues between Christophe and Hugonin:

> Christophe: "I regret nothing. I tried to put something in this ungrateful earth . . . I wanted to give them hunger and the need of perfection."
> Hugonin: "Hunger oh la la! Aren't they gulping it down, and I'm both gobbling up the king's ham and lapping up the king's wine; there's only one thing that remains: it's their big rancid odor amongst the king's perfume."

Christophe: "Destroy, destroy, ruin. I stored up for them; stored up for wind and want. For ruins and dust!"
Hugonin: "The people live day by day, Majesty."
Christophe: "I wanted to force the enigma of this people that lags behind."
Hugonin: "The people move at their own pace, Majesty, their secret pace." (III, 6)

Christophe's failure is marked in terms of time and distance. If illness has minimized his palatial vantage point, the incomprehension of peasant time has magnified his distance from them. As he sits upon high, Christophe's defiance turns to resignation, indicated by the repeated use of the past tense, "j'ai voulu." Furthermore, the temporal distance not only signals the end of his rule, it also *explains* it: even with his binoculars, Christophe cannot see that the people's understanding of "hunger" and "need" operates at a different pace. In contrast to the oppressive, perfected time span he set for the nation, the people live "day by day." Christophe has run out of time precisely because he failed to understand the rupture between this "secret pace" and an accelerated national project.

The space between rupture and continuity is the drama of Haitian history; the movement between them is the dramatic force of Césaire's theater. Earlier in the play, Métellus had fatefully crossed the space from revolution to nation and back to rebellion. Once a historical hero, a condemned Métellus later mythologizes the ideals of the Haitian Revolution in a long speech before being executed, "outside the scene." Before he falls, Métellus invokes revolutionary battles, "Bedoret, Ravine à Couleuvres, la Crête-à-Pierrot, Plaisance...," sites now memorialized. For Césaire, this Haitian cartography is the link between history and myth. As he hears the drumbeat of the *mandoucouman*, or the "sacred and military drum of retreat" (Walker 197), Christophe knows it is *time* for him to go. The rhythmic drumbeat signals his crossing over from a debilitating physical space to the world of spirits. The king orchestrates a Vodou ceremony and calls on the *loas*, only to succumb to a final hallucination: he evokes Africa and instructs a page to remove his clothes and to cleanse him. This is the last time the spectator sees Christophe alive, as he takes hold of the revolver attached to a chain around his neck.

As he had done with Toussaint, Césaire places Christophe at a sacrificial crossroads. Having invoked *Legba Atibon*, the *loa* of the crossroads of the human and the divine, Christophe prepares to communicate with the Gods. Paralyzed during the Assumption, Christophe rejects Western religion and makes a dying call to the syncretic cosmology of Africa and Haiti. According to Harris, at the suggestion of the African actors Césaire revised the ending to make Christophe the reincarnation of Shango, the Yoruba god of thunder (112). The addition of the West African Yoruba *orisha*, Shango and Ogun, does more than respond to similarities between the tragic hero and these deities. The study of anthropology and religion that went into the play was significant; several critics have carried out in-depth analyses of this dimension to argue that Césaire had carefully worked through the relationships between Shango,

Ogun, and their counterparts in Haitian Vodou.²⁶ In Yoruba mythology, Shango was originally a king of Oyo, the ancient capital of the Yoruba; upon his death—he, too, committed suicide—he was venerated as god of thunder. Ogun, god of iron and war, symbolizes the relationship between creation and destruction. Both Shango and Ogun are divinities that incarnate the dual power of natural forces and are essential to the balance of historical and mythological structures that Césaire cultivated throughout the play.

La tragédie du roi Christophe achieves dramatic tension between a historic human condition and the Gods and Spirits that symbolically represent it. In the final analysis, what kind of tragedy will occur at the crossroads? Will Christophe experience human solitude and pain, or will he be exalted as a divine king? In either case, the spectator-reader moves to the edge of the seat, as Hugonin, drunk and crazier than ever, begins chanting of Ogoun Badagry, or the rendering of Ogun in Haitian Vodou. Increasingly unintelligible, Hugonin invokes this *loa* of war and of the sword in a direct, if excessively dramatic, reference to his master's war with History, just as a gunshot rings out in the king's bedroom (instead of showing Christophe's death, Césaire leaves a stage direction). Hugonin declares, "The king is dead . . . Bernard Juste Hugonin/Baron-Samedi at your service" (III, 8). Before Hugonin can expound further on the attempt of the blacksmith-king to forge his people into productive citizens, he is interrupted by Christophe's suicide. In an ironic twist, Hugonin's folly leads him to assume the figure of Baron Samedi, the *loa* of death. The horror of tragedy comes to two men, a king and his fool, whose lives, it appears, are now in the hands of the Gods.

The greater tragedy is that it will be up to the people to complete, and give meaning to, the death of their king. The final scene moves from the palace to the path on the way to the Citadel. As porters carry Christophe's body uphill, he appears to be on the path to a monumental resting place fit for a *loa*-king. Along the way, however, the porters remark that he is getting heavier, perhaps "more like a king." The king's weight is a reminder that the struggle of the people continues. The porters do not bury him in the ground; instead, they leave his body upright. The African page declares that he has placed Christophe in Ifé (a city in southwestern Nigeria and a sacred site of origin for the Yoruba) and evokes Shango. Christophe-Shango will not have the last word, however, as it falls to Vastey, loyal scribe to the end, to mediate the significance of the king's final, suicidal gesture. In an intimate second person, Vastey addresses the (body of the) king: "And here you are again a king upright, suspended over the abyss of your own memorial table" (III, 9). Upright yet suspended, neither human nor spirit, Christophe has, in the end, led his people to a tragic place, and though they are now freed of a liberator-tyrant, their lives, too, hang over an abyss.

Between Politics and Playwriting

Many have interpreted the final scene as an apotheosis. The development of a syncretic cosmology in the concluding act and the final evocation of the golden phoenix rising from the ashes make this a plausible analysis. But it is also true that these are human voices calling for the Gods to make sense of their fate. It is significant that Vastey mediates the final appeal to the Gods. To play up the deification of Christophe is to ignore the careful balance that Césaire staged between the king and his people; in the end, it is to dismiss the symbolic place of the abyss and the warning it contained for people coming out from under the yoke of colonial rule.

The interaction between History and Myth—or, to return to the question of narrative with which I began this chapter, their capacity to mediate each other—delivers Césaire's reflection on the painful transformation from the slave's bondage to the citizen's freedom.[27] The turn to theater allowed him the opportunity to draw on a wide range of European, Caribbean, and African religious and dramatic traditions to develop further his artistic and historiographical sensibilities. For Césaire, the agonizing coming to universal freedom that emerged in the Haitian Revolution was archetypal; as he had announced in "Poetry and Knowledge," it is a past that represents the "old, ancestral depths," an inaugural core that would continue to reveal itself over time (*Tropiques* 12, 167). The roughly twenty-five years between the first publication of the *Cahier* and *Christophe*, which encompassed World War II and several African independence movements, was an intense period of the reactivation of history. He discovered that the founding moments of Haiti were shaped by conflicting idealist projects that had sacrificed much to achieve basic freedoms. Most important, in the wake of departmentalization, he understood that these early-nineteenth-century ideals had yet to be fully realized. As he reflected on Toussaint and Christophe, he became acutely aware of his own relationship to the people he represented. Returning to Nietzsche's insistence on the fundamental place of the spectator on the stage of tragedy, we might see Césaire, the poet-playwright-statesman, engrossed in his own "surfeited contemplation." Whether in his seat in the archives, his writing desk in Fort-de-France, or his deputy's chair, Césaire was his own chorist.

With the passage of the law of departmentalization, Césaire was in the position of giving voice to a people (colonized Martinicans *becoming* French citizens) and carrying them across to new rights and a new government. Departmentalization removed the inequities of colonial law and brought economic protection, but it was also a compromise that did little to improve racial and social equality on the island. Césaire consistently stated that the law was a political necessity, but it could also be argued that it was far-reaching: like Toussaint before him, he proposed to "take the Declaration of the Rights of Man at its word" (*Toussaint Louverture* 344). Thirteen years later his founding of a new political party called for a reevaluation of the politics of decolonization. At the same time, Césaire's rise to prominence brought the spotlight to him. The playwright picked up where the essayist left off, and so the scholarly and dramatic retrieval of historical leaders (from colonial to postcolonial) served as a critical reflection on his leadership. In this sense, the self-critique is split by the reasoned analyses of the essayist and the searing drama of the artist. To imagine Césaire peering through the looking glass, one has only to go back to the essays and the plays that spanned more than a decade.

And it is in the space between the essay and the theater to which I now return to the dead Christophe atop the Citadel. By way of the short essay Césaire wrote on Sékou Touré in the months following the Second International Congress of Black Writers and Artists in Rome in spring 1959, I offer one final reflection on the intersection of art and politics in Césaire's writing. In "La pensée politique de Sékou Touré," Césaire praised the first president of Guinea, who had also given a speech in Rome. He glorified the "quasi-carnal liaison" between Touré and "the masses whose language [*langue*] and, more important, whose way of speaking [*langage*] he himself speaks" (66). He argued that Touré refused to treat the people as an abstraction, precisely because he humanized Marxism by "Africanizing" it. "Abstraction is the mother of all scleroses," Césaire continued, "of the spirit as of the heart" (70). By rejecting de Gaulle's New Community a year earlier and opting for independence, Touré defined the needs of his community and the rights of his people. In this political assessment, Césaire saw in the president's "grandiose perspective" the possibility of the enactment of the universal, "opening onto . . . the re-establishment in the world of a pariah continent and the enrichment of the universal human" (74). This evaluation fits seamlessly into the context of his research on the Haitian Revolution, and could even be read as a prologue to *Toussaint Louverture*; in fact, a similar encomium reappears a year later: "when Toussaint came, . . . it was to show that there is no pariah race; that there is no marginal country; that there are no outcast people [*peuple d'exception*]" (344). Touré's negative response to the 1958 French referendum was a singular moment, if only for a short time, and even the violence that Touré would do to the politics of the universal would not, for Césaire, diminish its initial promise.

"La Pensée politique de Sékou Touré" also provides another way to read the fate of Christophe. If Césaire praised Touré's political ideas in glowing terms that announced the analysis of the Haitian Revolution, it was the insistence on the strength of the Guinean's character that brought the playwright to evoke the tragic authoritarianism of Christophe. "I have spoken of the ideas of Sékou Touré," he wrote, "it is now necessary to say the essential: his passion. He is a man supported by an immense force, which is very precisely a passion: the passion of Africa" (72). For the reader-spectator of *La tragédie du roi Christophe*, what should leap out on the page here is the dramatic exchange between Christophe and Pétion in the opening act: "I've spoken of principles, and you persist in speaking of your person," stated Pétion. In the space of four years, the "passion" that Césaire celebrated in Touré and his "Africa" found new meaning, it could be argued, in the suffering of Christophe and his people. In this damaging light, the agony of Christophe is not about the apotheosis of a tragic hero; it is a painful critique of the ideological deformation of negritude. The tree that Césaire had planted with such hope in "Conscience raciale" and replanted outside the field of the French Communist Party in the *Lettre à Maurice Thorez* had now petrified in Guinea, where, by 1963, Touré had already imposed a single-party regime and had already built the notorious Camp Boiro, where thousands of political prisoners would perish.[28]

In hindsight, it is hard to read the celebration of Touré as the "decisive" African leader. But it would be unfair to judge Césaire with what the world later learned about the despotism of Touré. The degeneration of negritude under Touré did not mean that the tree planted by Césaire could not have grown elsewhere. Césaire signaled the possible transformation of the radical universal into violence and petrifaction in the doubled language that both praised Touré (and Toussaint) and portrayed Christophe's tragic downfall. The essayist wrote first of passion as devotion (Touré), then as sacrifice (Toussaint), while the dramatist evoked passion as the suffering of a tyrant (Christophe). As I have argued throughout this book, these meanings mediate each other, such that it is impossible to witness the suspended agony of the Haitian king without rereading the praise of the Guinean president.

At the beginning of this chapter, I set out to explore *La tragédie du roi Christophe* as a dramatization of the solitude of power faced with the problem of postrevolutionary freedom. I have argued that, during his study of Toussaint, Césaire had a crisis of representation, both political and aesthetic. In the effort to work through the immobility of departmentalization, a state of dependency of which he was coauthor, he undertook the task of going to the root of the problem, one that had imprisoned Toussaint in the mountains of France, and had suspended Christophe between the Citadel and the heavens. But where did it leave Césaire? As the scribal-politician, he was not the political double of Christophe; he did not seek to be the heroic incarnation of the will of the people; he was not an architect-king. He was a leader with limited and conflicting powers, one who represented Martinique to a French authority but also to the greater authority of the historical Caribbean. As a politician, he was prepared to accept departmentalization as a "failure" but only because the French failed to honor the full reach of universal rights. As a playwright, he mediated the problem of freedom both to the people and to Caribbean and African leaders of his day. The great triumph of the play was its unflinching representation of spectacular political promise and failure, past and present. It is the work of an artist who peered into the future to see the unfinished politics of departmentalization, still hanging over the abyss, the legacy of a challenge first put forward in the Haitian Revolution.

Conclusion

Artisans of Free and French

THIS BOOK HAS brought together Toussaint Louverture and Aimé Césaire to examine their historical expressions of "free and French." Over the years, metropolitan representatives of the French Republic tried to translate and contain their voices. If the relationships between various French governments and the two overseas leaders were often tumultuous during their life spans, in death, both men would be brought back into the fold. In a more circumspect way, one might say that the French officially recognized their redacted contributions to the Republic. On 27 April 1998, the French government brought Toussaint into the Pantheon, the national monument to "Great Men from a Grateful Country" (as reads the inscription above its main entrance). The date was auspicious, as it also marked the 150th anniversary of the 1848 decree of the French abolition of slavery. Toussaint, who was inducted along with Louis Delgrès, the Guadeloupean martyr, was remembered with a plaque that reads, "Combattant de la liberté, artisan de l'abolition de l'esclavage, héros haïtien mort déporté au Fort de Joux en 1803 [Combatant of liberty, artisan of the abolition of slavery, Haitian hero deported to the Fort de Joux, dead in 1803]." The inscription is on the hallway that leads to the tombs of Victor Schœlcher and Félix Eboué, the colonial administrator from Guyana. Then minister of justice, Elisabeth Guigou, praised Toussaint and Delgrès as "heroes of the Republic" and "precursors of decolonization."[1] Thirteen years later, on 6 April 2011, President Sarkozy presided over the commemoration of Césaire, whose plaque was placed in the crypt between Caves XXV and XXVI, just down the hall from Toussaint. The plaque memorialized Césaire as an "inlassable artisan de la décolonisation [tireless artisan of decolonization]." This national homage, which included the presence of Césaire's family and the projection of a short film by fellow Martinican Euzhan Palcy, saw President Sarkozy honor the poet and statesman as a man "so profoundly Martinican and, at the same time, so profoundly French."[2] On this day, the official memory of Césaire, joining that of Toussaint, was engraved into the walls of the Pantheon.

The circumstances of these commemorations speak to the enormous difficulties that each man confronted upon his unique articulation of freedom under French supervision. The plaques mark a symbolic resting place, since the bodies of Toussaint and Césaire remain elsewhere. Toussaint died in prison, decidedly not free, his bones scattered anonymously in a field near the Fort de Joux, while Césaire was interred in Martinique.[3] The official nature of commemoration, a carefully mediated event, works to remake the image of the hero and to redefine his legacy as part of the larger national story. As Dubois has remarked, even the placement of the plaques of Toussaint and Césaire—*on the way* to Schœlcher—tethered the two men to the narrative of abolition represented by the 1848 decree.[4] It was not enough, it seems, that their struggles for liberty be defined so neatly for the audience; the French orchestrated the complicated understandings of freedom embodied by Toussaint and Césaire for future visitors as well. In his address, President Sarkozy declared, "At no moment in his life did he speak against France." This was an astounding statement, given Césaire's numerous public denunciations; as a result, we could read the president's speech as an attempt to elide Césaire's well-known critiques of the French narrative of republicanism, most famously in the *Discours sur le colonialisme*.[5] Césaire's historical stance against commemoration, and particularly the official remembrance of the 1848 decree, is another glaring example of his having spoken against a certain idea of France. In a speech on 27 April 1948 at the Sorbonne, ostensibly to honor the centennial of the decree, Césaire instead offered a withering critique of the historical and contemporary racism and violence of republicanism.[6] Even though he never rejected the Republic outright, Césaire accused the French time and again of ignoring and/or rewriting its past.

The process of commemoration, which sets the past into stone, cannot capture the elusive movement between "free and French" as it was conceived by Toussaint and Césaire. The ceremonial acts of remembrance in 1998 and 2011 raise questions about the French desire to reclaim them in a manner that erased moments when they staked positions contrary to metropolitan discourse and interests. Through a series of analyses that follow the migration of "free and French" across the diverse forms of the writings of Toussaint and Césaire, and across generations, this book is intended as a counterpoint to official memory. Instead of assuming that the two attributes are indivisible, I have argued for a marked tension between them. The commemorative plaques themselves hint at a more ambiguous reading of the ideas expressed by Toussaint and Césaire, and of a French Republic split between a "here" (metropolitan France) and "elsewhere" (Haiti and Martinique). Moreover, the 2005 French Law on Colonialism, especially its controversial Article 4, requiring the teaching of the "positive role of the French presence overseas," remains a troubling mediator of both ceremonies: it called into question the memory of Toussaint preserved in 1998 and, in crucial ways, predicted the sanitized revision offered by President Sarkozy in 2011. By performing open-ended analyses of departmentalization, the *Discours sur le colonialisme*, and the *Lettre à Maurice Thorez*, the speech cited passages ambiguously without going to the heart of Césaire's critique.

The recuperative work of commemoration is facilitated by ceremonies that are, as a matter of course, abridged. It is important to recognize the political motivation behind all acts of public commemoration; therefore, a certain amount of bias comes with the territory. Indeed, it is for this reason that I do not wish to make too much of the Pantheon moments of Toussaint and Césaire. Alternatively, I would like to close by reappropriating one meaningful word that quite rightly, and, perhaps contrary to the national narratives proposed to the audiences of 1998 and 2011, found space on both plaques: Toussaint and Césaire were "artisans." This word, so apt and precise, allows me to turn away from inscriptions on a wall and back to the texts through which both men worked and reworked the terms of freedom and sovereignty. An artisan is someone who makes something; according to the *Trésor de la langue française*, he is also someone who is "author" of something. The artistic origins of this word—whether the craftsman fashioning an object by hand, the apprentice learning a trade, or even the poet working with words on a page—call to mind the determined efforts of Toussaint and Césaire to create their respective *œuvres*. "Artisan" recalls the tropes of "blacksmith" and "poet" so dear to Césaire; it also conjures up the theatrical ownership of *Louverture*, in the sense of a man who exercised his military and political craft with such skill that he made an "opening" everywhere.

The commemorative plaques to Toussaint and Césaire betray a countermemory that circulates in the pages of their writings: in their own ways, they were artisans of liberty and decolonization who transformed the limited freedom always extended to them by the French. Yet any balanced analysis must also acknowledge that while they created anew, in important ways they were also apprenticed to the discourse of French republicanism. Throughout this book, I have examined the deeper historical circumstances shared by Toussaint's writing during the Haitian Revolution and Césaire's authorship of the 1946 law of departmentalization; I have endeavored to bring out important differences between Saint-Domingue at the close of the eighteenth century and Martinique following World War II. The filiation that structures the two parts of this book depends on a series of proper historical analyses of key problems (of assimilation, constitutional standing, citizenship, and so on) encountered from Toussaint to Césaire, as well as within the generations of each man's life. The brief readings above of the commemorations of 1998 and 2011 must then be understood in terms of the multiple iterations of "free and French" that developed over time.

Toussaint and Césaire were artisans who responded to evolving historical conditions with an array of narrative tools. I have focused on the varied narrative structures of their writings and argued that the value of a literary treatment of Toussaint's largely political writings comes through in the attention to the construction of family in his correspondence, to literacy as agency, and to the blend of justification and prosecution that made the *Mémoire* neither a chronicle of service nor an autobiography but rather a report for Bonaparte. In the absence of newly discovered documents, scholars of the archives are well served by the consideration of the literary art that gives shape to historical texts. But there is more to understanding the narrative frame of an individual text of Toussaint or Césaire. I have also insisted on the mediation that takes place between multiple texts. Toussaint readdressed his Constitution in the *Mémoire*; Césaire redirected his essayistic walk through the archives for the stage. Such generic shift alters the expression of ideas from one text to the next, and enjoins the reader-spectator to rethink the past for the present and future.

My focus throughout this book has been on the textual and historical dimensions of the expression of "free and French" that Toussaint inaugurated and that Césaire redeployed nearly 150 years later. There is an artisanal quality to the complicated stories they wove concerning the consequences and promise of freedom, as well as the historical resiliency of the French Caribbean. Toussaint's rebellious attachment to France led to his death; he did not live to witness the near future of emancipation and independence, and, in any event, it is not at all clear that he had such a future in mind. Césaire lived the passage from colonized to overseas citizen, but his vision of Martinican autonomy within a greater France willing to take responsibility for a transformed republicanism was always deferred. Both men thrived in the space between loyalty and opposition.

The 2009 strikes in Guadeloupe and Martinique and the international "partnerships" formed in and with Haiti following the earthquake speak to the continued failure of France and the United States to translate these relationships in terms outside of their own interests. Today, the discourses of neoliberalism and humanitarianism pervade the French Caribbean and Haiti, and both directly impact the kinds of freedom and sovereign power that its citizens are able to exercise. Much humanitarian work begins with, and thrives on, a pedagogical bond in which charitable organizations exist to tutor their needy charges. Similarly, neoliberalist trade practices too often end up restructuring the Caribbean, and Haiti in particular, for the benefit of its larger, more powerful neighbors. The historical writings examined in this book are evidence of the simple truth that today's problems are not new. The texts of Toussaint and Césaire do not offer resolution; however, they are a narrative background that is critical to any project that seeks to learn from the past before rebuilding and transforming the future.

Notes

Introduction

1. The Indian Ocean colony of Réunion was also included in the law of departmentalization. On the history and legacy of departmentalization, see Fred Constant and Justin Daniel, eds., *1946–1996: Cinquante ans de Départmentalisation Outre-Mer* (Paris: L'Harmattan, 1997). Another Indian Ocean island, Mayotte, became a fifth overseas department in March 2011 after a controversial referendum passed by a large majority in March 2009. Backed by the African Union, the Comoros Islands, which include the three islands of the archipelago that voted for independence from France in 1975, declared that the referendum was illegal. Mayotte was the lone island in the archipelago to remain with France. The Comoros claim that Mayotte is still part of its union as per a 1960 resolution of the United Nations. See Robert Aldrich and John Connell, *The Last Colonies* (Cambridge: Cambridge University Press, 1998).

2. Here and throughout I follow the standard practice of referring to Toussaint by his given first name.

3. The official French report on the revolt in Saint-Domingue, prepared by French Deputy Jean-Philippe Garran-Coulon, was the four-volume *Rapport sur les troubles de Saint-Domingue* (1799). The report came out of a lengthy investigation during the 1794–95 trial of the French Republican commissioners, Sonthonax and Polverel. In addition, there is the anonymous *Histoire des désastres de Saint-Domingue* (1795) and the vast collection of documents compiled by the colonial committee of the French revolutionary assemblies, now housed in the Dxxv series of the Centre Historique des Archives Nationales (hereafter, AN), which contains several boxes on the "Troubles de Saint-Domingue." Boxes 79–82, in particular, hold hundreds of "réclamations" of Chambers of Commerce that line the French Atlantic Coast. One from the "citizens of Bayonne" is representative of the lot: "of all the parts of the empire, a cry rises, 'our colonies ravaged, French commerce is lost.'" AN, Dxxv, 79. In all these documents, "troubles" or "disaster" referred not only to the violence witnessed by the authors but also to the threat to French rule delivered by the violence.

4. For an example of how the desire to help the suffering met the need to explain the tragedy, see David Brooks, "The Underlying Tragedy," *New York Times*, 14 January 2010, http://www.nytimes.com/2010/01/15/opinion/15brooks.html (accessed 7 June 2010). Brooks's controversial column—in which he wrote, "Haiti suffers from a complex web of progress-resistant cultural influences"—reads more like an exercise in assigning blame than a genuine effort to understand the historical scope of the earthquake. Predicting Brooks's tired argument, Peter Hallward offered compelling evidence that the disaster was "another thoroughly manmade outcome of a long and ugly historical sequence." See Hallward, "Our Role in Haiti's Plight," *The Guardian*, 13 January 2010, http://www.guardian.co.uk/commentisfree/2010/jan/13/our-role-in-haitis-plight (accessed 7 June 2010).

5. See Suzanne Dracius, Jean-François Samlong, and Gérard Théobald, eds., *La crise de l'outre-mer français: Guadeloupe, Martinique, Réunion* (Paris: L'Harmattan, 2009); Gilles Lubeth, "Between Past and Present, Roadblocks and Negotiation: The Guadeloupe 2009 Crisis," *International Journal of African Renaissance Studies* 4.1 (2009): 80–90; and Yarimar Bonilla, "Guadeloupe Is Ours: The Prefigurative Politics of the Mass Strike in the French Antilles," *Interventions: International Journal of Postcolonial Studies* 12.1 (March 2010): 125–37.

6. The strike spread to all French overseas departments, Martinique, Guyana, and Réunion. Bonilla writes, "Each of these movements took shape in response to the particular social and political

context in which they were embedded; they were in contact with each other, but did not strategize or negotiate collectively" (129).

7. "Discours de M. Nicolas Sarkozy, Président de la République, prononcé à Petit-Bourg, Guadeloupe," January 9, 2011, http://www.2011–annee-des-outre-mer.gouv.fr/annee-des-outres-mer/edito-du-president-de-la-republique.html (accessed 10 August 2011).

8. For the complete list of demands, see http://www.lkp-gwa.org/ revendications.htm (accessed 10 August 2011).

9. See Thomas A. Hale and Kora Véron, "Is There Unity in the Writings of Aimé Césaire?" *Research in African Literatures* 41.1 (Spring 2010): 54.

10. In a speech delivered to the "elite of African youth" on July 26, 2007, at the Cheikh Anta Diop University in Dakar, Sarkozy proclaimed: "The drama of Africa is that the African has not sufficiently entered history." See "Allocution de M. Nicolas Sarkozy, Président de la République, prononcée à l'Université de Dakar," 26 July 2007, http://www.elysee.fr/elysee/elysee.fr/francais/interventions/2007/juillet /allocution_à_l_université_de_dakar.79184.html. The speech was consistent with the spirit of a campaign promise Sarkozy made to put an end to "repentance." On the evening of his election, Sarkozy gave his first official speech in which he asserted, "I am going to give back to the French the pride of France. I am going to finish with the repentance that is a form of self-hatred and with the competition of memories that nourishes hatred of others" ("Verbatim: La France a choisi le changement," *Le Monde*, 8 May 2007).

11. I analyze this scene of *La tragédie du roi Christophe* in chapter 6.

12. "Accord Regional Interprofessionnel sur les Salaires en Guadeloupe—Accord Jacques Bino." Signed at Pointe-à-Pitre, 26 February 2009, http://www.lkp-gwa.org (accessed 10 August 2011).

13. Elie Domota is also secretary general of the Union Générale des Travailleurs de Guadeloupe.

14. "Les Guadeloupéens voulaient une autre société," *Libération*, 29 December 2010, http://www.liberation.fr/societe/01012310468–les-guadeloupeens-voulaient-une-autre-societe (accessed 10 August 2011).

15. Lubeth argues that, for Domota, "the issue at hand was not the political status of Guadeloupe, but social equality and justice" (86).

16. There is a website for the Estates General, but the latest updates date back to October 2009: http://www.etatsgenerauxdeloutremer.fr/ (accessed 17 August 2011).

17. For a good summary of the aftermath of the strike, see "État des lieux des Antilles, deux ans après la crise sociale," *RFI*, 7 January 2011, http://www.rfi.fr/france/20110107–antilles-deux-ans-apres-crise-sociale (accessed 17 August 2011).

18. I am attempting here to build on Bonilla's notion of a prefigurative politics, which she develops from a number of critics, including Gary Wilder, whose reading of Césaire's politics and rhetoric of decolonization plays a pivotal role in this book. See "Untimely Vision: Aimé Césaire, Decolonization, Utopia," *Public Culture* 21.1 (Winter 2009): 101–40.

19. See Charles Forsdick, "Haiti and Departmentalization: The Spectral Presence of Toussaint Louverture," *International Journal of Francophone Studies* 11.3 (2008): 327–44; E. Anthony Hurley, "Is He, Am I, a Hero?," in Doris L. Garraway, ed., *Tree of Liberty: Cultural Legacies of the Haitian Revolution in the Atlantic World* (Charlottesville: University of Virginia Press, 2008): 113–33; Víctor Figueroa, "Between Louverture and Christophe: Aimé Césaire on the Haitian Revolution," *French Review* 82.5 (April 2009): 1006–21; and Wilder, "Untimely Vision."

20. Michel-Rolph Trouillot, *Silencing the Past: Power and the Production of History* (Boston: Beacon Press, 1995); and Sibylle Fischer, *Modernity Disavowed: Haiti and the Cultures of Slavery in the Age of Revolution* (Durham, NC: Duke University Press, 2004).

21. Historical works include David Geggus, *Haitian Revolutionary Studies* (Bloomington: Indiana University Press, 2002); Laurent Dubois, *Avengers of the New World: The Story of the Haitian Revolution* (Cambridge, MA: Harvard University Press, 2004); Jeremy Popkin, *Facing Racial Revolution:*

Eyewitness Accounts of the Haitian Insurrection (Chicago: University of Chicago Press, 2008), and *You Are All Free: The Haitian Revolution and the Abolition of Slavery* (Cambridge: Cambridge University Press, 2010). For a literary and cultural studies approach, see Deborah Jenson, *Beyond the Slave Narrative: Politics, Sex and Manuscripts in the Haitian Revolution* (Liverpool: Liverpool University Press, 2011); Doris Garraway, ed., *Tree of Liberty* (2008); Nick Nesbitt, *Universal Emancipation: The Haitian Revolution and the Radical Enlightenment* (Charlottesville: University of Virginia Press, 2008); and Fischer. See also two special editions: *Research in African Literatures* 35.2 (2004), "Haiti, 1804–2004: Literature, Culture, and Art"; and *Yale French Studies* 107 (2005), "The Haiti Issue: 1804 and Nineteenth-Century French Studies."

22. Charles Forsdick, "Situating Haiti: On Some Early Nineteenth-Century Representations of Toussaint Louverture," *International Journal of Francophone Studies* 10 (2007): 17–34.

23. See, among others, Thomas Madiou, *Histoire d'Haïti* (Port-au-Prince: Imprimerie de J. Courtois, 1847–48); Beaubrun Ardouin, *Études sur l'histoire d'Haïti suivies de la vie du général J. M. Borgella* (Paris: Dézobry, Magdeleine et Cie, 1853–60); and H. Pauléus Sannon, *Histoire de Toussaint-Louverture*, 3 vols. (Port-au-Prince: Héraux, 1920–33). See Geggus, *Haitian Revolutionary Studies*, for an excellent bibliography.

24. C. L. R. James, *The Black Jacobins: Toussaint L'Ouverture and the San Domingo Revolution* (New York: Vintage, [1938] 1963); Jean Price-Mars, *Silhouettes de nègres et de négrophiles* (Paris: Présence Africaine, 1960); Édouard Glissant, *Monsieur Toussaint* (Paris: Editions du Seuil, 1961); and Aimé Césaire, *Toussaint Louverture: La Révolution française et le problème colonial* (Paris: Présence Africaine, [1962] 1981).

25. In "The Spectral Presence of Toussaint Louverture" Forsdick writes of Césaire's essay and Glissant's play as "the core of a nexus of texts that interpret the implications of Toussaint for contemporary debates regarding decolonization and the nature of postcolonial cultures" (332).

26. An amnesia both well documented and, ironically, present in the Debray Report. See Régis Debray, *Haïti et la France* (Paris: Broché, 2004). For an insightful analysis, see Chris Bongie, "Chroniques de la francophonie triomphante: Haiti, France, and the Debray Report," in *Tree of Liberty*, 153–76.

27. "Liberté ou la Mort, Jean Jacques Dessalines, Gouverneur Général des habitants d'Haïty, Quartier général du Cap, 23 avril 1804, première année de l'indépendance," AN, AF IV 1213, 85.

28. André Breton, "Un grand poète noir," in *Martinique charmeuse de serpents* (Paris: Pauvert, 1972), 93–111.

29. Aimé Césaire, *La tragédie du roi Christophe* (Paris: Présence Africaine, 1963).

30. Twice, in fact. The first time occurred when French Republican commissioner, Sonthonax, declared a local emancipation in August 1793; the second time took place in February 1794, when the French National Convention ratified Sonthonax's proclamation. Napoleon rescinded this decree less than ten years later.

31. The Constitution de la Colonie française de Saint-Domingue (1801) is reprinted in both the appendix to Pierre Pluchon, *Toussaint Louverture: Un révolutionnaire noir d'ancien régime* (Paris: Fayard, 1989), 573–87; and Claude Moïse, *Le Projet national de Toussaint Louverture et la Constitution de 1801* (Montreal: Editions du CIDIHCA, 2001), 97–123.

32. Aimé Césaire, introduction to Daniel Guérin, *Les Antilles décolonisées* (Paris: Présence Africaine, 1956).

33. Geggus followed the pioneering research of Gabriel Debien, whose prolific work centers on case studies of plantation life in the prerevolutionary periods. See Debien, *Les esclaves aux Antilles françaises, XVIIe et XVIIIe siècles* (Basse-Terre: Société d'histoire de la Guadeloupe, 1974). Another key moment was the publication of Carolyn E. Fick's *The Making of Haiti: The Saint Domingue Revolution from Below* (Knoxville: University of Tennessee Press, 1990). In addition to a plethora of essays on the prerevolutionary period in Saint-Domingue, Geggus has edited two collections of essays:

The Impact of the Haitian Revolution in the Atlantic World (Columbia: University of South Carolina Press, 2001) and, with Norman Fiering, *The World of the Haitian Revolution* (Bloomington: Indiana University Press, 2009); and for two recent works on the influence of the Haitian Revolution and the United States, see Ashli White, *Encountering Revolution: Haiti and the Making of the Early Republic* (Baltimore: Johns Hopkins University Press, 2010); and Matthew J. Clavin, *Toussaint Louverture and the American Civil War: The Promise and Peril of a Second Haitian Revolution* (Philadelphia: University of Pennsylvania Press, 2010).

34. Toussaint Louverture, *Mémoires du général Toussaint Louverture, écrits par lui-même*, ed. Joseph Saint-Rémy (Paris: Pagnerre, 1853). Saint-Rémy's edition was reissued as *Mémoires du Général Toussaint-Louverture. Commentées par Saint-Rémy*, Préface de Jacques de Cauna (Paris: La Girandole, 2009); Louis-Joseph Janvier, *Les Constitutions d'Haïti* (1886); Jean Fouchard, *Les Marrons de la liberté* (Paris: Editions de l'École, 1972); Victor Schoelcher, *Vie de Toussaint Louverture* (Paris: Karthala, [1889] 1982); see also David Nicholls, *From Dessalines to Duvalier: Race, Colour, and National Independence in Haiti* (Cambridge: Cambridge University Press, 1979).

35. This is one of the main points of Yves Bénot, *La Révolution française et la fin des colonies* (Paris: La Découverte, 1987).

36. "Général de Brigade Kerverseau au Citoyen Bruix, Ministre de la Marine et des Colonies, le premier Ventôse, l'an 7 [19 February 1799]," Centre Historique des Archives Nationales d'Outre-Mer (hereafter, CAOM), Fonds Ministériels, Colonies, sous-série CC9B23 (Saint-Domingue et Îles sous le Vent). Among the generals who left memoirs, reports, and observations of their tours of duty on Saint-Domingue, Kerverseau was one of the most prolific. Pluchon relies heavily on Kerverseau for his portrait of Toussaint as a figure of the ancien régime.

37. Perhaps the most notable example of such collaboration is the Haiti Lab at the John Hope Franklin Humanities Institute at Duke University. See http://www.fhi.duke.edu/labs/haiti-lab (accessed 10 August 2011). Codirected by Laurent Dubois and Deborah Jenson, it is remarkable for the variety of its research, course offerings, and symposia, all of which engage scholars and students in a number of different fields, including the humanities, social sciences, public health, and the law.

38. In addition to thosed cited above (Jenson, Nesbitt, and Garraway) this group includes Brent Hayes Edwards, *The Practice of Diaspora: Literature, Translation, and the Rise of Black Internationalism* (Cambridge, MA: Harvard University Press, 2003); and Christopher L. Miller, *The French Atlantic Triangle: Literature and Culture of the Slave Trade* (Durham, NC: Duke University Press, 2008).

39. I am grateful to Gary Wilder for helping me to work through this argument.

40. Pamphile de Lacroix. Pierre Pluchon, ed., *La Révolution de Haïti* (Paris: Karthala, 1995), 244. I take up the genre of the *mémoire* in chapter 4.

41. Hayden White, *Metahistory: The Historical Imagination in Nineteenth-Century Europe* (Baltimore: Johns Hopkins University Press, 1973); *Tropics of Discourse: Essays in Cultural Criticism* (Baltimore: Johns Hopkins University Press, 1978); *The Content of the Form: Narrative Discourse and Historical Representation* (Baltimore: Johns Hopkins University Press, 1987). For a critique of *Metahistory* and White's subsequent publications, see David Scott, *Conscripts of Modernity: the Tragedy of Colonial Enlightenment* (Durham, NC: Duke University Press, 2004), 45–51, 233 n. 50.

42. William Cronon, "A Place for Stories: Nature, History, and Narrative," *Journal of American History* 78.4 (March 1992): 1347–76.

43. Geggus writes, "Secrecy and duplicity were perhaps too integral a part of Toussaint's character, some might say, for his actions ever to be satisfactorily explained" (*Haitian Revolutionary Studies* 120).

44. Fick's *The Making of Haiti* is an exception to the overpriviledging of Toussaint's role.

45. Madison Smartt Bell, *Toussaint Louverture: A Biography* (Pantheon Books, 2007), 298.

46. Charles Forsdick, "Madison Smartt Bell's Toussaint at the Crossroads: The Haitian Revolutionary between History and Fiction," *Small Axe* 23 (June 2007): 197.

47. See *Aimé Césaire à l'œuvre: Actes du colloque international*, sous la direction de Marc Cheymol et Philippe Ollé-Laprune (Paris: Editions des Archives Contemporains, 2010).

48. Mireille Rosello, "'A Thousand Bamboo Fangs Down My Throat: Césaire's *Cahier d'un retour au pays natal*," *PMLA* 125.3 (May 2010): 755.

49. Thomas A. Hale and Kora Véron, "Les Écrits d'Aimé Césaire: Nouvelle Bio-bibliographie commentée," in *Aimé Césaire à l'œuvre*, 221–22.

50. In the introduction to the *Actes* of the colloquium, Bernard Cerquiglini observed, "Finally, the œuvre. Indeed, what is 'at work [à l'œuvre]' in this colloquium is the complete works of Aimé Césaire in the edition that you are preparing" (4).

51. Aimé Césaire, *Discours sur le colonialisme* (Paris: Présence Africaine, 1955). Jacqueline Leiner explains that it was never a speech. Césaire was asked by editors of *Chemin du Monde* in 1948 to write an article on the French Union. Leiner wrote, "Aimé Césaire seized upon this unexpected occasion to challenge [the French]." See Leiner, *Aimé Césaire, le terreau primordial* (Tübingen: Gunter Narr Verlag, 1993), 81.

52. Aimé Césaire, *Lettre à Maurice Thorez* (Paris: Présence Africaine, 1956). I take up this letter in chapter 5.

53. This is the gist of Wilder's thesis in "Untimely Vision," one, as I mention above, to which Bonilla turns to fill out her analysis of the "prefigurative politics" of the LKP strikers in Guadeloupe in 2009. For Wilder, Césaire exercised "an enacted and concrete utopia," an "untimely intervention that looked simultaneously backward, to emancipate futures past, and forward, to anticipate futures to come" (124).

54. Aimé Césaire, preface to Sékou Touré, *Expérience guinéenne et unite africaine* (Paris: Présence Africaine, 1962).

55. For a recent summary of the one-sided criticism of Césairean *négritude*—including how Césaire's view of Haiti functioned as a substitute for Africa—see Miller, *The French Atlantic Triangle*. I draw out this problem in chapter 5.

56. A. James Arnold, *Modernism and Negritude: The Poetry and Poetics of Aimé Césaire* (Cambridge, MA: Harvard University Press, 1981); and "D'Haïti à l'Afrique: *La Tragédie du roi Christophe* de Césaire," *Revue de Littérature Comparée* 60.2 (1986): 133–48; Bernadette Cailler, *Proposition poétique: Une lecture de l'œuvre d'Aimé Césaire* (Sherbrooke: Naaman, 1976); Gregson Davis, *Aimé Césaire* (Cambridge: Cambridge University Press, 1997); Aimé Césaire, *Cahier d'un retour au pays natal*, edited, with introduction, commentary, and notes by Abiola Irele (Columbus: Ohio University Press, 1999); M. a M. Ngal, *Aimé Césaire: Un homme à la recherche d'une patrie* (Paris: Présence Africaine, 1975); Aliko Songolo, *Aimé Césaire: Une poétique de la découverte* (Paris: L'Harmattan, 1985); and Régis Antoine, *La Littérature franco-antillaise* (Paris: Karthala, 1992).

57. In Francophone and Anglophone studies, there is an abundance of scholarship on the topic. For an excellent collection of essays of postcolonial studies in the francophone context, see Charles Forsdick and David Murphy, eds., *Francophone Postcolonial Studies: A Critical Introduction* (London: Hodder Arnold, 2003).

58. See Chris Bongie, *Islands and Exiles: The Creole Identities of Post/Colonial Literature* (Stanford: Stanford University Press, 1998). Bongie writes, "two words and worlds appear uneasily as one, joined together and yet also divided in a relation of (dis)continuity" (12).

59. See Gary Wilder, "Race, Reason, Impasse: Césaire, Fanon, and the Legacy of Emancipation," *Radical History Review* 90 (Fall 2004): 31–61.

60. Wilder borrows the phrase "problem of freedom" from Thomas C. Holt, *The Problem of Freedom: Race, Labor, and Politics in Jamaica and Britain, 1832–1938* (Baltimore: Johns Hopkins University Press, 1992). I discuss Holt in chapter 3.

61. Isaac Louverture, "Bordeaux, le 17 août 1822," CAOM, Archives privées de colonies, Papiers Isaac Louverture (1817/1824), 6 APC 1. This folder contains several letters related to the

complaint brought by Isaac against Placide. Isaac was furious that Placide took the name even though he was not the legitimate son of Toussaint (by birth), but of Suzanne and a mulatto, Jean-Marie Clerc. From an archival perspective, what is fascinating about this legal dispute, which apparently dragged on for a few years, is that it might have also been responsible for the collection of the documents concerning the education of the boys in the Institution nationale des colonies (which I take up in chapter 1). According to a letter by Beauchamp, the *chef du* Dépôt des Archives et Chartes de la Marine et des Colonies, the documents were brought together during a petition by Placide in 1823 to certify that the sons of Toussaint were granted a French education. Is it possible that what we now know of their education in France was due to Placide's attempts to prove he was Toussaint's son?

62. The self-proclaimed "epigones of Césaire," Patrick Chamoiseau, Raphaël Confiant, and Jean Bernabé penned the manifesto on Creoleness to mark a filial break with Césairean *négritude*. See *L'Éloge de la créolité* (Paris: Gallimard, 1989).

63. See Mireille Rosello, "The 'Césaire Effect,' or How to Cultivate One's Nation," *Research in African Literatures* 32.4 (Winter 2001): 77–91. In particular, Rosello expresses caution with the paradigm of filiation because of the "complexity of reactions" it engenders (77).

Chapter 1

1. Joseph Borromé, "Toussaint Louverture: A Finding List of His Letters and Documents in Archives and Collections (Public and Private) of Europe and America." This unpublished inventory is now housed at the New York Public Library's Schomburg Center for Research in Black Culture. Borromé's incredible efforts led to a list of 1,662 entries.

2. WorldCat database lists the book under Krieger Publishing in 1986. However, a representative confirmed to me that the book was never published. Andre Elizee, curator of the Division of Manuscripts, Archives and Rare Books at the Schomburg Center—where Borromé bequeathed part of his papers upon his death in 2002—suspects that Borromé never completed the book. The collection at the Schomburg Center contains but a seven-page introduction to the proposed book.

3. See Doris L. Garraway, "'*Légitime Défense*': Universalism and Nationalism in the Discourse of the Haitian Revolution," in *Tree of Liberty*. Garraway observes, "Toussaint's royalism leaves open the question of whether his use of universal rights discourse could have founded an emancipation project independent from French interests" (72).

4. Geggus, *Haitian Revolutionary Studies*, 119–36.

5. While several historians and biographers have cited many of Toussaint's letters, to my knowledge, there have been only two attempts at an annotated collection, and both cases are limited to Toussaint's epistolary exchange with Laveaux. The first was Gérard Laurent, *Toussaint Louverture à travers sa correspondance, 1794–1798* (Madrid, 1953). This collection was recently updated by Antonio M. Baggio and Ricardo Augustin, eds., *Lettres à la France: Idées pour la libération du Peuple Noir d'Haïti (1794–1798)* (Paris: Nouvelle Cité, 2011). While these collections are vital to restoring Toussaint's voice, a more complete collection of his general correspondence is sorely needed. As early as 1960, in his preface to Césaire's *Toussaint Louverture*, the colonial historian Charles-André Julien wrote of this necessity: "As long as his general correspondence remains unpublished, we will draw only temporary conclusions because his texts, still new, have the potential to turn upside down the hierarchy of values [of our studies]" (9).

6. In the spirit of Albert Camus, one must imagine Borromé happy.

7. Isaac Louverture, "Notes historiques sur l'expédition de Leclerc à St Domingue et sur la famille Louverture," CAOM, Archives privées de colonies, Papiers Isaac Louverture (1817/1824), 6 APC 1. On 3 January 1819, Métral wrote to Isaac, "I consider your work a precious gift. Please be convinced, Sir, that I will put it to worthy use." See also Antoine Métral, *Histoire de l'expédition*

des français à Saint-Domingue, sous le consulat de Napoléon Bonaparte, suivie des Mémoires et Notes d'Isaac Louverture, sur la même expedition, et sur la vie de son père (Paris: Fanjat Ainé, 1825).

8. For an overview of Toussaint's slave background, see the groundbreaking essay by Gabriel Debien, Jean Fouchard, and Marie Antoinette Menier, "Toussaint Louverture avant 1789: Légendes et réalités," *Conjonction, Revue Franco-Haïtienne* 134 (June–July 1977): 67–80; see also Geggus's overview in *Haitian Revolutionary Studies*, 5–29.

9. "Rapport sur la Partie française de St. Domingue depuis la promotion de Toussaint Louverture au Général en chef jusqu'au 1er germinal, an 9, François-Marie Périchou Kerverseau, Général de Brigade et Commissaire au Directoire Exécutif de la partie ci-devant Espagnole de Saint-Domingue, au Bruix, Ministre de la Marine & des Colonies, 21 mars 1801," CAOM, Fonds Ministériels, Colonies, sous-série CC9B23.

10. Métral, *Histoire de l'expédition*, 326. However, in his "Notes" Isaac makes no mention of this. Debien, Fouchard, and Menier write that this story comes from Métral himself (67).

11. See Debien, Fourchard, and Menier. See also, among others, James, 19–20; Geggus, *Haitian Revolutionary Studies*, 16; and Dubois, *Avengers of the New World*, 171–72.

12. Geggus, *Haitian Revolutionary Studies*, 16.

13. Mirbeck, Roume, and Saint-Léger arrived in Le Cap on 29 November 1791. They were originally commissioned to enforce the Constituent's decree of 15 May 1791, which granted rights to free men of color whose parents had also been free.

14. Cited in Dubois, *Avengers of the New World*, 125.

15. Ibid. Dubois cites the *Moniteur Général* of 22 November 1791. See also Lacroix, 114.

16. The full title is *Récit historique sur les événements qui se sont succédés dans les camps de la Grande-Rivière, du Dondon, de Ste.-Suzanne et autres, depuis le 26 octobre 1791 jusqu'au 24 décembre de la même année: Par M. Gros, procureur-syndic de Valière, fait prisonnier par Jeannot, chef des brigands* (Cap Français: Parent, impr., au coin des rues Royale et Notre-Dame, 1793). Cited in Popkin, *Facing Racial Revolution*. Popkin states that the *Moniteur Général de Saint Domingue* noted a 1792 publication; he also cites the Paris edition, *Isle de Saint-Domingue: Précis historique* (L. Potier de Lille, 1793), and the English translation, *Historick Recital* (Baltimore: S. & J. Adams, 1793). See also Dubois, "Avenging America."

17. Popkin supports this claim by noting the narrative's influence on the summaries of the slave revolt published by colonists, whose reports were compiled by the colonial committee of the French revolutionary assemblies and are now housed in the AN, series Dxxv. In addition, Popkin points out that Gros's account had an impact on Garran-Coulon's official report and on the Haitian historian Beaubrun Ardouin's *Études sur l'histoire d'Haïti, suivis de la vie du Général J.-M. Borgella* (1853). See *Facing Racial Revolution*, 106, 377, notes 5 and 7.

18. Both Popkin and Dubois comment on the significant revision Gros made in a supplement to the English version of the *Récit*, in which he offered a much less sympathetic view of the black rebels by foregrounding accounts of violence and terror.

19. For these addresses, see AN, Section Moderne, sous-série DXXV, Comité des Colonies, 1, Dossier 4.

20. See Lacroix, 114–17; Pluchon, 72–73; James, 104–5; and Césaire, *Toussaint Louverture*, 200–201.

21. See Pluchon's editorial note 4 to Lacroix, 118.

22. Toussaint Louverture to "Brothers and friends," 29 August 1793, AN, Section Moderne AA 53/1490. Geggus notes the "printed versions of Pauléus Sannon, *Histoire de Toussaint-Louverture*, 1:138–139, and Schœlcher, *Vie de Toussaint-Louverture*, 94, are neither complete nor accurate" (*Haitian Revolutionary Studies* 268). See James, 125; Dubois, *Avengers of the New World*, 176; and Garraway, "'Légitime Défense,'" 72.

23. Bell writes, "Some suggest that it [the name Louverture] comes from a small gap Toussaint is supposed to have had between his two front teeth. Others claim it derives from Polverel's reaction to Toussaint's string of lightning attacks in 1793 and 1794" (56). Bell may have in mind Thomas Madiou's *Histoire d'Haïti*, I, 90. Bell also refers to the alleged remark of French Republican Commissioner Polverel, who, marveling at the speed of Toussaint's military victories, is said to have declared, "This man makes an opening everywhere." In a note to his *Vie de Toussaint Louverture*, Schœlcher attributes the remark to Laveaux. Schœlcher goes on to state, "Toussaint, informed of this remark, is said to have seized upon the word, Ouverture, to make a name of it in an act of bravado" (94–95). He claims to have found weak support for the legend in a note in the Archives but does not cite a specific folder. In any case, he is unconvinced of the truth of any version of the legend. In a short note, James attributes the remark to "either Laveaux or Polverel" (126).

24. "I'm spending quite a bit on this double-dealer [*fourbe*], Toussaint Louverture." Personal correspondence of Joseph Boromé, "À Madeleine, le 23 février 1976," Papers of Joseph A. Boromé, Columbia University, Rare Book and Manuscript Library, Unprocessed Collection, Box 15, folder 1.

25. See Charles Forsdick, "Madison Smartt Bell's Toussaint at the Crossroads: The Haitian Revolutionary between History and Fiction," *Small Axe* 23 (June 2007): 194–208.

26. See Jenson, "Toussaint Louverture, Spin Doctor?" in *Tree of Liberty*, 60.

27. "Toussaint Louverture, Général en chef de l'Armée de Saint-Domingue, A ses chers enfants, Isaac et Placide Louverture, à Paris," Au Cap, le 22 prairial, l'an sixième de la République française, une et indivisible [10 June 1798]." AN, AF III 210, Dossier 963, folio 29.

28. The majority of the documents pertaining to the Institution Nationale des Colonies are located at the CAOM, Fonds Ministériels, Premier Empire Colonial, Documents Divers, sous-série F2C 1645/1847. F2C13, in particular, contains the documents concerning Isaac and Placide at the school from 1795 to 1802. See Michel Roussier, "L'éducation des enfants de Toussaint Louverture et l'Institution nationale des colonies," *Revue Française d'Histoire d'Outre-Mer* 236 (1977): 308–49. This article was first given as a conference at the Société française d'histoire d'outre-mer on 9 March 1977. Reprinted in de Cauna, ed., *Toussaint Louverture et l'indépendance d'Haïti* (Paris: Karthala, 2004). See also Bernard Gainot, "La Décade et la 'colonisation nouvelle,'" *Annales Historiques de la Révolution Française* 339 (janvier–mars 2005): 99–116; and "Un projet avorté d'intégration républicaine: L'Institution nationale des colonies (1797–1802)," *Dix-huitième Siècle* 32 (2000): 371–401.

29. On his "Finding List," Boromé notes five letters from Toussaint to Isaac and Placide, between 3 June 1798 and 14 February 1801, including the letter of 10 June that I cite above. I have been unable to locate additional letters. However, it seems possible that there are more, given the number of references that Toussaint and his sons make to other letters. It is known that Isaac and Placide were away from their father from August 1796 to January 1802.

30. "Au Citoyen La Révellière, Président du Directoire exécutif, 9 nivôse an 7 [29 December 1798]," AN, AF III 210, Dossier 963, folio 32. I have translated *colon* as "student," or as one who "cultivates," in the spirit of the Republican ideology to which Coisnon subscribed. In his *Opinion* on the 1795 Constitution, Dufay writes, "The word *colon* does not only mean inhabitant of the colonies but even more so he who cultivates. Such colonists are much more useful to the State than the rich landowners, who can do nothing without them," Bibliothèque Nationale (hereafter BN), Le (45) 2154, *Opinion de Dufay sur le titre III de la résolution soumise au Conseil des Anciens, concernant l'organisation de la Constitution dans les colonies*. Cited in Gainot, "La Naissance des départements d'Outre-Mer: La loi du 1er janvier 1798," *Revue d'Histoire des Mascareignes et de l'Océan Indien* 1 (1998): 70.

31. I will comment further on the dramatic reunion between Toussaint, his sons, and Coisnon in chapters 2 and 4. A brief description is warranted as it raises important questions here. Coisnon addressed a detailed summary of the encounter to General Decrès, minister of the navy and colonies, on 18 February 1802. The consensus among historians is that before engaging in an all out battle

with Toussaint and his generals, Bonaparte sent the boys and Coisnon to remind him of French support and to convince him of his intentions to keep him in power. Isaac and Placide delivered the message, and so the boys were used as a sign of Bonaparte's goodwill. Bonaparte also gave Coisnon a letter assuring Toussaint that he would not reestablish slavery on Saint-Domingue. To appreciate the diverse interpretations of the scene at Ennery, see Métral, II:52–62; Lacroix, 308–12; Schœlcher, 326–30; Pluchon, 481–82; and Dubois, *Avengers of the New World*, 251–52, 267.

32. Roussier and Gainot are notable exceptions. Roussier cites a letter from Toussaint to his sons on 15 prairial, year six [3 June 1798] (de Cauna, 219); Schœlcher appended a letter of 25 germinal, year seven [14 April 1799] (437–38).

33. See Gainot, "Un projet avorté d'intégration républicaine."

34. In the letter of 3 June 1798, Toussaint had expressed concern for the "impressionable" character of his sons.

35. Housed in the *Fonds français* section (12102–104) of the Bibliothèque Nationale, the *Correspondance du Général Laveaux* includes hundreds of letters from Toussaint to Laveaux over the four-year period, 1794–98. It is the largest collection of his writings. For the letter cited above, see "Toussaint Louverture, Commandant en Chef le Cordon de l'Ouest, à Étienne Laveaux, Général en Chef de St. Domingue, 28 ventôse 1796," BN, Correspondance du Général Laveaux, Fonds français 12104, folio 131. Also cited in Laurent, 347. On Toussaint's relationship with Laveaux, see James, 158–61; Schœlcher, 183; and Bell, 108–9.

36. Sigmund Freud, "Family Romances," in *The Standard Edition of the Complete Works of Sigmund Freud*, vol. 9 (1906–8), trans. James Strachey (London: Hogarth Press, 1959). In German, the term was first written as "Der familienroman der neurotiker," and the focus was on problems in the psychic development of "neurotics." The essay first appeared as a short chapter in Otto Rank's *Der Mythus von der Geburt des Helden* (1909).

37. Lynn Hunt, *The Family Romance of the French Revolution* (Berkeley: University of California Press, 1992).

38. Hunt notes that she is indebted to Fredric Jameson's theory of the "political unconscious," although only insofar as she supports his claim that "the structure of the psyche is historical and has a history." Fredric Jameson, *The Political Unconscious: Narrative as a Socially Symbolic Act* (Ithaca: Cornell University Press, 1981), 62. Had I more space here, I would develop further Hunt's appeal to Jameson. It is no coincidence that the language employed by Jameson to define the concept of the "political unconscious" is borrowed from the psychoanalytic register of Freud. Jameson unlocked the validation of desire from an individual subject to the expression of a community. It would be revealing to reconsider his argument that "all literature must be read as a symbolic meditation on the destiny of community" in light of Toussaint's (and for that matter, Césaire's) transformation of the colonial discourse of sovereign profit to that of universal liberty (*The Political Unconscious*, 70).

39. Hunt mentions Saint-Domingue and the relationship of real slaves and masters but once, and does not inquire how the colonial relationship might influence her conception of family romance.

40. *Decret de la Convention Nationale*, 5 thermidor, an 3 [23 July 1795], cited in Laurent, 242–43.

41. "Toussaint Louverture, Commandant en Chef le Cordon de l'Ouest, à Étienne Laveaux, Général en Chef de St. Domingue," le 30 prairial, l'An 3 de la République Française, une et indivisible, [18 June 1795], BN, 12103, folio 97.

42. "Laveaux to Toussaint, 6 germinal [26 March]," BN, 12104, folio 104.

43. Cited in Schœlcher, 159; and Pluchon, 119.

44. For the notable historical accounts, see Madiou, 234–38; Lacroix, 193–94; Schœlcher, 155–69; Pluchon, 116–30; Laurent, 349–60; and Dubois, *Avengers of the New World*, 199–203.

45. "Henry Perroud au Ministre plénipotentiaire et Consuls de la République auprès des États-Unis de l'Amérique, le 10 Germinal, an quatrième de la République française [30 March 1796]," CAOM, Fonds Ministériels, Colonies, sous-série CC9A/12 (Saint-Domingue); Perroud, *Précis des*

derniers troubles qui ont eu lieu dans la partie du nord de Saint-Domingue, addressé au Ministre de la Marine et des colonies (Le Cap, 1796), 2–4.

46. Although their interpretations differ significantly, both Pluchon and Schœlcher argue that race played a central role. Pluchon leans heavily on his pursuit of Toussaint as self-absorbed with his own power in the manner of a despot of the ancien régime. He also writes, "While all races fought indistinctly with each other, Laveaux concentrates his analysis and his hatred on the mixed race" (121). Schœlcher reads more of a personal struggle between two jealous adversaries in Toussaint and Villatte and laments that they both fell victim to the "fatal prejudice of color, the source of so much evil" (169). For his part, Madiou writes, "The event of 30 ventôse, one of the most important in our history, resulted in the definitive establishment of the supremacy of the blacks in the North and in the Artibonite" (237).

47. Later on Laurent restates, "The principal cause [of the Affair of 30 ventôse] was a rivalry between two chiefs who coveted the highest echelon of power" (375).

48. Bell argues that the period from 1794, when the Convention ratified the abolition of slavery, up to the Villatte Affair of 1796 was empowering for both the people of color and the *anciens libres*, like Toussaint, who had been free before the decree of emancipation. He closes: "the *gens de couleur* of the north had reason to believe that they had finally inherited the kingdom of their fathers" (132).

49. James argues that for the laborers, "Toussaint's word by 1796 was law—the only person in the North whom they could be depended upon to obey" (154).

50. Lacroix, 193; Schœlcher, 172.

51. By order of the same decree, Villatte, who had fled to France, was arrested and imprisoned in Rochefort, where he was eventually acquitted by a military tribunal.

52. "Suzanne Toussaint L'Ouverture au Citoyen Sonthonax, Délégué de la République française aux Îles sous le Vent, D'Ennery le 15 messidor l'an IV [3 July 1796]," CAOM, F2C13, Dossier l'an IV.

53. Although born in Paris, Dufay was a white landholder on Saint-Domingue and clerk of the court in Le Cap. He played a crucial role in the early revolutionary debates over colonial representation in the National Constituent Assembly. Along with Mills and Belley, he was an emissary on behalf of Sonthonax, who sent to him to Paris in September 1793 with the task of convincing the National Convention to ratify the abolition of slavery decreed on Saint-Domingue in August. See Louis-Pierre Dufay, *Compte rendu sur la situation actuelle de Saint-Domingue* (Paris: Imprimérie Nationale, 1794). For an account of the dangerous journey to Paris and of his powerful speech before the Convention in February 1794, see Dubois, *Avengers of the New World*, 169. See also Elizabeth Colwill, "Sex, Savagery, and Slavery in the Shaping of the French Body Politic," in Sara E. Melzer and Kathryn Norberg, eds., *From the Royal to the Republican Body: Incorporating the Political in Seventeenth- and Eighteenth-Century France* (Berkeley: University of California Press, 1998), 198–223.

54. "Dufay, Représentant du peuple au Corps Législatif, au Ministre de la Marine et des Colonies, le 21 brumaire l'an V [11 November 1796],"; "Dufay au Ministre, le 12 frimaire l'an V [2 December 1796]," CAOM, F2C13.

55. "Dufay au Ministre, le 12 frimaire [2 December]."

56. Ibid.

57. Dufay's letters would seem to be one possible answer to a question posed by Jenson: "Were the boys sent to France as hostages from the start?" (Jenson, "Kidnapping(s)," 178).

58. Of course, Isaac and Placide had never been slaves, but Sonthonax's statement underscored not only the continued presence of slavery and slave-trading in the British Caribbean and in the United States but also the fear of elements within the French government that desired a return to a slave regime on Saint-Domingue.

59. An excerpt from the speech of the son of Lechat, adjudant general of Le Cap. Cited in P. Roussier, 213.

60. See Gainot, "*La Décade*," 99. Gainot draws support from Yves Bénot.

61. On 18 fructidor, year five [4 September 1797], the members of the Directory, backed by the military, staged a coup that removed royalists from both councils and purged the legislative bodies of counterrevolutionaries. While the coup rid the councils of those who wished to see the old order restored in the colonies, it had the ominous side effect of empowering the Directory, and particularly the presidency, over the legislative bodies.

62. Gainot, "La Naissance des départements d'Outre-Mer," 51. Gainot includes "principal provisions" of the law, which was printed over several days in the *Moniteur*, beginning on 19 nivôse, year six (8 January 1798) (55–60).

63. It also requires, Gainot contends, that scholars take a long, hard look at the received wisdom concerning the "duplicity" of the French revolutionaries. See Gainot, "La Naissance," 63–64. In chapter 5, I contrast Gainot's analysis of some of these debates and reports, particularly the report to the Convention by Boissy d'Anglas in August 1795, with Césaire's interpretation of these same debates.

Chapter 2

1. "Toussaint Louverture, Général de Division et Commandant en Chef du Département de l'Ouest, à Étienne Laveaux, Général en Chef de St.-Domingue, 30 thermidor, l'an 4 [17 August 1796]," BN, 12104, folio 333.

2. "Toussaint Louverture, Général de Division et Commandant en Chef du Département de l'Ouest, à Étienne Laveaux, Général en Chef de Saint-Domingue, le 14 fructidor, l'an 4 [31 August 1796]," BN, 12104, folio 344.

3. Toussaint wrote a letter to the Minister of the Navy and Colonies on 1 February 1797 requesting Sonthonax's delayed departure to France. Cited in Pluchon, 171.

4. Bell located the letter in the private collection of Gérard Barthélemy.

5. "Des officiers généraux de l'armée de St. Domingue au Commissaire Sonthonax, le 3 fructidor an 5 [20 August 1797]" AN, AF III 210, Dossier 961, folio 13.

6. AN, AF III 210, Dossier 961. Folios 19–36 contain a series of letters pertaining to this power struggle between Toussaint, Sonthonax, and Raimond. For additional correspondence of Raimond concerning the affair, see CAOM, Fonds Ministériels, Colonies, sous-série CC9B17.

7. Toussaint Louverture, "Rapport au Directoire Exécutif, Toussaint Louverture, Général en Chef de l'Armée de St.-Domingue, Cap français, le 18 fructidor, l'an 5 [4 September 1797]," AN, AF III 210, Dossier 961, folio 1.

8. *Philadelphia Gazette*, October 7, 1797. Cited in Jenson, *Beyond the Slave Narrative*, 94.

9. Dubreuil writes, "The capacity to change form according to the nature of his word marks each one of Toussaint's texts, which elect, then exhaust linguistic forms" (120).

10. "Léger-Félicité Sonthonax au Directoire Exécutif, Bayonne, le 17 nivôse, l'an 6 [6 January 1798]," AN, AF III 210, Dossier 963. The flair for the dramatic was evidently not limited to Toussaint!

11. "Observations présentées au Directoire Exécutif sur mon départ de St.-Domingue, Paris, le 8 pluviôse, l'an 6 [27 January 1798]," AN, AF III 210, Dossier 962. Sonthonax appended seven letters of support by various "citizen commanders." See folios 15–22.

12. Concerning Toussaint's writing, Schœlcher stated unequivocally: "contrary to received opinion . . . he knew how to write fluently" (347); Jenson writes, "Read aloud, the texts sound close to conventional French. Toussaint had in effect learned enough French, and enough writing, to create his own linguistic system for transcribing the complex political and military discourses of his environment" (*Beyond the Slave Narrative* 79).

13. My reading of Toussaint's practice of mediation owes much to Jenson, who writes, "But his idiosyncratic rendition of French—his personal reconstruction in writing of the sophisticated military and political discourses in which he had been immersed verbally—constitutes a unique and unmistakable signature" (*Beyond the Slave Narrative* 27).

14. James wrote that Toussaint dictated "his thoughts in the crude words of a broken dialect, written and rewritten by his secretaries until their devotion and his will hammered them into adequate shape" (197–98).

15. Emmanuel de Las Cases, *Le Mémorial de Sainte-Hélène*, 2 vols., ed. Gérald Walter (Paris: Gallimard, Bibliothèque de la Pléiade, 1956).

16. In the preface to *Le Mémorial de Sainte-Hélène*, André Maurois wrote, "There is an unmistakable tone. Only a man who had commanded and governed could speak like the hero of the *Mémorial*" (vii).

17. Srinivas Aravamudan, *Tropicopolitans: Colonialism and Agency, 1688–1804* (Durham: Duke University Press, 1999).

18. Viénot de Vaublanc, *Discours sur l'état de Saint-Domingue et sur la conduite des agents du Directoire*, le 10 prairial, l'an 5 [29 May 1797]; cited in Toussaint Louverture, *Réfutation de quelques assertions d'un Discours prononcé au Corps Législatif le 10 prairial, an cinq par Viénot Vaublanc*, signé le 8 brumaire, l'an 6 [29 October 1797], BN, microfiche LK12–536. Hereafter *Réfutation*. See also Pluchon, 178–80.

19. Jean-Baptiste Donatien de Vimeur, Comte de Rochambeau, *Précis sur la colonie de Saint-Domingue*, AN, AF IV 1213, Dossier 4, folio 20.

20. See Malick Ghachem, "The Colonial Vendée," in Geggus and Fiering, eds., *The World of the Haitian Revolution*, 156–76.

21. "Toussaint Louverture, Général en Chef de l'armée de St.-Domingue, au Citoyen Laveaux, Général de Division, Membre du Conseil des Anciens, le 3 vendemiaire, l'an 7 [24 September 1798]," BN, 12104, folio 401.

22. See Pluchon, 214–15; Dubois, *Avengers of the New World*, 216–17.

23. "Hédouville au Directoire Exécutif, nivôse, an 7 [December 1798]," AF III 210, Dossier 962.

24. "Toussaint Louverture, Général en chef de l'Armée de St.-Domingue, au Directoire Exécutif, 22 brumaire, l'an septième [12 November 1798]," AN, AF III 210, Dossier 962.

25. Anonymous, *Précis historique des annales de la colonie française de Saint-Domingue depuis 1789*, BN, Nouvelles acquisitions françaises 14878–14879. Geggus makes a strong case that the anonymous author was most likely Pélage-Marie Duboys; see *Haitian Revolutionary Studies*, 43–44.

26. "Toussaint Louverture, Général en chef de l'Armée de St.-Domingue, au Général et agent particulier du Directoire à Saint-Domingue, l'an sixième," AN, AF III 210, Dossier 962, 30–32.

27. "Rapport aux Consuls de la République, an 8," CAOM, F2C13.

28. It is important to remember that the decree did not apply to the territories and colonies that had accepted the 1794 abolition. While the May 1802 decree did not specifically cover Saint-Domingue, it certainly was a catalyst for the all-out war of independence.

29. As I argue in the next chapter, in the 1801 Constitution Toussaint navigated the colonial *and* the postcolonial.

30. Aravamudan defines the catachrestical structure through Gayatri Spivak: "concept metaphors for which no historically adequate referent may be advanced from postcolonial space" (5). See Spivak, *Outside the Teaching Machine* (New York: Routledge, 1993), 281.

Chapter 3

1. The language scholars have used to describe this climactic event has varied greatly. Despite the language of his local captor, little emphasis has been placed on the fact that he was taken. In a letter to Bonaparte on 11 June, Leclerc writes, "Toussaint est enlevé." This verb contains multiple meanings, but the sense here is clearly "to remove by force." See Paul Roussier, ed., *Lettres du Général Leclerc* (Paris: Librairie Ernest Leroux, 1937), 171. Lacroix writes barely a paragraph on the arrest and only two sentences on Toussaint's death. Schœlcher cites Lacroix's account but offers the following

embellishment: "All resistance being impossible, he resigned himself to his fate, calm and in control of himself, as if he had been raised in the school of the Stoics" (349). James paraphrases Toussaint's own account: "They bound him like a common criminal, arrested his aide-de-camp, arrested his wife, son and niece, treating them with every indignity" (334). Pluchon writes of an "arrest" and a "deportation" but couches these in the following terms: "For the first time, Louverture lost the dangerous game of deception" (498).

2. "6202–Décret, 4 thermidor an X [23 juillet 1802]," *Correspondance de Napoléon Ier* (Paris: Plon, 1861), VII:530; hereafter, *Napoléon* VII. The French expression, "le nommé," is typical of the insulting language that Bonaparte used to refer to Toussaint.

3. See Louis Marie Auguste Fortuné, Comte d'Andigné de la Blanchaye, *Mémoires du Général D'Andigné* (Paris: Plon, 1901), II:118.

4. The two men escaped on 16 August 1802. In "Prisons and Exile" (72–79), d'Andigné gives a meticulous description of the Fort. *Le Journal de M. de Suzannet* is appended to d'Andigné's *Mémoires*. Royalists who had fought in the Vendée War, d'Andigné and Suzannet were imprisoned by Bonaparte in December 1800.

5. D'Andigné wrote, "Among other things, we said that the arrival of new prisoners, which had been announced to us, had hastened our departure" (II:117).

6. "6316–Au Général Caffarelli, Paris 22 fructidor an X [9 September 1802]," *Correspondance de Napoléon Ier*, vol. VIII (Paris: Plon, 1861), 30; hereafter *Napoléon*.

7. "Général Caffarelli au Général Bonaparte, à Pontarlier le 29 fructidor an 10 [16 September 1802]," AN, AF 1213, 11.

8. In his chapter, "Toussaint in Chains," Bell provides a moving description. Geggus discusses the treatment of Toussaint at the Fort de Joux in the context of an essay on his fellow prisoner, Jean Kina. He writes, "The story of their [Kina and his son] imprisonment, like that of Toussaint, is one of petty bureaucratic meanness" (*Haitian Revolutionary Studies*, 151). For his part, Pluchon writes, "The penitentiary regime of the Fort de Joux tested morale more than body" (534). Two documentary films capture the Fort de Joux: see Laurent Lutaud and Georges Nivoix, dirs., *Toussaint Louverture, Haïti et la France* (DVD, L'Harmattan, 2006); and Noland Walker, dir., Edwige Danticat, narr., *Égalité for All: Toussaint Louverture and the Haitian Revolution* (DVD, PBS Home Video, 2009).

9. AN, AF IV 1213, 25. This text was found postmortem, folded and sewn into a handkerchief that Toussaint wore on his head. This passage reappears, in slightly altered forms, in each version of the *Mémoire*. As I discuss in the next chapter, it is evidence of his state of mind as well as the process of writing that characterizes the prison letters.

10. CAOM, CC9B18. Two letters from Amiot, Toussaint's jailer at the time of his death, accompany the autopsy report in the archives. Shortly before Toussaint's death, Amiot noted that even as he was dying, Toussaint never called for a doctor. "Amiot au Ministre de la Marine et des Colonies, 28 Ventôse, an 11 [18 March 1803]." Amiot also announced Toussaint's death on 17 germinal, an 11 [7 April 1803].

11. "4455—Aux Citoyens de Saint-Domingue," Paris, 4 nivôse an VIII [25 December 1799], *Napoléon* VI:42. In *Toussaint Louverture*, Césaire argued that Toussaint "was not fooled by this verbiage" (278). According to Césaire, Toussaint was well aware that Bonaparte's tangled web of decrees could not cover over plans to invade Saint-Domingue. Bonaparte would later notoriously urge Leclerc: "Rid us of these gilded Africans, and we will having nothing left to desire" ("6154–"Au Capitaine Général Leclerc, Commandant en Chef de l'Armée de Saint-Domingue," Paris 12 messidor an X [1 July 1802], *Napoléon* VII:503–4.

12. Constitution de la colonie française de Saint-Domingue (1801). The full text is reprinted in Moïse, *Le Projet national de Toussaint Louverture et la Constitution de 1801* (2001), 97–123. It is also appended to Pluchon, *Toussaint Louverture*, 573–87. Moïse's book remains the most extensive analysis of Toussaint's constitution.

13. In *The French Imperial Nation-State*, Gary Wilder has argued persuasively for the "founding antinomy" of universality and particularity that underlay French republicanism. He underscores the problem of "the nation-state as a doubled political form founded upon both universality and particularity: abstract human rights and concrete national rights enable and entail each other" (13).

14. "Procès-verbal de la Cérémonie qui a lieu au Cap-Français, le 18 messidor, l'an neuvième [8 July 1801] de la République française, une et indivisible, jour de la Proclamation de la Constitution," *Extrait des registres de l'Administration municipale du Cap-Français*, CAOM CC9B18. This 12-page document, signed by the principal authorities and administrators in attendance, is an official register that was meant to attest to, or to be proof of, the remarks and events that occurred throughout the day of the ceremony.

15. See Pluchon, 371–74.

16. *Constitution de 1791 Titre VII, De la révision des décrets constitutionnels*, Article 8. All of the French constitutions can be found on the website of the Conseil Constitutionnel, http://www.conseil-constitutionnel.fr/conseil-constitutionnel/francais/la-constitution/les-constitutions-de-la-france/constitution-de-1791.5082.html (accessed 10 February 2010).

17. Duboys, *Précis historique*, II:202; Dubreuil, 119.

18. "Napoléon Bonaparte au Général Toussaint Louverture, 27 brumaire an X [18 November 1801]," *Napoléon* VII:322.

19. "Au Premier Consul de la République française," 27 Messidor, an 9 [16 July 1801], cited in Schœlcher, 303–4.

20. Toussaint Louverture, General en Chef de l'Armée de Saint-Domingue, "Règlement relatif à la culture, 20 vendemiaire [12 October 1800]," CAOM, CC9B18. Toussaint spelled out the regulations that will form the basis of the above articles in the Constitution. This regulation was not new. As early as March 1795, Toussaint addressed to his "brothers and sisters in Verrettes" a decree, the sixth article of which is an early version of Article 16 of the Constitution: "All laborers, twenty-four hours after the publication of the present proclamation, will return to engage themselves in all agricultural work on the plantations to which they belong." Cited in Schœlcher, 127–28.

21. This is the approach taken by Nesbitt, who juxtaposes what he terms "primary articles" (because principled) that are the grounding of universal freedom, with the "subsidiary articles," or the "paternalistic and exploitative empirical system" (157). The latter, he argues, "is a priori *invalidated* by their betrayal of the grounding, unqualified right to human autonomy" (ibid.; original emphasis).

22. Dubois argues that Toussaint's preparation for war with the French goes back to his secret treaty with the British General, Maitland: "Louverture was making sure. . . . But he was also doing more. He was preparing for the possibility of open conflict with the French government" (223).

23. Césaire will follow his reading of the tragic connection between revolution and dictatorship with a meditation on the dual representation of the Citadel in *La tragédie du roi Christophe*.

24. In the *Précis historique*, Duboys recounts the brutal execution of "several blacks" including one Jean Pineau and Sainte-Jésus-Maman-bondieu, for being ardent followers of Vodou. According to Duboys, a total of twenty-three persons were executed by a firing squad, without any trial, on the Drouillard-Lamare plantation. See II:226–27.

25. Eric Williams, *Capitalism and Slavery* (Chapel Hill: University of North Carolina Press, 1944); and David Brion Davis, *The Problem of Slavery in the Age of Revolution, 1770–1823* (Ithaca: Cornell University Press, 1975). See also Rebecca J. Scott, *Slave Emancipation in Cuba: The Transition to Free Labor, 1860–1899* (Princeton: Princeton University Press, 1985).

26. This is part of Carolyn Fick's argument in *The Making of Haiti*; see 207–8. Fick expanded on her analysis of freedom and citizenship in multiple Haitian Constitutions in "The Haitian Revolution and the Limits of Freedom: Defining Citizenship in the Revolutionary Era," *Social History* 32.4 (November 2007): 394–414.

27. "Au Premier Consul de la République française," 6 fructidor, an 9 [23 August 1801]," AN, AF IV 1213, 3.
28. Ibid.

Chapter 4

1. "Au Général et Premier Consul, au Cachot du Fort de Joux, le 17 vendémiaire an 11 [8 October 1802]," AN, AF IV 1213, 24.
2. "A bord du Héros, le Général Toussaint Louverture au Général Bonaparte, le premier thermidor, an dix [20 July 1802]," AN, AF 1213, 9.
3. "Au Général et Premier Consul, au Cachot du Fort de Joux, le 17 vendémiaire an 11 [8 October 1802]," AN, AF IV 1213, 24. Bell notes the "weirdly similar tone" in plaintive letters written by Leclerc to Bonaparte (268–69). Leclerc beseeched his brother-in-law to "come to his rescue" by sending reinforcements. Ironically, Leclerc died of yellow fever on Saint-Domingue on 1 November 1802, five months before Toussaint succumbed to pneumonia in the Fort de Joux.
4. Daniel Désormeaux is a notable exception. His recent edition updates the first published version, *Mémoires du général Toussaint Louverture, écrits par lui-même*, ed. Joseph Saint-Rémy (Paris: Pagnerre, 1853). Saint-Rémy's edition was reissued as *Mémoires du Général Toussaint-Louverture. Commentées par Saint-Rémy*, Préface de Jacques de Cauna (Paris: La Girandole, 2009).
5. "Ménard, au Ministre de la Guerre, 6 frimaire an 11 [27 November 1802]," AN, AF IV 1213, 12.
6. The copies in the Archives Nationales are located in AF IV 1213, Dossier 1 ("Le Général Toussaint Louverture"). Folios 17–18 are the original manuscript entirely of Toussaint's hand and whose pagination is 11 folios, recto and verso, with a faint numbering on the upper right, also possibly in Toussaint's hand; folio 20 is likely the first draft of dictation to the secretary. This copy does not include the addendum in Toussaint's hand, and several passages are rephrased in folio 21, which is the revised copy of folio 20. In addition to these copies, there are also five loose sheets that could have been drafts: Boromé noted that these sheets, "served T.L. for clarifying his expression. Some of them were inserted into the final copy." The copy in the Archives Nationales d'Outre-Mer is located in EE 1743, Dossier Toussaint Louverture, Dossier 02–Général de Division. As of July 2012, all seven dossiers of EE 1743 are still in the process of being made available online.
7. Boromé added: "A copy of 42 pp. folio was sold at Sotheby's (London) 1 April 1957. Another copy of 79 pp. declared to be of an original in the handwriting of Martial Besse and in the War Ministry, was made for Hippolyte de Saint Anthoine in January 1866. It is in NWU" (328). Boromé typed detailed notes (later annotated in pencil) concerning the handwriting and expression of the various copies. I have been unable to locate any of these additional copies: "NWU" is unfortunately not listed as an archival site in his index. There is an "NWN" for Northwestern University, but if it is a typo, I have not been able to locate the copy that he referenced. De Cauna argues that none of the dictated versions of the *Mémoire* could have come from Martial Besse. See "Préface à l'Édition 2009" (21).
8. "General et premier consul, Au ca chou du for jout, 30 fructidor an 10 [16 September 1802]," AN, AF IV 1213, 23.
9. According to de Cauna, this was done to "authenticate his *Mémoire*" (267). The Girandole publication reproduces Saint-Rémy's annotated edition of the *Mémoire* (published as *Mémoires*) but appends a re-transcription of Toussaint's hand-written document that also integrates the Aix copy "in the case of missing words or added paragraphs during the dictation" (211). De Cauna adds that it was necessary to print the "original document in Toussaint's hand in particular to be able to gauge the noticeable differences with what Saint-Rémy published" (23).
10. This passage is cited by James, who translates *soldat* as "servant" and thus read the idea of soldier as one "in service" to a leader or a state (364).

11. Marc Fumaroli, *La diplomatie de l'esprit: de Montaigne à La Fontaine* (Paris: Gallimard, 1998), 183. See chapter 6, "Les Mémoires au carrefour des genres en prose," and chapter 7, "Les Mémoires, ou l'historiographie royale en procès."

12. In *Avengers of the New World*, Dubois borrows from Bell, who titled his novel *Master of the Crossroads* (2000), to argue that Toussaint "would draw on both experiences [as master and slave] in governing the evolving colony of Saint-Domingue" (176). Dubois also noted that "in Haitian Vodou the crossroads are the symbolic site where the *lwa* (gods) intersect with the living" (331).

13. Pierre Nora, ed., *Les Lieux de mémoire*, 7 vols. (Paris: Gallimard, 1992). The first four volumes were published between 1984 and 1986; Gallimard published the final three volumes, along with the four initial ones, in 1992. The English translation was split into two volumes, *Realms of Memory*, 3 vols., ed. Lawrence B. Kritzman and trans. Arthur Goldhammer (New York: Columbia University Press, 1996–98); and *Rethinking France*, 4 vols., ed. David P. Jordan and trans. Mary Trouille (Chicago: University of Chicago Press, 2001). See Pierre Nora, "Memoirs of Men of State: From Commynes to De Gaulle," in *Rethinking France*, vol. 1, *The State*, 401–51.

14. See Ann Laura Stoler, "Colonial Aphasia: Race and Disabled Histories in France," *Public Culture* 23.1 (2011): 121–56.

15. Pierre Nora, "General Introduction," trans. Richard C. Holbrook, in *Rethinking France*, 1:18.

16. Fumaroli cites Blaise de Montluc, *Commentaires 1521–1576* (Paris: Gallimard, 1964). Montluc wrote, "because historians write only to the honor of kings and princes" (in Fumaroli, 190–91).

17. Nora and Fumaroli do not so much disagree on the importance of the memoir as they do on what constitutes History; and even then it appears to be more of a semantic difference. Nora pulls the memoir out of the margins by contrasting it with official historiography: "All memoirs are antihistories first and foremost" (417). Fumaroli emphasizes the marginal place of the memoir but does not devalue its ethical role in the creation of alternate histories.

18. This is consistent with Fumaroli's finding that in the last half of the seventeenth century memoir writing became a "spiritual exercise," invoking the notion of "debts contracted to divine grace" (206).

19. Here and throughout this chapter, I cite the version written in Toussaint's hand housed in AN, AF IV 1213. In the case of missing or illegible words, I refer to the dictated versions housed in both AN and CAOM. The translations are my own. Finally, because the version in Toussaint's hand contains no paragraphs, I have deferred to the structure of the dictated version in CAOM.

20. Antoine Furetière, *Dictionnaire Universel* (1694), http://gallica.bnf.fr/ark:/12148/bpt6k5542578m.image.r=mémoire.f883.langEN.hl (accessed 10 March 2010); Émile Littré, *Dictionnaire de la langue française* (1876); *Le Trésor de la langue française informatisé* (1971–94), http://atilf.atilf.fr.

21. Desormeaux draws on this link through Philippe Ariès, "Pourquoi écrit-on des Mémoires?" in Noémi Hepp and Jacques Hennequin, eds., *Les Valeurs chez les mémorialistes français du XVIIe siècle avant la Fronde* (Paris: Éditions Klincksieck, 1979), 12–20.

22. This is the title of the copy written in Toussaint's own hand. All of the dictated versions are titled *Mémoire pour le Général Toussaint Louverture*.

23. It should be noted that Schœlcher refers to it as "un long mémoire justificatif" (347); Pluchon writes "the mémoire . . . which contains a fierce indictment of Leclerc" (529).

24. The description is from de Cauna's preface to Saint-Rémy's edition of the *Mémoire* (2009), 24.

25. Generals Lacroix, Kerverseau, and Vincent left exemplary *Mémoires pour servir*. General Kerverseau, in particular, left a plethora of documents (*rapports*, *précis*, and *observations*) that would seem to fit Furetière's lowercase distinction of *mémoires*. See, for example, "Observations politiques et militaires sur la Colonie de St. Domingue et sur les moyens les plus analogues aux circonstances de venir à son secours, Paris, le 30 Brumaire an 13 [21 November 1804]," AN, AF 1213, Dossier 9, 67. In

this long report, Kerverseau aimed to provide both a rationale and a method in support of an attempt to reconquer Saint-Domingue (French *and* Spanish sides). Although he is clearly outraged by reports of Dessalines's summary executions of white colonists who remained on Saint-Domingue after the declaration of Haitian independence, Kerverseau gives free rein to the kind of thinking that will isolate Haiti for some time: "I repeat, it is necessary to exterminate the monster [a reference to an earlier description in the document of Africans as "barbarous hordes"] or muzzle it. . . . I will conclude this report by saying that either we must abandon the Antilles or eradicate the current generation on St. Domingue, kill more efficiently [*tuer mieux*] if it can spare bloodletting [in the future]."

26. Fumaroli underscores the "climate of a settling of scores" (198), a "political drama" that "encouraged the appearance of this polyphonic form of History" (214). For his part, Desormeaux contends that Toussaint follows the model of "war memoirs from the sixteenth and seventeenth centuries [that] indirectly evoke the unreimbursable nature of the debts contracted during the momentous negotiations and military campaigns waged victoriously under a monarch's banner" (133).

27. "5867–"Au Général Toussaint Louverture, Paris 27 brumaire an X [18 November 1801]," *Napoléon* VII:322.

28. "5868–"Au Capitaine Général Leclerc, Paris 28 brumaire an X [19 November 1801]," *Napoléon* VII:325.

29. "5874–"Exposé de la Situation de la République, Paris, le 1er frimaire an X [22 November 1801]," *Napoléon* VII:331.

30. "6154–"Au Capitaine Général Leclerc, Paris, le 12 messidor an X [1 July 1802]," *Napoléon* VII:504.

31. See "5997–"Au Capitaine Général Leclerc, Paris, 25 ventôse an X [16 March 1802]," *Napoléon* VII:413–14; and "6053–56–"Au Consul Cambacérès, Paris, le 7 floréal an X [27 April 1802]," *Napoléon* VII:444–47.

32. Schœlcher, Pluchon, Dubois, and James all bring up this connection.

33. Stoler includes a brief but damning analysis of Nora's first book, *Les Français d'Algérie* (Paris: René Julliard, 1961), which he wrote after returning to Paris from a teaching assignment in Oran, Algeria. Stoler points out that Charles-André Julien, the colonial historian who, a year earlier, had prefaced Césaire's *Toussaint Louverture*, also wrote the preface to Nora's first book.

34. It is also tempting to equate the scholarly omission of Saint-Domingue in *Les Lieux de mémoire* with Bonaparte's silencing of Toussaint, who was soon deprived of pen and paper at the Fort de Joux. However, as Susan Buck-Morss argues in her influential essay, "Hegel and Haiti," the historical silence was a political and ideological denial and isolation of Haiti because the revolution was "unthinkable." "Today," Buck-Morss continues, "when the Haitian Revolution might be more thinkable, it is more invisible due to the construction of disciplinary discourses through which knowledge of the past has been inherited." See "Hegel and Haiti," in *Hegel, Haiti, and Universal History* (Pittsburgh: University of Pittsburgh Press, 2009), 50.

Chapter 5

1. White acknowledges that there may be other modes, such as the epic. He continues: "A given historical account is likely to contain stories cast in one mode as aspects or phases of the whole set of stories emplotted in another mode. But a given historian is *forced* to emplot the whole set of stories making up his narrative in one comprehensive or archetypal story form" (*Metahistory*, 7–8; emphasis mine). For his definitions of these four modes of emplotment, see pp. 8–11.

2. See Scott, *Conscripts*, 48–49. Scott cites White's later revision in a discussion of Nazism and the "Final Solution," a story, White admitted, that the historian ought to emplot responsibly.

3. See White, "The Burden of History," in *Tropics of Discourse*, 40–41. White had previously published this essay in *History and Theory* 5.2 (1966).

4. In a sense this brings us back to Cronon's reading of White.

5. Aimé Césaire, *Nègre je suis, nègre je resterai: Entretiens avec Françoise Vergès* (Paris: Albin Michel, 2005), 16–17.

6. Aimé Césaire, *Discours sur le colonialisme, suivi de Discours sur la négritude* (Paris: Présence Africaine, 2004), 85–86.

7. Before Hurley, Wilder, Figueroa, and Forsdick, there was Gloria Nne Onyeoziri, who, as far as I can tell, wrote one of the first analyses of the essay. See "Le *Toussaint* d'Aimé Césaire: Réflexions sur le statut d'un texte," *L'Esprit Créateur* 32.1 (Spring 1992): 87–96.

8. See Césaire, introduction to Guérin's, *Les Antilles décolonisées*; "Culture et colonisation," *Présence Africaine* 8–10 (1956), 190–205; "L'homme de culture et ses responsabilités," *Présence Africaine* 24–25 (1959): 116–22; and "Crises dans les départements d'outre-mer ou crise de la départementalisation," *Présence Africaine*, no. 36 (1961): 109–11.

9. Pierre Mabille was a French doctor, writer, anthropologist, and close friend of André Breton. As cultural attaché in Haiti from 1940 to 1946, Mabille established the Institut français d'Haïti and took an active role in helping French intellectuals who had fled the German Occupation of France during World War II.

10. See Thomas A. Hale, *Les Écrits d'Aimé Césaire, Bibliographie Commentée*, in *Études Françaises* 14.3-4 (Montreal: Les Presses de l'Université de Montréal, 1978), 249.

11. René Depestre, interview by Frantz Leconte, 28 October 1995, http://www.lehman.cuny.edu/ile.en.ile/paroles/depestre_entretien.html (accessed 7 July 2010).

12. See Gérald Bloncourt and Michael Löwy, *Messagers de la tempête: André Breton et la révolution de janvier 1946 en Haïti* (Paris: Le Temps des Cérises, 2007).

13. Roumain's wife and brother published the novel after his death. See Leon-François Hoffman, "Présentation de *Gouverneurs de la Rosée*," http://www.lehman.cuny.edu/ile.en.ile/paroles/roumain_gouverneurs.html (accessed 7 July 2010). I have been unable to verify if Césaire met Roumain during his trip.

14. A close ally of the United States, Lescot declared war on Japan and, less than a week later, on Germany and Italy. The declaration of war allowed Lescot to declare a state of emergency in Haiti, which included censoring the press and suspending constitutional rights. In addition, one of the most unpopular policies was the "anti-superstition" campaign, by which the Catholic Church sought to ban the practice of Vodou.

15. See Niru Ratnam, "Surrealism's Other Side" in Paul Wood, ed., *Varieties of Modernism* (New Haven: Yale University Press, 2004).

16. See René Depestre, "André Breton à Port-au-Prince," *Opus International* 123–124, "André Breton et le Surréalisme International" (April-May 1991), reprinted in Bloncourt and Löwy, *Messagers*, 50–54. Also reprinted in Richardson and Fijalkowski, *Refusal of the Shadow*, 229-33. Depestre's remarkable statement confirms the temporal web of the revision of the past. In 1995, he mobilizes May 1968 to burnish the memory of January 1946.

17. In his interview, Césaire commented that his play on Christophe also owed much to a trip he took to Cap-Haïtien. However, he did not say when this visit took place.

18. Colin Dayan, "Out of Defeat: Aimé Césaire's Miraculous Words" *Boston Review* (September–October 2008), http://bostonreview.net/BR33.5/dayan.php (accessed 6 April 2009).

19. Henock Trouillot, "La présence d'Aimé Césaire en Haïti," in Jacqueline Leiner, ed., *Soleil éclaté* (Tübingen: Gunter Narr Verlag, 1984), 405–12. Trouillot places Césaire's visit in the context of increased intellectual activity in Haiti after the Allied Blockade was lifted: "Under the Presidency of Élie Lescot, foreign intellectuals were invited to give lectures in Port-au-Prince" (405). However, Trouillot does not mention the student agitation that was a part of this activity. He also states that the trip occurred in 1943, and "only for a few days" (406). I have been unable to confirm a 1943 trip, as all accounts point to May–December 1944 as the time when Césaire first visited Haiti. The Allied blockade of Martinique was in place until August 1943.

20. Apparently, that being in Haiti cleared Césaire's stutter was common knowledge: in a footnote Ngal wrote, "Corroborating witness testimony" (301).

21. See Hale, *Les Écrits*, 249–50.

22. *Tropiques* 12 (January 1945), reprinted in *Tropiques: 1941–1945. Collection complète* (Paris: Jean Michel Place, 1978).

23. Arnold refers here to Césaire's poem adapted for the theater, *Et les chiens se taisaient*, as well as to *Christophe*. Other studies of Césaire give little space to the essay. Nesbitt finds that it brings out the transformation of consciousness enabled by Toussaint. See Nesbitt, "Troping Toussaint, Reading Revolution," *Research in African Literatures* 35.2 (Summer 2004): 18–33; likewise, in his monograph, Gregson Davis states, "this excursion into historiography occupies a cardinal position in Césaire's intellectual evolution that has often been overlooked" (*Aimé Césaire*, 138–39); ironically, after a brief page, Davis moves on.

24. Nesbitt develops extensively the Hegelian dimension of Césaire's writing. See "Troping Toussaint"; *Voicing Memory: History and Subjectivity in French Caribbean Literature* (Charlottesville: University of Virginia Press, 2003); and *Universal Emancipation*.

25. Césaire's inconsistent citation of sources is well known. It is clear from the texts he cited, however, that he had access to French National and Colonial Archives, as well as eighteenth-century newspapers. Moreover, he appears to have sought a balance in the source materials. He relied on both French and Haitian authors from the eighteenth to the early twentieth century. He leaned heavily on Schœlcher (for his extensive recourse to the Laveaux Correspondence), Lacroix, and Ardouin. He cited James but once (234), yet it is obvious that *The Black Jacobins* influenced the writing of *Toussaint Louverture*.

26. As deputy, Césaire was part of the Commission des Territoires d'Outre-Mer and helped prepare a report to the French National Assembly. He was the *rapporteur* along with Gaston Monnerville, Léopold Bissol, and Raymond Vergès.

27. See chapter 1 for my discussion of this coup.

28. Gary Wilder, *The French Imperial Nation-State: Negritude & Colonial Humanism Between the Two World Wars* (Chicago: University of Chicago Press, 2005). See chapter 3, "Citizenship in Imperial Paris," for a detailed history of the plight of "racialized colonial subjects who did not enjoy full rights, genuine equality, or an unmolested freedom of civil association" (160).

29. See Nesbitt, "Departmentalization and the Logic of Decolonization," *L'Esprit Créateur* 47.1 (2007); and Wilder, "Untimely."

30. Césaire, "Nègreries: Jeunesse noire et assimilation," *L'Étudiant Noir: Journal Mensuel de l'Association des Étudiants Martiniquais en France* 1 (March 1935). Cited in Hale, *Les Écrits*, 223.

31. Christian Filostrat, *Negritude Agonistes: Assimilation against Nationalism in the French-Speaking Caribbean and Guyane* (Cherry Hill: Africana Homestead Legacy, 2008).

32. Aimé Césaire, "Conscience raciale et révolution sociale," *L'Étudiant Noir: Journal Mensuel de l'Association des Étudiants Martiniquais en France* 3 (May–June 1935): 1–2, in Filostrat, *Negritude Agonistes*, 123–26.

33. I have followed Miller's translation.

34. Translated by Arnold, *Modernism and Negritude*, 174. See also Toumson and Henry-Valmore, 122. Césaire explained the circumstances of his election to Ngal: "When Liberation arrived, the Communist Party came to ask me before the first elections—I was a man of the left, of course, but without being a registered member of the Party—if I would accept to run on the ticket the Party was presenting for the first municipal elections in 1945" (207).

35. Aimé Césaire, "Maurice Thorez parle," *Justice*, 4 May 1950. See Toumson and Henry-Valmore, 130–31.

36. My translation does not do justice to Césaire's poetic rhythm: "Le grand reproche que j'adresse au pseudo-humanisme: d'avoir trop longtemps rapetissé les droits de l'homme, d'en avoir

eu, d'en avoir encore une conception étroite et parcellaire, partielle et partiale et, tout compte fait, sordidement raciste."

37. See Wilder's introduction, "Working through the Imperial Nation-State," for the distinction he establishes, via LaCapra and Freud, between the psychoanalytic concepts of "acting out" and "working through": "Acting out would incorporate colonial societies into an expansionist national historiography that conflates republicanism and universalism. Alternatively, working through entails situating (not mastering or resolving) the sociopolitical dilemmas raised by French colonialism in relation to the nation-state as an imperial political form" (8).

38. Cilas Kemedjio is a notable exception. See "Aimé Césaire's *Letter to Maurice Thorez*: The Practice of Decolonization," *Research in African Literatures* 41.1 (Spring 2010): 87–108.

39. Kemedjio points out the Césaire understood this fraternalism to be a "counterpart of 'colonialist paternalism'" (98).

40. Aimé Césaire, "La pensée politique de Sékou Touré," *Présence Africaine* 29 (December–January 1959–60): 65–74.

Chapter 6

1. Aimé Césaire, *Les Armes miraculeuses* (Paris: Gallimard, [1946] 1970). In the absence of information regarding an earlier, theatrical version, Arnold writes, "*Et les chiens se taisaient* is a transitional work [*écrit-charnière*] for Césaire, one that allowed him to envision the possibility of theater." See Arnold, "D'Haïti à l'Afrique: *La Tragédie du roi Christophe* de Césaire," *Revue de Littérature Comparée* 2 (1986): 139.

2. Alex Gil, "Découverte de l'Ur-texte de *Et les chiens se taisaient*," in *Césaire à l'œuvre*, 145–56.

3. Rodney Harris, *L'Humanisme dans le théâtre d'Aimé Césaire: Études de trois tragédies* (Quebec: Naaman, 1973).

4. Chris Bongie, *Friends and Enemies: The Scribal Politics of Post/Colonial Literature* (Liverpool: Liverpool University Press, 2008).

5. Régis Debray, *Le Scribe: Genèse du politique* (Paris: Grasset, 1980).

6. According to Vergès, Césaire read aloud from the text. Personal email to author, 12 July 2011.

7. See John Conteh-Morgan, *Theater and Drama in Francophone Africa: A Critical Introduction* (Cambridge: Cambridge University Press, 1994), 85. The play was first performed under the direction of Jean-Marie Serreau in Austria at the Salzburg Festival on 4 August 1964. From there, it was put on in Berlin, Brussels, and at the Venice Biennale. In May 1965, the play had its first run in France at the Odeon Theater in Paris. According to André Alter, it was "one of the most beautiful *moments* of the spring of 1965. It has been a long time since we have been a part of such a convincing encounter of theater and poetry" (cited in Harris, 77; emphasis in original).

8. Friedrich Nietzsche, *The Birth of Tragedy, or Hellenism and Pessimism*, trans. William A. Haussman (Edinburgh: Edinburgh Press, [1872, 1886] 1909), 73.

9. See also Paola Martini, "Les Deux editions de *la Tragédie du roi Christophe* de Césaire," in *Césaire à l'œuvre*, 157–72.

10. See Régine Latortue, "Le Corps du roi: Christophe, le tragique architecte," *Œuvres et Critiques XIX*, 2 (1994): 295–300. It is also worth noting the transformation of the metaphor of the tree from "Conscience raciale" to the *Lettre à Maurice Thorez* and, finally, to *Christophe*.

11. This is especially true in that the slave trade, though legally abolished in 1807 by the United Kingdom and the United States, continued illegally in the Caribbean until the 1850s and within the United States (below the Mason-Dixon line) until 1865. Wilberforce was a member of parliament who actively campaigned for the British law. France abolished the slave trade in 1831.

12. See Geggus, "The Naming of Haiti," 215–17.

13. In his novel *Texaco* (Paris: Gallimard, 1992), Patrick Chamoiseau inscribes a fictional history of the resonance of the word "work [*travail*]" in "slavery [*esclavage*]." His narrator-scribe, the

"*marqueur de paroles*," has taken down the word of a *femme-matador*, Marie-Sophie Laborieux. In notebook number two, we read, "They used to say with their words: slavery [*l'esclavage*]. For us it was to hear: work [*l'estravaille*]. When they knew it and, in turn, said *l'estravaille* to speak to us at our level, we had already cut it down to the idea of work . . . hee hee hee, the word furrowed, Sophie, the word furrowed like a weapon" (65).

14. See Doris R. Kadish and Françoise Massardier-Kenny, eds., *Translating Slavery: Gender and Race in French Women's Writing, 1783–1823* (Kent, OH: Kent State University Press, 1994), particularly part 4, "Claire de Duras (1777–1828)." See also Christopher Miller, *The French Atlantic Triangle*, chapter 8, "Duras and Her Ourika, 'The Ultimate House Slave,'" 158–73; and A. James Arnold, "Recuperating the Haitian Revolution in Literature: From Victor Hugo to Derek Walcott" in *Tree of Liberty*, 179–99.

15. Claire de Duras, *Ourika: The Original French Text*, ed. Joan DeJean, introd. Joan DeJean and Margaret Waller (New York: Modern Language Association, [1826] 1994), 13.

16. Césaire thus provides a contrast to the model of English abolitionism espoused by Wilberforce.

17. Three years later, Césaire published a subsequent play, *Une saison au Congo* (Paris: Présence Africaine, 1966), the protagonist of which is the leader, Patrice Lumumba. However, the title of this play is significant for the attention taken away from the hero and placed on the country.

18. Nesbitt cites the seminal work of Lilyan Kesteloot and Barthélemy Kotchy, *Aimé Césaire: L'Homme et l'œuvre* (Paris: Présence Africaine, [1973] 1993).

19. *Magazine Littéraire* 34 (November 1969). Cited in Keith Q. Warner, "De l'écrivain devenu leader politique: à la recherche d'un héros antillais," in *Soleil éclaté*, 422. See also Ngal, 247; and Arnold, "D'Haïti à l'Afrique," 148.

20. See Arnold, "D'Haïti à l'Afrique"; Cailler; Antoine; Conteh-Morgan; Ngal; and Walker; see also Sandra Williams, "La Renaissance de la Tragédie dans l'œuvre dramatique d'Aimé Césaire," *Présence Africaine* 76 (1970): 63–81; and Marianne Wichmann Bailey, *The Ritual Theater of Aimé Césaire: Mythic Structures of the Dramatic Imagination* (Tübingen: Gunter Narr Verlag, 1992).

21. Conteh-Morgan discussed the "imperfect analog[ies]" (97) between Christophe and Prometheus, the Nietzschean "surhomme nègre," as well as the Yoruba god, Shango, which I address below.

22. According to Kesteloot and Kotchy, Césaire wrote *Et les chiens* after reading Nietzsche's essay. Cited in Cailler, 143. See also Arnold, "D'Haïti à l'Afrique," 137; and Harris, 28.

23. By contrast, Cailler sees Toussaint's attempt to raise the people's consciousness of the rights of man as a direct historical legacy for Christophe's desire to found a nation based on the freedom of the people. See *Proposition poétique*, 144.

24. See Jack Corzani, "Césaire et la Caraïbe oubliée . . . ," in *Soleil éclaté*, 89–99.

25. See Jean-François Brière, *Haïti et la France, 1804–1848: le rêve brisé* (Paris: Karthala, 2008).

26. Much of Césaire's descriptions of Vodou rites come from his study of Alfred Métraux, *Le vaudou haïtien* (Paris: Gallimard, 1959). See also Frederick Ivor Case, "Sango Oba ko so: Les Vodoun dans la Tragédie du roi Christophe," *Cahiers Césairiens* 2 (1975): 9–24.

27. Nesbitt argues that Césaire understood the movement between negation and existence as a dialectical process, one that he derived from Hegel's model of historical understanding in *Phenomenology of the Spirit*. He argues that Hegel's influence is essential to understanding Césaire's place in the pre- and postwar European intellectual fields of anticolonialism, existentialism, and Marxism (*Voicing Memory*, 118–22). Nesbitt's comparison of *Phenomenology* and *Christophe*—and, in particular, the articulation of the "historical, temporal development of mankind away from an existence of unconscious, brutal repetition toward a fully historical human existence" (131)—complements Arnold's reading of the interferences that structure the play.

28. See Manthia Diawara, *In Search of Africa* (Cambridge, MA: Harvard University Press, 1998).

Conclusion

1. Cited in Laurent Dubois, *A Colony of Citizens: Revolution & Slave Emancipation in the French Caribbean, 1787–1804* (Chapel Hill: University of North Carolina Press, 2004), 423.
2. "Discours de M. Nicolas Sarkozy, Président de la République, Cérémonie d'hommage solennel de la Nation à Aimé CÉSAIRE," 6 April 2011, http://www.elysee.fr/president/les-actualites/discours/2011/discours-ceremonie-d-hommage-solennel-de-la.11063.html (accessed 10 November 2011).
3. The French government later presented an urn filled with dirt from the grounds of the Fort de Joux as a symbolic gesture. Césaire's funeral, a long, communal procession accompanied by enormous crowds that sang and danced, took place in Fort-de-France on 20 April 2008.
4. For an exemplary reading of the commemoration of Toussaint and Delgrès, see the epilogue to Dubois, *A Colony of Citizens*, 423–27.
5. President Sarkozy's speech has also been read as a form of reconciliation following the disastrous law of 23 February 2005, whose Article 4 mandated that French high schools teach the "positive role of the French presence overseas." The law, "Loi n. 2005–158 du 23 février portant reconnaissance de la Nation et contribution nationale en faveur des Français rapatriés," was proposed by Sarkozy's political party, the Union for a Popular Movement. Article 4 was repealed less than a year later. When candidate Sarkozy visited Martinique, Césaire refused to meet with him.
6. Gaston Monnerville, Léopold Sédar-Senghor, and Aimé Césaire, *Commémoration du centenaire de l'abolition de l'esclavage: Discours prononcés à la Sorbonne le 27 avril 1948* (Paris: Presses Universitaires de France, 1948).

Bibliography

"Accord Régional Interprofessionel sur les Salaires en Guadeloupe–Accord Jacques Bino." Signed at Pointe-à-Pitre, February 26, 2009. http://www.lkp-gwa.org (accessed 10 August 2011).

Aldrich, Robert, and John Connell. *The Last Colonies*. Cambridge: Cambridge University Press, 1998.

Antoine, Régis. *La Littérature franco-antillaise*. Paris: Karthala, 1992.

Aravamudan, Srinivas. *Tropicopolitans: Colonialism and Agency, 1688–1804*. Durham: Duke University Press, 1999.

Ardouin, Beaubrun. *Études sur l'histoire d'Haïti suivies de la vie du général J. M. Borgella*. Paris: Dézobry, Magdeleine et Cie, 1853–1860.

Ariès, Philippe. "Pourquoi écrit-on des Mémoires?" In N. Hepp and J. Hennequin, eds., *Les Valeurs chez les mémorialistes français du XVIIe siècle avant la Fronde*, 12–20. Paris: Éditions Klincksieck, 1979.

Arnold, A. James. "D'Haïti à l'Afrique: *La Tragédie du Roi Christophe* de Césaire." *Revue de Littérature Comparée* 60.2 (1986): 133–48.

———. "Devenir Aimé Césaire: un itinéraire intellectuel et artistique." In M. Cheymol and P. Ollé-Laprune, eds., *Aimé Césaire à l'œuvre: Actes du colloque international*, 203–14. Paris: Editions des Archives Contemporains, 2010.

———. *Modernism and Negritude: The Poetry and Poetics of Aimé Césaire*. Cambridge, MA: Harvard University Press, 1981.

———. "Recuperating the Haitian Revolution in Literature: From Victor Hugo to Derek Walcott." In D. Garraway, ed., *Tree of Liberty: Cultural Legacies of the Haitian Revolution in the Atlantic World*, 179–99. Charlottesville: University of Virginia Press, 2008.

Baggio, Antonio M., and Ricardo Augustin, eds. *Lettres à la France: Idées pour la libération du peuple noir d'Haïti (1794–1798)*. Paris: Nouvelle Cité, 2011.

Bell, Madison Smartt. *Toussaint Louverture: A Biography*. New York: Pantheon Books, 2007.

Bénot, Yves. *La Révolution française et la fin des colonies*. Paris: La Découverte, 1987.

Bloncourt, Gérald, and Michael Löwy. *Messagers de la tempête: André Breton et la révolution de janvier 1946 en Haïti*. Paris: Le Temps des cérises, 2007.

Bonaparte, Napoleon. *Correspondance de Napoléon Ier, publiée par ordre de l'empéreur Napoléon III*. 32 vols. Paris: Plon, 1861.

Bongie, Chris. "Chroniques de la francophonie triomphante: Haiti, France, and the Debray Report." In D. Garraway, ed., *Tree of Liberty: Cultural Legacies of the Haitian Revolution in the Atlantic World*, 153–76. Charlottesville: University of Virginia Press, 2008.

———. *Friends and Enemies: The Scribal Politics of Post/Colonial Literature*. Liverpool: Liverpool University Press, 2008.

———. *Islands and Exiles: The Creole Identities of Post/Colonial Literature*. Stanford: Stanford University Press, 1998.

Bonilla, Yarimar. "Guadeloupe Is Ours: The Prefigurative Politics of the Mass Strike in the French Antilles." *Interventions: International Journal of Postcolonial Studies* 12.1 (March 2010): 125–37.

Boromé, Joseph. "Toussaint Louverture: A Finding List of his Letters and Documents in Archives and Collections (Public and Private) of Europe and America." Unpublished. Schomburg Center for Research in Black Culture, New York Public Library.

Breton, André. "Un grand poète noir." In A. Breton and A. Masson, eds., *Martinique charmeuse de serpents*, 93–111. Paris: Pauvert, 1972.

Brière, Jean-François. *Haïti et la France, 1804-1848: Le Rêve Brisé*. Paris: Karthala, 2008.

Brooks, David, "The Underlying Tragedy." *New York Times*, 14 January 2010, http://www.nytimes.com/2010/01/15/opinion/15brooks.html (accessed 7 June 2010).

Brown, Gordon. *Toussaint's Clause: The Founding Fathers and the Haitian Revolution*. Jackson: University Press of Mississippi, 2005.

Buck-Morss, Susan. *Hegel, Haiti, and Universal History*. Pittsburgh: University of Pittsburgh Press, 2009.

Cailler, Bernadette. *Proposition poétique: Une lecture de l'œuvre d'Aimé Césaire*. Sherbrooke: Naaman, 1976.

Case, Frederick Ivor. "Sango Oba ko so: Les Vodoun dans *la Tragédie du roi Christophe*." *Cahiers Césairiens* 2 (1975): 9–24.

Cauna, Jacques de, ed. *Toussaint Louverture et l'indépendance d'Haïti*. Paris: Karthala, 2004.

Césaire, Aimé. *Les armes miraculeuses*. Paris: Gallimard, 1946.

———. "Après interventions répétées ministre accepte revendications ouvrières salaires." *Justice* (16 February 1946).

———. *Cahier d'un retour au pays natal*. Ed. Abiola Irele. Columbus: Ohio University Press, 1999.

———. "Conscience raciale et révolution sociale." *L'Étudiant Noir: Journal Mensuel de l'Association des Étudiants Martiniquais en France* 3 (May–June 1935): 1–2.

———. "Crises dans les départements d'outre-mer ou crise de la départementalisation." *Présence Africaine* 36 (1961): 109–11.

———. "Culture et colonisation." Speech for the Premier Congrès International des Écrivains et Artistes Noirs, 19–22 September. 1956. *Présence Africaine* 8–10 (1956): 190–205.

———. *Discours sur le colonialisme*. Paris: Présence Africaine, 1955.

———. *Discours sur le colonialisme, suivi de Discours sur la Négritude*. Paris: Présence Africaine, 2004.

———. *Et les chiens se taisaient*. Paris: Présence Africaine, 1956.

———. "L'Homme de culture et ses responsabilités." Speech for the Deuxième Congrès International des Écrivains et Artistes Noirs, Rome, 26 March–1 April 1959. *Présence Africaine* 24–25 (1959): 116–22.

———. Introduction. *Les Antilles décolonisées*, by Daniel Guérin. Paris: Présence Africaine, 1956. 9–17.

———. Speeches. *Journal officiel de la République française, Documents de l'Assemblée nationale constituante*. (19 February 1946); (12 March 1946); (14 March 1946); (16 March 1948); (3 March 1950).

———. *Lettre à Maurice Thorez*. Paris: Présence Africaine, 1956.

———. "Maurice Thorez parle." *Justice* (4 May 1950).

———. "Mémoriel à Louis Delgrès." *Présence Africaine* 23 (December 1958–January 1959): 69–72.

———. *Nègre je suis, nègre je resterai: Entretiens avec Françoise Vergès*. Paris: Albin Michel, 2005.

———. "Nègreries: Jeunesse noire et assimilation." *L'Étudiant Noir: Journal Mensuel de l'Association des Étudiants Martiniquais en France* 1 (March 1935).

———. "La pensée politique de Sékou Touré." *Présence Africaine* 29 (December–January 1959–60): 65–74.
———. Preface. *Expérience guinéenne et unite africaine*, by Sékou Touré. Paris: Présence Africaine, 1962.
———. *Une saison au Congo*. Paris: Présence Africaine, 1966.
———. *Toussaint Louverture: La Révolution française et le problème colonial*. Paris: Présence Africaine, [1962] 1981.
———. *La tragédie du roi Christophe*. Paris: Présence Africaine, 1963.
———. *Tropiques, 1941–1945: Collection complète*. Dir. Suzanne Césaire and René Ménil. Paris: Jean-Michel Place, 1994.
Chamoiseau, Patrick. *Texaco*. Paris: Gallimard, 1992.
Chamoiseau, Patrick, Raphaël Confiant, and Jean Bernabé. *L'Éloge de la créolité*. Paris: Gallimard, 1989.
Cheymol, Marc, and Philippe Ollé-Laprune, eds. *Aimé Césaire à l'œuvre: Actes du colloque international*. Paris: Editions des Archives Contemporains, 2010.
Clavin, Matthew J. *Toussaint Louverture and the American Civil War: The Promise and Peril of a Second Haitian Revolution*. Philadelphia: University of Pennsylvania Press, 2010.
Colwill, Elizabeth. "Sex, Savagery, and Slavery in the Shaping of the French Body Politic." In S. Melzer and K. Norberg, eds., *From the Royal to the Republican Body: Incorporating the Political in Seventeenth- and Eighteenth-Century France*, 198–223. Berkeley: University of California Press, 1998.
Confiant, Raphael. *Aimé Césaire: Une Traversée paradoxale du siècle*. Paris: Stock, 1993.
Constant, Fred, and Justin Daniel, eds. *1946–1996: Cinquante ans de Départmentalisation Outre-Mer*. Paris: L'Harmattan, 1997.
Constitution de 1791. Titre VII, De la révision des décrets constitutionnels, Article 8. http://www.conseil-constitutionnel.fr/conseil-constitutionnel/francais/la-constitution/les-constitutions-de-la-france/constitution-de-1791.5082.html (accessed 10 February 2010).
Conteh-Morgan, John. *Theater and Drama in Francophone Africa: A Critical Introduction*. Cambridge: Cambridge University Press, 1994.
Corzani, Jack. "Césaire et la Caraïbe oubliée . . . " In J. Leiner, ed., *Soleil éclaté*, 89–99. Tübingen: Gunter Narr Verlag, 1984.
Cronon, William. "A Place for Stories: Nature, History, and Narrative." *Journal of American History* 78.4 (March 1992): 1347–76.
Davis, David Brion. *The Problem of Slavery in the Age of Revolution, 1770–1823*. Ithaca: Cornell University Press, 1975.
Davis, Gregson. *Aimé Césaire*. Cambridge: Cambridge University Press, 1997.
Dayan, Colin. "Out of Defeat: Aimé Césaire's Miraculous Words." *Boston Review* (September–October 2008), http://bostonreview.net/BR33.5/dayan.php (accessed 6 April 2009).
Debien, Gabriel. *Les Esclaves aux Antilles françaises, XVIIe et XVIIIe siècles*. Basse-Terre: Société d'histoire de la Guadeloupe, 1974.
Debien, Gabriel, Jean Fouchard, and Marie Antoinette Menier. "Toussaint Louverture avant 1789: Légendes et réalités." *Conjonction, Revue Franco-Haïtienne* 134 (June–July 1977): 67–80.
Debray, Régis. *Haïti et la France*. Paris: Broché, 2004.
———. *Le Scribe: Genèse du politique*. Paris: Grasset, 1980.
Depestre, René. "André Breton à Port-au-Prince." *Opus International* 123–124, "André Breton et le Surréalisme International" (April–May 1991).

———. Interview by Frantz Leconte, 28 October 1995. http://www.lehman.cuny.edu/ile.en.ile/paroles/depestre_entretien.html (accessed 7 July 2010).

Descourtilz, M. E. *Voyages d'un naturaliste à Saint-Domingue*. 3 vols. Paris: Dufart, 1809.

Desormeaux, Daniel. "The First of the (Black) Memorialists: Toussaint Louverture." *Yale French Studies* 107, "The Haiti Issue: 1804 and Nineteenth-Century French Studies" (2005): 131–45.

Diawara, Manthia. *In Search of Africa*. Cambridge, MA: Harvard University Press, 1998.

Dracius, Suzanne, Jean-François Samlong, and Gérard Théobald, eds. *La Crise de l'outre-mer français: Guadeloupe, Martinique, Réunion*. Paris: L'Harmattan, 2009.

Dubois, Laurent. *Avengers of the New World: The Story of the Haitian Revolution*. Cambridge, MA: Harvard University Press, 2004.

———. "Avenging America: The Politics of Violence in the Haitian Revolution." In D. Geggus and N. Fiering, eds., *The World of the Haitian Revolution*, 111–24. Bloomington: Indiana University Press, 2009.

———. *A Colony of Citizens: Revolution & Slave Emancipation in the French Caribbean, 1787–1804*. Chapel Hill: University of North Carolina Press, 2004.

Duboys, Pélage-Marie. *Précis historique des annales de la colonie française de Saint-Domingue depuis 1789*. BN, Nouvelles acquisitions françaises 14878–14879.

Dubreuil, Laurent. *L'Empire du langage: Colonies et francophonies*. Paris: Hermann Éditeurs, 2008.

Dufay, Louis-Pierre. *Compte rendu sur la situation actuelle de Saint-Domingue*. Paris: Imprimérie Nationale, 1794.

Duras, Claire de. *Ourika: The Original French Text*. Ed. Joan DeJean. New York: Modern Language Association, [1826] 1994.

Edwards, Brent Hayes. *The Practice of Diaspora: Literature, Translation and the Rise of Black Internationalism*. Cambridge, MA: Harvard University Press, 2003.

———. "Aimé Césaire and the Syntax of Influence." *Research in African Literatures* 36.2 (Summer 2005): 1–18.

———. "Introduction: Césaire in 1956." *Social Text* 103, 28.2 (Summer 2010): 115–25.

Les Etats Généraux de L'Outre-Mer. http://www.etatsgenerauxdeloutremer.fr/ (accessed 17 August 2011).

Fick, Carolyn, E. "The Haitian Revolution and the Limits of Freedom: Defining Citizenship in the Revolutionary Era." *Social History* 32.4 (November 2007): 394–414.

———. *The Making of Haiti: The Saint Domingue Revolution from Below*. Knoxville: University of Tennessee Press, 1990.

———. "The Saint-Domingue Slave Revolution and the Unfolding of Independence, 1791–1804." In D. Geggus and N. Fiering, eds. *The World of the Haitian Revolution*, 177–95. Bloomington: Indiana University Press, 2009.

Figueroa, Víctor. "Between Louverture and Christophe: Aimé Césaire on the Haitian Revolution." *French Review* 82.5 (April 2009): 1006–21.

Filostrat, Christian. *Negritude Agonistes: Assimilation against Nationalism in the French-Speaking Caribbean and Guyane*. Cherry Hill: Africana Homestead Legacy, 2008.

Fischer, Sibylle. *Modernity Disavowed: Haiti and the Cultures of Slavery in the Age of Revolution*. Durham, NC: Duke University Press, 2004.

Forsdick, Charles. "De la plume comme des pieds: The Essay as a Peripatetic Genre." In C. Fordsick and A. Stafford, eds., *The Modern French Essay: Movement, Instability, Performance*, 45–59. Bern: Peter Lang, 2005.

———. "Haiti and Departmentalization: the Spectral Presence of Toussaint Louverture." *International Journal of Francophone Studies* 11.3 (2008): 327–44.
———. "Madison Smartt Bell's Toussaint at the Crossroads: The Haitian Revolutionary between History and Fiction." *Small Axe* 23 (June 2007): 194–208.
———. "Situating Haiti: On Some Early Nineteenth-Century Representations of Toussaint Louverture." *International Journal of Francophone Studies* 10.1–2 (2007): 17–34.
Forsdick, Charles, and David Murphy, eds. *Francophone Postcolonial Studies: A Critical Introduction*. London: Hodder Arnold, 2003.
Fortuné, Louis Marie Auguste, comte d'Andigné de la Blanchaye. *Mémoires du Général D'Andigné*. Paris: Plon, 1901.
Fouchard, Jean. *Les Marrons de la liberté*. Paris: Editions de l'École, 1972.
Freud, Sigmund. "Family Romances." In *The Standard Edition of the Complete Works of Sigmund Freud*, vol. 9 (1906–1908). Trans. James Strachey. London: Hogarth Press, 1959.
Fumaroli, Marc. *La Diplomatie de l'esprit: de Montaigne à La Fontaine*. Paris: Gallimard, 1998.
Furetière, Antoine. *Dictionnaire Universel* (1694). http://gallica.bnf.fr/ark:/12148/bpt6k5542578m.image.r=mémoire.f883.langEN.hl (accessed 10 March 2010).
Gainot, Bernard. "*La Décade* et la 'colonisation nouvelle.'" *Annales Historiques de la Révolution Française* 339 (Janvier–Mars 2005): 99–116.
———. "La naissance des départements d'Outre-Mer: La Loi du 1er janvier 1798." *Revue d'Histoire des Mascareignes et de l'Océan Indien* 1 (1998): 51–74.
———. "Un projet avorté d'intégration républicaine: l'institution nationale des colonies (1797–1802)." *Dix-huitième Siècle* 32 (2000): 371–401.
Garran-Coulon, Jean-Philippe. *Rapport sur les troubles de Saint-Domingue*. 4 vols. Paris, 1799.
Garraway, Doris L. *The Libertine Colony: Creolization in the Early French Caribbean*. Durham, NC: Duke University Press, 2005.
———. "'Légitime Défense': Universalism and Nationalism in the Discourse of the Haitian Revolution." In D. Garraway, ed., *Tree of Liberty: Cultural Legacies of the Haitian Revolution in the Atlantic World*, 63–88. Charlottesville: University of Virginia Press, 2008.
Gaspar, David Berry, and David Patrick Geggus, eds. *A Turbulent Time: The French Revolution and the Greater Caribbean*. Bloomington: Indiana University Press, 1997.
Geggus, David Patrick. *Haitian Revolutionary Studies*. Bloomington: Indiana University Press, 2002.
———. *The Impact of the Haitian Revolution in the Atlantic World*. Columbia: University of South Carolina Press, 2001.
Geggus, David Patrick, and Norman Fiering, eds. *The World of the Haitian Revolution*. Bloomington: Indiana University Press, 2009.
Ghachem, Malick. "The Colonial Vendée." In D. Geggus and N. Fiering, eds., *The World of the Haitian Revolution*, 156–76. Bloomington: Indiana University Press, 2009.
Gil, Alex. "Découverte de l'Ur-texte de *Et les chiens se taisaient*." In M. Cheymol and P. Ollé-Laprune, eds., *Aimé Césaire à l'œuvre: Actes du colloque international*, 145–56. Paris: Editions des Archives Contemporains, 2010.
Glissant, Edouard. *Le Discours antillais*. Paris: Gallimard, 1981.
———. *Monsieur Toussaint*. Paris: Editions du Seuil, 1961.
Gros, M. *Historick Recital*. Baltimore: S. & J. Adams, 1793.
———. *Isle de Saint-Domingue: Précis historique*. Paris: L. Potier de Lille, 1793.
———. *Récit historique sur les événements qui se sont succédés dans les camps de la Grande-Rivière, du Dondon, de Ste.-Suzanne et autres, depuis le 26 octobre 1791 jusqu'au 24

décembre de la même année: Par M. Gros, procureur-syndic de Valière, fait prisonnier par Jeannot, chef des brigands. Cap Français: Parent, impr., au coin des rues Royale et Notre-Dame, 1793.

Hale, Thomas A. "Les Écrits d'Aimé Césaire, Bibliographie Commentée." Études françaises 14.3–4 (1978).

Hale, Thomas A., and Kora Véron. "Les Écrits d'Aimé Césaire: Nouvelle Bio-bibliographie commentée." In M. Cheymol and P. Ollé-Laprune, eds., Aimé Césaire à l'œuvre: Actes du colloque international, 215–24. Paris: Editions des Archives Contemporains, 2010.

———. "Is There Unity in the Writings of Aimé Césaire?" Research in African Literatures 41.1 (Spring 2010): 46–70.

Hallward, Peter. Absolutely Postcolonial: Writing between the Singular and the Specific. Manchester: Manchester University Press, 2001.

———. "Our Role in Haiti's Plight." The Guardian, January 13, 2010. http://www.guardian.co.uk/commentisfree/2010/jan/13/our-role-in-haitis-plight (accessed 7 June 2010).

Harris, Rodney. L'Humanisme dans le théâtre d'Aimé Césaire: Études de trois tragedies. Quebec: Naaman, 1973.

Hector, Michel, ed. La Révolution française et Haïti: Filiations, ruptures, nouvelles dimensions. Port-au-Prince: Editions H. Deschamps, 1995.

Holt, Thomas C. The Problem of Freedom: Race, Labor, and Politics in Jamaica and Britain, 1832–1938. Baltimore: Johns Hopkins University Press, 1992.

Hunt, Lynn. The Family Romance of the French Revolution. Berkeley: University of California Press, 1992.

Hurley, E. Anthony. "Is He, Am I, a Hero?" In D. Garraway, ed., Tree of Liberty: Cultural Legacies of the Haitian Revolution in the Atlantic World, 113-33. Charlottesville: University of Virginia Press, 2008.

James, C. L. R. The Black Jacobins: Toussaint L'Ouverture and the San Domingo Revolution. New York: Vintage, [1938] 1963.

Jameson, Fredric. The Political Unconscious: Narrative as a Socially Symbolic Act. Ithaca: Cornell University Press, 1981.

Janvier, Louis-Joseph. Les Constitutions d'Haïti. Paris, 1886.

Jenson, Deborah. Beyond the Slave Narrative: Politics, Sex and Manuscripts in the Haitian Revolution. Liverpool: Liverpool University Press, 2011.

———. "Kidnapping(s)." Yale French Studies 107, "The Haiti Issue: 1804 and Nineteenth-Century French Studies" (2005): 162–86.

———. "Toussaint Louverture, Spin Doctor?" In D. Garraway, ed., Tree of Liberty: Cultural Legacies of the Haitian Revolution in the Atlantic World, 41–62. Charlottesville: University of Virginia Press, 2008.

Jordan, David P., ed. Rethinking France. 4 vols. Trans. Mary Trouille. Chicago: University of Chicago Press, 2001.

Kadish, Doris R., and Françoise Massardier-Kenny, eds. Translating Slavery: Gender and Race in French Women's Writing, 1783–1823. Kent, OH: Kent State University Press, 1994.

Kemedjio, Cilas. "Aimé Césaire's Letter to Maurice Thorez: The Practice of Decolonization." Research in African Literatures 41.1 (Spring 2010): 87–108.

Kesteloot, Lilyan and Barthélemy Kotchy. Aimé Césaire: L'Homme et l'œuvre. Paris: Présence Africaine, [1973] 1993.

Koffi, Sylvie. "Etat des lieux des Antilles, deux ans après la crise sociale." *RFI*, 7 January 2011. http://www.rfi.fr/france/20110107-antilles-deux-ans-apres-crise-sociale (accessed 17 August 2011).

Kritzman, Lawrence B., ed. *Realms of Memory*. 3 vols. Trans. Arthur Goldhammer. New York: Columbia University Press, 1996–98.

Lacroix, Pamphile de. *La Révolution de Haïti*. Ed. Pierre Pluchon. Paris: Karthala, 1995.

Las Cases, Emmanuel de. *Le Mémorial de Sainte-Hélène*. 2 vols. Ed. Gérald Walter. Paris: Gallimard, Bibliothèque de la Pléiade, 1956.

Latortue, Régine. "Le Corps du Roi: Christophe, le tragique architecte." *Œuvres et Critiques* 19.2 (1994): 295–300.

Laurent, Gérard. *Toussaint Louverture à travers sa correspondance, 1794–1798*. Madrid, 1953.

Le Touzet, Jean-Louis. "'Les Guadeloupéens voulaient une autre société' *Libération*, 29 December 2010. http://www.liberation.fr/societe/01012310468-les-guadeloupeens-voulaient-une-autre-societe (accessed 10 August 2011).

Le Trésor de la langue française informatisé (1971–94). http://atilf.atilf.fr.

Leiner, Jacqueline. *Aimé Césaire, le terreau primordial*. Tübingen: Gunter Narr Verlag, 1993.

———, ed. *Soleil éclaté: Mélanges offerts à Aimé Césaire à l'occasion de son 70e anniversaire*. Tübingen: Gunter Narr Verlag, 1984.

Littré, Émile. *Dictionnaire de la langue française* (1876).

Louverture, Toussaint. "La Constitution de la colonie française de Saint-Domingue" (1801).

———. *Mémoire du Général Toussaint Louverture* (1802).

———. *Mémoires du Général Toussaint Louverture, écrits par lui-même*. Ed. Joseph Saint-Rémy. Paris: Pagnerre, 1853.

Lubeth, Gilles. "Between Past and Present, Roadblocks and Negotiation: The Guadeloupe 2009 Crisis." *International Journal of African Renaissance Studies* 4.1 (2009): 80–90.

Lutaud, Laurent, and Georges Nivoix, dirs. *Toussaint Louverture, Haïti et la France*. DVD. L'Harmattan, 2006.

Madiou, Thomas. *Histoire d'Haiti*. Port-au-Prince: Imprimerie de J. Courtois, 1847–48.

Martini, Paola. "Les deux editions de *la Tragédie du roi Christophe* de Césaire." In M. Cheymol and P. Ollé-Laprune, eds., *Aimé Césaire à l'œuvre: Actes du colloque international*, 157–72. Paris: Editions des Archives Contemporains, 2010.

Métral, Antoine Marie Therese, and Isaac Toussaint Louverture. *Histoire de l'expédition des Français à Saint-Domingue*. Paris: Imprimé Chez Paul Renouard, 1825.

Métraux, Alfred. *Le Vaudou haïtien*. Paris: Gallimard, 1959.

Miller, Christopher L. *The French Atlantic Triangle: Literature and Culture of the Slave Trade*. Durham, NC: Duke University Press, 2008.

———. "The (Revised) Birth of Negritude: Communist Revolution and 'the Immanent Negro' in 1935." *PMLA* 125.3 (May 2010): 743–49.

Moïse, Claude. *Le Projet national de Toussaint Louverture et la Constitution de 1801*. Montreal: Editions du CIDIHCA, 2001.

Monnerville, Gaston, Léopold Sédar-Senghor, and Aimé Césaire. *Commémoration du centenaire de l'abolition de l'esclavage: Discours prononcés à la Sorbonne le 27 avril 1948*. Paris: Presses Universitaires de France, 1948.

Montluc, Blaise de. *Commentaires 1521–1576*. Paris: Gallimard, 1964.

Nesbitt, Nick. "Departmentalization and the Logic of Decolonization." *L'Esprit Créateur* 47.1 (2007): 32–43.

———. "The Idea of 1804." *Yale French Studies* 107, "The Haiti Issue: 1804 and Nineteenth-Century French Studies" (2005): 6–38.

———. "The Incandescent I, Destroyer of Worlds." *Research in African Literatures* 41.1 (Spring 2010): 121–41.

———. "A Singular Revolution." In A. G. Hargreaves, ed., *Memory, Empire, and Postcolonialism: Legacies of French Colonialism*, 37–50. Lanham, MD: Lexington Books, 2005.

———. "Troping Toussaint, Reading Revolution." *Research in African Literatures* 35.2 (Summer 2004): 18–33.

———. *Universal Emancipation: The Haitian Revolution and the Radical Enlightenment*. Charlottesville: University of Virginia Press, 2008.

———. *Voicing Memory: History and Subjectivity in French Caribbean Literature*. Charlottesville: University of Virginia Press, 2003.

Nietzsche, Friedrich. *The Birth of Tragedy, or Hellenism and Pessimism*. Trans. William A. Haussman. Edinburgh: Edinburgh Press, [1872, 1886] 1909.

Ngal, M. a M. *Aimé Césaire: Un homme à la recherche d'une patrie*. Paris: Présence Africaine, [1975] 1994.

Nicholls, David. *From Dessalines to Duvalier: Race, Colour, and National Independence in Haiti*. Cambridge: Cambridge University Press, 1979.

Nora, Pierre. *Les Français d'Algérie*. Paris: René Julliard, 1961.

———. "General Introduction." Trans. Richard C. Holbrook. In D. Jordan, ed., *Rethinking France*, Vol. 1: *The State*, vii–xxii. Chicago: University of Chicago Press, 2001.

———. "Memoirs of Men of State: From Commynes to de Gaulle." Trans. M. Trouille. In D. Jordan, ed., *Rethinking France*, Vol. 1: *The State*, 401–51. Chicago: University of Chicago Press, 2001.

Nora, Pierre, ed. *Les Lieux de mémoire*. 7 vols. Paris: Gallimard, 1992.

Onyeoziri, Gloria Nne. "Le *Toussaint* d'Aimé Césaire: Réflexions sur le statut d'un texte." *L'Esprit Créateur* 32.1 (Spring 1992): 87–96.

Perroud, Henry. *Précis des derniers troubles qui ont eu lieu dans la partie du nord de Saint-Domingue, addressé au Ministre de la Marine et des colonies*. Le Cap, 1796.

Pluchon, Pierre. *Toussaint Louverture: Un révolutionnaire noir d'ancien régime*. Paris: Fayard, 1989.

Popkin, Jeremy. *Facing Racial Revolution: Eyewitness Accounts of the Haitian Insurrection*. Chicago: University of Chicago Press, 2008.

———. *You Are All Free: The Haitian Revolution and the Abolition of Slavery*. Cambridge: Cambridge University Press, 2010.

Price-Mars, Jean. *Silhouettes de nègres et de négrophiles*. Paris: Présence Africaine, 1960.

Ratnam, Niru. "Surrealism's Other Side." In P. Wood, ed., *Varieties of Modernism*, 53–71. New Haven: Yale University Press, 2004.

Richardson, Michael, and Krzysztof Fijalkowski, trans. *Refusal of the Shadow: Surrealism and the Caribbean*. London: Verso, 1996.

Rosello, Mireille. "The 'Césaire Effect,' or How to Cultivate One's Nation." *Research in African Literatures* 32.4 (Winter 2001): 77–91.

———. "'A Thousand Bamboo Fangs Down My Throat: Césaire's *Cahier d'un retour au pays natal*." *PMLA* 125.3 (May 2010): 750–55.

Roussier, Michel. "L'Éducation des enfants de Toussaint Louverture et l'Institution nationale des colonies." *Revue Française d'histoire d'outre-mer* 236 (1977): 308–49. Reprinted in de Cauna, ed. *Toussaint Louverture et l'indépendance d'Haïti* (Paris: Karthala, 2004).

Roussier, Paul, ed. *Lettres du Général Leclerc*. Paris: Librairie Ernest Leroux, 1937.
Sannon, H. Pauleus. *Histoire de Toussaint-Louverture*. 3 vols. Port-au-Prince: Héraux, 1920–33.
Sarkozy, Nicolas. "Allocution de M. Nicolas Sarkozy, Président de la République, prononcée à l'Université de Dakar." 26 July 2007., http://www.elysee.fr/elysee/elysee.fr/francais/interventions/2007/juillet /allocution_à_l_université_de_dakar.79184.html (accessed 10 August 2011).
———. "Discours de M. Nicolas Sarkozy, Président de la République, prononcé à Petit-Bourg, Guadeloupe." January 9, 2011. http://www.2011–annee-des-outre-mer.gouv.fr/annee-des-outre-mer/edito-du-president-de-la-republique.html (accessed 10 August 2011).
———. "Discours de M. Nicolas Sarkozy, Président de la République, Cérémonie d'hommage solennel de la Nation à Aimé CÉSAIRE." 6 April 2011. http://www.elysee.fr/president/les-actualites/discours/2011/discours-ceremonie-d-hommage-solennel-de-la.11063.html (accessed 10 November 2011).
Scharon, Faine. *Toussaint Louverture et la Révolution de St-Domingue*. 2 vols. Port-au-Prince: Imprimerie de l'État, 1959.
Schœlcher, Victor. *Vie de Toussaint Louverture*. Paris: Karthala, [1889] 1982.
Scott, David. *Conscripts of Modernity: the Tragedy of Colonial Enlightenment*. Durham, NC: Duke University Press, 2004.
Smith, Matthew J. *Red & Black in Haiti: Radicalism, Conflict, and Political Change, 1934–1957*. Chapel Hill: University of North Carolina Press, 2009.
Songolo, Aliko. *Aimé Césaire: Une poétique de la découverte*. Paris: L'Harmattan, 1985.
Spivak, Gayatri. *Outside the Teaching Machine*. New York: Routledge, 1993.
Stein, Robert Louis. *Léger Félicité Sonthonax: The Lost Sentinel of the Republic*. Rutherford: Associated University Presses, 1985.
Stoler, Ann Laura. "Colonial Aphasia: Race and Disabled Histories in France." *Public Culture* 23.1 (Winter 2011): 121–56.
Toumson, Roger, and Simonne Henry-Valmore. *Aimé Césaire: Le nègre inconsolé*. Paris: Syros, 1993.
Trouillot, Henock. *L'Itinéraire d'Aimé Césaire*. Port-au-Prince: Imprimerie des Antilles, 1968.
———. "La présence d'Aimé Césaire en Haïti." In J. Leiner, ed., *Soleil éclaté*, 405–12. Tübingen: Gunter Narr Verlag, 1984.
Trouillot, Michel-Rolph. *Silencing the Past: Power and the Production of History*. Boston: Beacon Press, 1995.
Vergès, Françoise. *Monsters and Revolutionaries: Colonial Family Romance and Métissage*. Durham, NC: Duke University Press, 1999.
Walker, Keith L. "Art for Life's Sake: Rituals and Rights of Self and Other in the Theatre of Aimé Césaire." In P. Harrison and G. Edwards, eds., *Black Theater: Ritual Performance in the African Diaspora*, 181–208. Philadelphia: Temple University Press, 2002.
Walker, Noland, dir., and Edwige Danticat, narr. *Égalité for All: Toussaint Louverture and the Haitian Revolution*. DVD. PBS Home Video, 2009.
White, Ashli. *Encountering Revolution: Haiti and the Making of the Early Republic*. Baltimore: Johns Hopkins University Press, 2010.
White, Hayden. *The Content of the Form: Narrative Discourse and Historical Representation*. Baltimore: Johns Hopkins University Press, 1987.
———. *Metahistory: The Historical Imagination in Nineteenth-Century Europe*. Baltimore: Johns Hopkins University Press, 1973.
———. *Tropics of Discourse: Essays in Cultural Criticism*. Baltimore: Johns Hopkins University Press, 1978.

Wichmann Bailey, Marianne. *The Ritual Theater of Aimé Césaire: Mythic Structures of the Dramatic Imagination.* Tübingen: Gunter Narr Verlag, 1992.

Wilder, Gary. *The French Imperial Nation-State: Negritude and Colonial Humanism between the Two World Wars.* Chicago: University of Chicago Press, 2005.

——. "Race, Reason, Impasse: Césaire, Fanon, and the Legacy of Emancipation." *Radical History Review* 90 (Fall 2004): 31–61.

——. "Untimely Vision: Aimé Césaire, Decolonization, Utopia." *Public Culture* 21.1 (Winter 2009): 101–40.

Williams, Eric. *Capitalism and Slavery.* Chapel Hill: University of North Carolina Press, 1944.

Williams, Sandra. "La Renaissance de la tragédie dans l'œuvre dramatique d'Aimé Césaire." *Présence Africaine* 76 (1970): 63–81.

Index

Page numbers in italic refer to illustrations.

abolition: Britain, 76–77; Césaire and, 113–14, 177n16; commemorations of, 6, 18; emancipation and, 17, 76, 115–16; French decree of, 117, 153–54; French Revolution and, 43, 166n48; Law of 1848, 117, 153–54; narratives of, 19, 128, 154; second movement of, 139; Sonthonax and, 37, 71; Toussaint and, 26, 28, 46, 68, 72–73, 77–79, 168n28; universal freedom and, 8, 26, 78
Adet, 38–39
Affaire du 30 ventôse, 38–39
Agency: literacy as, 54–55, 156; Toussaint and, 55–56, 63–64, 99, 102, 104
agent particulier, 52, 55, 60, 62
Alexis, Jacques Stephen, 107
ancien libre, 28, 40. See also *gens de couleur libre*
ancien régime, 12, 20, 43, 88, 128, 160n36, 166n46
Andigné, General d', 65–66, 169nn4–5
Anglas, Boissy d', 116–17, 122, 167n63
anticolonialism. See Colonialism
Aravamudan, Srinivas, 55–56, 64, 103, 168n30
archives: research of, 8–9, 11–12, 112, 156; Archives Nationales, 82; Archives Nationales d'Outre-Mer, 82
Ardouin, Beaubrun, 8, 163n17, 175n25
Ardouin, Céligny, 8
armes miraculeuses, Les, 125, 176n1
Arnold, A. James, 110–11, 119, 144, 146, 175n23, 175n34, 176n1, 177n27
assimilation: Boissy d'Anglas and, 116–17; Caribbean autonomy and, 2–3, 5, 7, 15, 72; Césaire and, 20, 99–100, 117–18; critique of, 120, 122–23; Toussaint and, 72.
Augereau, General, 57

Baptiste, Pierre, 27
Bauvais, Louis-Jacques, 37
Bell, Madison Smartt, 12, 48–49, 106, 164n23, 166n48, 167n4, 169n8, 171n3
Berthier, General, 65
Biassou, 28–29
Bino Accord, 3–4
Black Jacobins, The, 16, 20, 100–103, 105–6, 113, 175n25. See also James, C. L. R.
Blanchelande, Governor, 28
Bloncourt, Gérald, 107

Bonaparte, Napoleon: French sovereignty and, 68, 78, 89; memoir of, 54, 96; slavery and, 15, 65–68; Toussaint and, 19–20, 25, 63–71, 73–92, 96, 115, 132, 156, 165n31, 169n2, 169n11
Bongie, Chris, 127–30, 161n58
Borgella, J.-M., 70, 73
Boromé, Joseph, 25–26, 31, 81–82, 162nn1–2, 164n24, 164n29, 171n6, 171n7
Bourbon Restoration, 139, 145
Boyer, 134, 147
Bréda Plantation, 27–29, 47–48
Brest, 65
Breton, André, 7, 107–8, 125, 174n9
Britain: Césaire and, 112, 118; Hispaniola and, 6, 40, 42, 166n58; imperialism, 100–101; Toussaint and, 19, 37, 58–59, 68, 76, 79
Bruix, 9, 27
Brunet, General, 103

Caffarelli, General, 66–67, 82, 126
Cahier d'un retour au pays natal (Césaire), 7, 13, 99, 106, 109–10, 118–19, 125
Camp Boiro, 152
Cap, Le, 27–29, 37–41, 47–48, 59–60, 68, 70, 144
Carpentier, Alejo, 107
Cauna, Jacques de, 81–82, 171n7, 171n9
Chanlatte, 134, 147
Christophe, 15, 21, 45, 48, 75–76, 118, 123. See also *Tragédie du roi Christophe, La*
Citadel, 21, 75–76, 130, 133, 136, 138, 140–41, 147, 151–52, 170n23
citizens of color. See *gens de couleur libre*
Code Henry, 138
Code Noir, 18, 114
Coisnon, abbé, 33
Cold War, 101–2
Collège de la Marche. See Institution Nationale des Colonies
colonial aphasia, 95
Colonial Assembly, 28–29
colonial problem, 7, 106, 116, 119
colonialism: anti-, 16–17, 99, 101–4, 131, 177n27; Césaire's critique, 14, 119–22, 141; discourse of, 7–8, 31, 34–35, 63, 69, 165n38; French law on (2005), 154–55; neo/new, 4, 43–44, 54, 64, 101, 122;

189

old, 52; post-, 16, 106, 111, 126, 128–29, 145, 159n25; racism and, 18, 55, 92, 114, 121; republicanism and, 6, 18, 26, 63, 68–69, 82, 95, 112
Confiant, Raphaël, 109–10, 162n62
Complete Works of Aimé Césaire, 13
Comte de Suzannet, 65–66, 169n4
Congrès International de Philosophie, 107
Constitution, de la colonie française de Saint-Domingue (1801), 105, 126, 132; Césaire and, 74–75, 114, 132–33; European/American discourse and, 67–69; *discours préliminaire*, 72; freedom and power in, 60, 67–68, 72–78, 89; French authority and, 67, 73, 78–79; narratives of, 19–20, 26, 53; precedent, 70–71; religion and, 73–74; Toussaint's defense of, 92, 95
Constitution, Dessalines (1805), 71
Constitution, French (1795), 33, 37, 69–72, 41, 44, 57–58, 164n30
Constitutional Organization of the Colonies, 44, 116–17. *See also* Departmentalization
Conteh-Morgan, John, 132, 142, 177n21
Council of Elders, 33, 44
Council of Five Hundred, 33, 42, 52, 56
Coup of Brumaire, 67
Coup of Fructidor. *See* Fructidor
Cronon, William, 11–12

Datty uprising, 40–41, 55–56
Davis, David Brion, 76
Dayan, Colin, 108
Debray, Régis, 130, 159n26
De Bry, Jean, 65
Décade Philosophique, La, 43
Déclaration des droits de l'homme et du Citoyen de 1789, 69. *See also* Constitution, French
Declaration of the Rights of Man, 14, 44, 68, 71, 113, 150
Delgrès, Louis, 15, 153
departmentalization: 122, 152; Césaire and, 5, 7, 14–17, 99–100, 105–6, 111, 119–20, 124, 130, 150, 152; disappointment with, 6, 119–20, 122; First Law of (1798), 44, 55, 69, 116–17, 124; narratives of, 11; Second Law of (1946), 1–2, 18, 117, 150, 157n1; trans-Caribbean relationship, 1–3, 6, 20
Départements d'outre-mer, 44, 116
dépassement, 106, 111–12
Depestre, René, 107–8, 174n16
Descourtilz, M. E., 54
Desormeaux, Daniel, 54, 81, 84–85, 88
Dessalines, Jean-Jacques, 7, 60, 71, 128, 144, 173n25
devoir de mémoire, 129
dialectic, 13, 85, 112–13, 177n27

directory. *See* French Directory
Discours sur le colonialisme, Le (Césaire), 14, 16, 106, 109, 119, 154–55, 161n51
doubled memory, 129–30, 136
Dubois, Laurent, 9, 39, 69, 154, 160n37, 163n18, 170n22, 172n12
Duboys, Pélage-Marie, 59–60, 71, 77, 168n25, 170n24
Dubreuil, Laurent, 31, 50, 71, 169n9
Dufay, Louis-Pierre, 31, 42–44, 164n30, 166n53, 166n57
Duvalier, François, 143

Eboué, Félix, 153
École de Liancourt, 42
Edwards, Brent Hayes, 10, 119–20
emancipation. *See* abolition
emplotment, 10, 33, 68, 79, 95, 103–4, 173n1
Ennery, 34, 63, 90, 126
Et les chiens se taisaient (Césaire), 125
Étudiant noir, L', 99, 117, 118, 121,
Expérience guinéenne et unité africaine (Touré), 15
Exposé de la situation de la République, 89

family romance: colonial, 31, 40, 52, 63, 130; colonial tropology and, 55; French Revolution and, 35–36; Freud and, 35–36; republican, 44; of Saint-Domingue, 130, 133; Toussaint and, 36, 49, 63, 78, 91, 105, 156
Fanon, Frantz, 18, 117
Festival of Negro Arts, 131
Fick, Carolyn E., 115, 170n26
filiation: discursive, 17, 31, 34, 36; legacy of, 34; narratives of, 105, 155; Toussaint and Césaire, 7, 15, 17–18, 100, 130; Toussaint and sons, 31–34
Filostrat, Christian, 118
First Civil Commission, 28
First Conference between the Commissioner Sonthonax and the General Toussaint Louverture, 49
First Consul, 66–67, 69, 78, 80, 84, 89, 91
Fischer, Sibylle, 9, 71
Flaville, Joseph, 38
Forsdick, Charles, 12, 112, 159n25
Fort-de-France, 7, 108–9, 150, 178n3
Fort de Joux, 65–67, 126, 153–54
Fouchard, Jean, 8, 163n10
Fourth Republic, 108
Fraternalism, 121, 176n39
French blockade of Haiti, 144–45
French Communist Party, 102, 108, 118–19, 121–22
French Directory, 33, 41–44, 46, 48–49, 52, 54, 58, 60, 63, 67, 108, 110
French Guyana, 1, 58, 116, 153, 157n6

French National Convention, 33, 108, 116, 159n30
French republicanism: ideology, 63–64, 105, 155; narratives of, 33–36; pro-slavery factions, 69; racism, 55, 92, 95, 116–17, 154
French Revolution, 2, 8, 14, 36, 43, 55, 58, 69, 112–14, 167n63
Fructidor: coup of, 44, 48, 52, 117; Fructidorization, 48; post-, 116–17
Frye, Northrop, 10, 103
Fumaroli, Marc, 83–84, 172n17, 173n26
Furetière, Antoine, 85, 88, 172n25

Gainot, Bernard, 43–44, 116–17, 165n32, 167nn62–63
Garraway, Doris, 72, 162n3
genealogy, 105–6
genre: Césaire and, 124; essay as peripatetic, 123; historical reenactment, 131–32, 146; letters, 121; literary, 111, 115; Myth, 30–31, 126, 141, 143–44, 146, 150; parody, 139, 145; *pièce de théâtre*, 49; poetry, 15; theater, 131–32, 148; tragedy, 50, 124–25, 132–33, 135, 141–42
gens de couleur libres, 6, 28, 69, 112–13
Geggus, David, 8, 25, 27, 29–31, 159n33, 160n43, 163n22, 168n25, 169n8
Ginguené, Pierre-Louis, 43
Glissant, Édouard, 6, 18, 106, 159n25
Gonaïves, 38, 39
Grégoire, abbé, 114
Gros, 28–29, 54
Guadeloupe, 3–5, 17–18, 109, 116, 136, 153
Guérin, Daniel, 120, 122
Guigou, Elisabeth, 153
Guinea, 15, 151–52
Guyana. *See* French Guyana

hagiography, 115, 124; Toussaint as martyr, 126
Harris, Rodney, 125, 133, 142–43, 147–48
Hédouville, General, 37, 55, 58–60, 63–64, 66, 92, 110, 117
Henry-Valmore, Simonne, 109–10
Histoire philosophique et politique des établissements et du commerce des Européens dans les deux Indes, 54
historiography: connection to memoir, 84–85, 172n17; method, 2, 6, 5, 10, 101–6, 176n37; narrative art of, 30, 100
Holt, Thomas C., 18, 76
hostage of fidelity, 56, 64
Hughes, Langston, 107
Hugonin, 134, 145, 147–49
Humanisme dans le théâtre d'Aimé Césaire, L', 125. *See also* Harris, Rodney

Hunt, Lynn, 35–36
Hurston, Zora Neale, 107

Île de la Réunion, 116, 157n1, 157n6
Institution Nationale des Colonies, 33, 37, 43, 54, 64
International Congress of Negro Writers and Artists: first, 120; second, 123
Itinéraire d'Aimé Césaire, L' (Trouillot), 109

James, C. L. R., 6, 8, 16, 20, 28–30, 58, 100–106, 115, 123, 166n49, 168n14, 169n1, 171n10. *See also Black Jacobins, The*
January Revolution, 107
Janvier, Louis-Joseph, 8
Jean-François, 28–29, 57
Jeannot, 28
Jenson, Deborah, 49–50, 61, 127–28, 160n37, 166n57, 167nn12–13
Jura, 19, 65–66, 75, 83, 133

Kerverseau, General, 9, 27, 59–60, 92, 160n36, 172n25
Kesteloot, Lilyan, 140, 177n22
Kotchy, Barthélémy, 140, 177n22

Lacroix, Pamphile de, 8, 10, 41, 54, 63, 132, 168n1, 172n25
Lam, Wifredo, 107, 110
Laveaux, General, 34, 37–42, 46–48, 59, 74, 105, 117, 121, 164n23, 165n35, 166n46
Le Cap. *See* Cap, Le
Le Héros, 80, 85, 126
Le Progressiste, 14
Lear, Tobias, 68
Leclerc, General, 27, 33, 80–81, 85, 88–92, 96, 168n1, 169n11, 171n3
legacy, 8, 13, 18, 96, 111, 130, 133, 152, 154, 157n1, 177n23
Legba Atibon, 148
Lescot, Élie, 107, 174n14
Lettre à Maurice Thorez (Césaire), 14, 16, 106, 120–21, 123, 151, 155, 176n10
Léveillé, Pierre, 38
Lhérisson, Camille, 107
Libertat, Bayon de, 27–28, 47–48
L'Indien, 48
literacy. *See* agency; trope
Littré, Emile, 85
Liyannage Kont Pwofitasyon (LKP), 3–5, 17, 161n53
Loa, 148–49
Louis XVIII, 145
L'Ouverture: Toussaint's use of, 30–31
Louverture, Isaac, 18, 26–27, 31, 32, 33–34, 41–43, 53, 55–56, 63–64, 161n61, 162n7, 163n10, 164nn28–29, 165n31, 166n58

Louverture, Placide, 18, 26–27, 31, 32, 33–34, 41–43, 53, 55–56, 63–64, 161n61, 164nn28–29, 165n31, 166n58
Louverture, Suzanne, 41–42
loyal opposition, 18, 20, 121
Lumumba, 15, 177n17

Mabille, Pierre, 107, 110, 174n9
Madiou, Thomas, 8, 39, 47, 166n46
Maitland, General, 37, 59
Martinique, 1, 3, 6, 14–15, 90, 107–9, 116, 139, 152, 155–56, 157n6, 174n19, 178n5
Marxism, 15, 118–19, 121, 151
mediation: of History and Myth, 150, 152; intertextual, 104–5, 127–28, 156; of political power, 128–30; theories of, 127–28; Toussaint's, 128
Mémoire: etymology of, 85; history and, 83; types of, 83–95
Mémoire du Général Toussaint Louverture, 19, 20, 143; defense of 1801 Constitution, 92; form, 88–89; as juridical document, 81, 85, 88; multiple copies of, 82; narrative strategies of, 82–83, 156; universal freedom and French sovereignty, 92, 95
Mémorial de Sainte-Hélène, Le. *See* Bonaparte, Napoleon
memory: as historiographical site, 95–96; as reputation after death, 85
Ménard, General, 81–82
Ménil, René, 110, 141
mère-patrie, 34, 36, 40, 42, 64, 116
metaliteracy, 55–56
Métellus, 140, 147–48
Métral, Antoine, 27, 63
Michel, Pierre, 38
Miller, Christopher, 109–10, 118–19, 139
Moïse, 48, 60; execution of, 76
Monsieur Toussaint, 106
Montaigne, 112
monumenta, 85
Mulatto, 56, 112–14, 162n61
myth. *See* genre

narrative: allegory, 143–44; Césaire's language and rhetoric, 114–15; of French republicanism, 154; forms of history, 103, 150; of heroic resistance, 102; linguistic modes, 134; metaphors, 137; Toussaint's strategies of, 68, 123
National Constituent Assembly: First, 28, 108; Second, 116
négritude, 10, 15, 106, 109–11, 118–20, 125, 151–52, 161n55, 162n62

Nesbitt, Nick, 71–75, 111, 140–41, 170n21, 175nn23–24, 177n27
Ngal, M. a M., 109, 119, 125, 175n20, 175n30
Nietzsche, Friedrich, 133, 142–43, 146, 150, 177nn21–22
Nogéré, 78
Nora, Pierre, 83–84, 88, 95, 172n17, 173n33
nouveaux libres, 37, 43, 47

Ogun, 148–49
Onyeoziri, Gloria Nne, 111, 114–15, 174n7
Ourika, 138–39

Palcy, Euzhan, 154
pantheon, 153–54
Parti Communiste Français (PCF). *See* French Communist Party
Parti Progressiste Martiniquais (PPM), 14, 102, 122
Pascal, 8
pedagogy, 53–55, 64, 130
pères-ennemis, 130
Perroud, Henry, 37–39
Pétion, 128–29, 133–35, 140, 143–45, 147, 151
Philadelphia Gazette, 49
pièce de théâtre. *See* Genre
Pierrot, General, 42
Pluchon, Pierre, 8, 29, 31, 39, 49, 55–56, 68, 74, 106, 160n36, 166n46, 169n1, 169n8, 172n23
Polverel, 47, 157n3, 164n23
Popkin, Jeremy, 28–29, 81, 163nn16–18
postcolonialism. *See* Colonialism
Pourquoi je suis communiste, 119
Price-Mars, Jean, 6, 108
pwofitasyon, 4, 8

Raimond, Julien, 43, 47–50
Raynal, 41, 54–55
Réfutation du Discours de Viénot Vaublanc, 16, 56–59, 70
republicanism. *See* French republicanism
Réunion. *See* Île de la Réunion
Rigaud, André, 7, 19, 37, 45, 60, 63, 68, 92
Rochambeau, 56–57, 92
Rochefort, 42, 166n51
Rosello, Mireille 13, 162n63
Roumain, Jacques, 107–8, 174n13
Roume, 59, 63, 163n13
Roussier, Michel, 42, 81, 165n32
Ruche, La, 107–8

Saint-Louis-du-Nord, 39–41, 56, 77
Saint-Rémy, Joseph, 8, 88, 171n9
Sainton, Jean Pierre, 4

Saison au Congo, Une, 15
Sannon, Pauléus, 8, 81
Sarkozy, Nicolas 3–5, 18, 136, 153–55, 158n10, 178n5
Say, Jean-Baptiste, 43
Schœlcher, Victor, 8, 15, 39, 47, 74, 106, 153–54, 164n23, 166n46, 167n12, 168n1, 172n23
Scott, David, 16–17, 100–102, 104
Senegal, 131, 139
Serreau, Jean-Marie, 133, 176n7
Shango, 148
Société haïtienne d'études scientifiques, 107
Sonthonax, 1, 25, 37, 42–43, 46–50, 51, 52–55, 58–60, 64, 69, 71, 121, 159n30, 166n53, 166n58, 167n3, 167n11
Sorbonne, 106
sovereignty: Bonaparte and, 68, 73; shared, 79; Toussaint and, 67, 68; universal rights and, 122
Spain: Civil War, 101; Hispaniola and, 37; Toussaint and, 37, 58–59; triangular trade, 114, 139
Stoler, Ann Laura, 95, 173n33

Taino, 136
Third Commission, 41, 48
Thorez, Maurice, 102, 119–22. See also *Lettre à Maurice Thorez*
Toumson, Roger, 109–10
Touré, Sekou, 15, 151–52
Toussaint Louverture: La Révolution française et le problème colonial (Césaire), 105, 112, 134, 142
Tragédie du roi Christophe, La (Césaire), 13, 110, 118, 124–34, 135–52
tragedy. See genre
tragic hero, 115, 124–25, 148

Treaty of Bâle, 37
trope, 11, 55, 112, 155; family, 105–6; and Hayden White, 103–5; literacy as, 54–56
Tropicalization, 55–56
Tropicopolitans (Aravamudan), 55
Tropiques (Césaire), 110
Trouillot, Henock, 108–9, 174n19
Truguet, 41, 43

United States: Césaire and, 119; open trade with, 68, 75; Toussaint and, 58–59

Vastey, 138–40, 145, 149–50
Vaublanc, Viénot, 47, 56–57, 64
Vendéens, 52, 58, 60, 66, 169n4
Vergès, Françoise, 36, 105–6, 123, 131, 134, 175n26, 176n6
Vie de Toussaint Louverture (Schœlcher), 106
Villate, Jean-Louis, 37–41, 166n46, 166n51
Villate Affair, 40–41, 47, 166n48
Vincent, Colonel, 78
Vodou, 73, 148–49, 170n24, 172n12, 174n14, 177n26

Walker, Keith L., 137, 139–40
Watigny, 42
White, Hayden, 10–12, 55, 100, 103–5, 173nn1–2
Wilberforce, 118, 131, 135–36, 146, 176n11, 177n16
Wilder, Gary, 18, 120, 123, 158n18, 161n53, 161n60, 170n13, 176n37
Williams, Eric, 76
World War II, 1, 7, 116–17, 150, 155, 174n9

Yoruba, 148–49

JOHN PATRICK WALSH is Assistant Professor of French and Francophone Studies at the College of Charleston in South Carolina. Research interests include the literature and history of Haiti, as well as the French Caribbean. He has published articles in *Research in African Literatures*, *Transition Magazine*, *The French Review*, *Small Axe*, and the *Journal of Haitian Studies*.

www.ingramcontent.com/pod-product-compliance
Lightning Source LLC
Chambersburg PA
CBHW070843160426
43192CB00012B/2288